WE ARE THE VOICE
OF THE GRASS

WE ARE THE VOICE OF THE GRASS

Interfaith Peace Activism in Northern Uganda

David A. Hoekema

OXFORD
UNIVERSITY PRESS

OXFORD
UNIVERSITY PRESS

Oxford University Press is a department of the University of Oxford. It furthers
the University's objective of excellence in research, scholarship, and education
by publishing worldwide. Oxford is a registered trade mark of Oxford University
Press in the UK and certain other countries.

Published in the United States of America by Oxford University Press
198 Madison Avenue, New York, NY 10016, United States of America.

CIP data is on file at the Library of Congress
ISBN 978–0–19–092315–0

1 3 5 7 9 8 6 4 2

Printed by Sheridan Books, Inc., United States of America

To the leaders of the Protestant, Catholic, and Muslim communities of the Acholi region of northern Uganda for demonstrating that words and deeds of faithfulness, patience, and collaboration are far more powerful than weapons of war.

CONTENTS

List of Abbreviations and Acronyms   ix

Introduction   xi

1. How the World Sees Uganda   1

2. From Kingdoms to Protectorate to New Nation   20

3. Politicians and Prophets   60

4. Religion and Culture in Uganda   99

5. Conflict, Displacement, and Interfaith Activism   119

6. Peace Comes to Northern Uganda   155

7. Perpetrators and Victims Return Home   187

8. Healing Conflict and Building Community   231

References   269

Index   281

LIST OF ABBREVIATIONS
AND ACRONYMS

———◆———

ARLPI   Acholi Religious Leaders Peace Initiative

HSM   Holy Spirit Movement (Lakwena's movement)

HSMF   Holy Spirit Military Force (Lakwena's army)

IDP   Internally Displaced Person (as in "IDP camp")

IRIN   Integrated Regional Information Network (formerly a UN agency, now independent)

LRA   Lord's Resistance Army (Joseph Kony's movement)

NRA   National Resistance Army (Museveni's militia, then the national army until 1995)

NRM   National Resistance Movement (Museveni's political party)

UNHCR   United Nations High Commissioner for Refugees

UPDA   Ugandan People's Democratic Army (a short-lived rebel movement, 1986–1988)

UPDF   Uganda People's Defence Force (Ugandan national army, renamed in 1995)

USAID   United States Agency for International Development

INTRODUCTION

―――――❖―――――

The conflict in northern Uganda is the biggest forgotten, neglected humanitarian emergency in the world today. . . . We should ask ourselves: how can we as an international community accept that a war is continuing that is directed and targeted against children . . . who are abducted, brainwashed and made into child soldiers or sex slaves and forced to attack and kill their own families in their own villages? . . . I know of no place in the world where such a bad situation has so little international presence and so little international relief.

—Jan Egeland,
UN Undersecretary-General for Humanitarian Affairs
(Al-Jazeera 2003)

We had to build trust, and we did not take sides. We tried to be completely neutral in talking to both sides, first the government and then the rebels. You know when two elephants are fighting, it is the grass that suffers. The government and the LRA, of course, are the two elephants, and the people are the grass. And the grass is crying out, "I am innocent! I am innocent!" And we are the voice of this grass.

—Bishop Matthew Odong,
Vicar General, Diocese of Northern Uganda (Odong 2014)

In this study I relate the story of a remarkable enterprise undertaken by residents of northern Uganda in response to a protracted and devastating civil conflict between a national government and a rebel army. It was a conflict that in many ways fit right into the prevailing Western picture of Africa today: a continent of bloody and bitter ethnic conflict, a region where human life has little value, and rapacious dictators and powerful warlords build their personal fiefdoms by exploiting, imprisoning, and murdering helpless populations. This picture is, of course, grossly exaggerated—no less so than 19th-century explorers' depictions of murderous savages devouring each other's entrails. And yet the depredations committed during the quarter-century when Joseph Kony and the Lord's Resistance Army (LRA) maintained a reign of terror over the people of northern Uganda seemed all too often to validate the stereotype.

I will trace the rise of the LRA in this study, describing the profound disruption that it inflicted on Ugandan communities and the unspeakable suffering of individuals and families that resulted from its rebellion. But I will tell that story in order to tell another, a story that in the end is even more important, both for those who live in Africa and for those who look at it from afar. And in that remarkable story we can find reasons for hope, not despair, about the future.

It is the story of the Acholi Religious Leaders Peace Initiative (ARLPI), a coalition of leaders in the Catholic, Protestant, and Muslim communities of the Acholi region of northern Uganda. This organization was created by a few courageous and persistent individuals at a time when the LRA rebellion had already held the region in its grip for more than a decade. Its founders came from religious communities whose relationship with each other had sometimes involved competition, sometimes open hostility, and seldom any sort of direct cooperation. But in the face of the LRA challenge, their relationship changed dramatically. Overcoming past mistrust, setting aside their isolation from each other, leaders of the major religious groups of northern Uganda resolved to work together. If they did so, they hoped, they could not only ameliorate the destruction caused by the continuing civil war but might also be able to help bring the government and the rebels together to work toward a resolution and an end to conflict. Even more distant, but no less important, was the goal of rebuilding communities and families when at last the conflict would come to an end and peace would return to northern Uganda.

To most Ugandans, and to the few outsiders who were aware of the suffering caused by LRA dominance, these goals appeared naïve and unrealistic. Progress toward their achievement was slow, and achievements of one month often disappeared in the next. Rebels viewed the religious leaders as covert agents of the government campaign to destroy them, whether as duplicitous collaborators with the regime or merely as its unwitting dupes. Military and political authorities regarded the priests, pastors, and imams who founded ARLPI as rebel sympathizers, and they believed the religious leaders' judgment was clouded by their Acholi ethnic identity. Why, they asked, did they not simply support the elected leaders of Uganda and the national army in their effort to defeat the LRA? Despite this atmosphere of mistrust on all sides, and despite the lack of visible progress in the early years, ARLPI leaders carried on their efforts in both advocacy and assistance.

The story of ARLPI demonstrates just how much can be accomplished by a small group of dedicated community leaders, in a situation where decades of military force and international pressure have yielded little relief. It shows, too, that centuries of antipathy and mistrust between Christian and Muslim communities in Africa can be overcome. And it offers dramatic evidence of the extraordinary consequences that can ensue when individuals who have won the trust of local communities—not politicians, nor government administrators, nor foreign advisors, nor military commanders, nor NGO workers, but respected leaders who have arisen from within their local communities—set out to find solutions to a seemingly intractable and interminable civil war.

Two Stories, and a Third

My goal in this study is to tell two important narratives about East Africa in the late 20th and early 21st centuries. The first is the story of how the Lord's Resistance Army emerged from the many-sided armed conflicts of Uganda's first decades as an independent nation and how it came to dominate the lives of residents in large portions of northern

Uganda. In recounting this story I will draw on a number of published and broadcast accounts—some of them careful and accurate, others reflecting the sources' preconceptions more than the actual history. These will be supplemented by first-hand accounts of Ugandans who lived through the worst periods of the conflict, some of them observing the LRA movement from the embattled cities and towns of the regions, others from within the movement itself.

The second story, one that has only been hinted at in published accounts by journalists and aid workers, is the emergence of an interfaith movement dedicated to pursuing resolution of the civil war between the LRA and the forces of the Ugandan government and to rebuilding lives and communities devastated by decades of conflict. The sources on which I base this account include a few published sources, documents disseminated by ARLPI during the three decades since its founding, and personal interviews with many of those who created the organization and oversee its activities today.

In order to tell these two stories effectively, it is essential first to look back to key events in the prior history of Uganda, not just as an independent nation but also as a British protectorate and, reaching back even further, as a region that was home to several large kingdoms and to many smaller population groups. Understanding the ethnic and linguistic origins of present-day Uganda, and examining the reasons why Great Britain sought to control this portion of the African continent in the late 19th century and then granted independence in the middle of the next century, will provide important clues to the character of the Ugandan state today and the ways in which the northern region relates to the more heavily populated regions to the south. This story will be recounted briefly on the basis of a number of historical and anthropological accounts.

I will begin with the third story that provides essential background for the first two. An outline of the ways in which my study will be organized may be helpful to orient a reader, especially a reader with a special interest in one part of my account.

The first chapter will provide some vignettes of Uganda as it is seen by outsiders, both through the writings of a European explorer of the 19th century and though an online video and social media campaign of young activists in the 21st century. The two perspectives are far removed in time, but not so distant in the assumptions they make concerning East Africa as a region where the ignorance and suffering of the people cries out for relief and assistance that Westerners alone can bring. We will also hear the voices of two women who were deeply affected by the northern conflict. One of them told me in an interview about her years in a rebel camp, where she was assigned to be the third wife and bear the children of an LRA commander. The other, interviewed by another writer, recounts her efforts to obtain release for her daughter—and her refusal to consider any arrangement that would leave others behind in captivity. These women's accounts of the suffering endured during the conflict, and of the courage and resilience with which they endured it, offer a very different picture of Uganda today from that of the explorer or the activist.

In the next chapter we will turn to the history of modern Uganda, in order to make it possible to set both the LRA movement and the countermovement of peace activists in an appropriate context. To make sense of these developments it is important to understand how the nation of Uganda came into being and how different populations have related to each other in its history, before and during the period of European colonization. Against this background we can understand better how the LRA was able to dominate a large region of the nation for a quarter-century. We will turn next to the attainment of independence and the tumultuous history of the new nation in the 1960s and 1970s. During this period, we will see, successive governments established different forms of essentially autocratic rule, some of them comparatively benign, others viciously malevolent.

Against this political and religious historical background, Chapter 3 will focus on the actions of three individuals who have most profoundly influenced the events of the Acholi region. The first is Uganda's current president, who was himself the leader of a rebel military force when he came to power in 1986 and who has remained in power ever since. The other two are the leaders of two successive rebel movements in the north, prophetess and military leader Alice Lakwena and her successor Joseph Kony, creator and commander of a far larger and more lasting internal struggle.

This political history of Uganda will be supplemented by an account of its religious history, the subject of the next brief chapter.

The events of the 19th century, including rivalry between Catholic and Protestant missionaries and the horrific slaughter of young men that brought them together, set the background for the complex ways that religion, ethnicity, and politics have influenced each other ever since.

Chapters 5 and 6 will recount the history of the LRA insurrection from the 1980s until the early 2000s, when armed conflict at last came to an end, and LRA forces withdrew. It was in this period that the persistent and courageous work of the religious leaders of the Acholi region most deeply influenced the course of events, succeeding where decades of military interventions had failed. A seemingly intractable conflict between a reclusive rebel commander and a government unable to win either effective control of the region or support from its residents came to a decisive, albeit complicated and protracted, conclusion, and northern Uganda was at last at peace. In these two chapters, then, two parallel stories will be recounted: the rise of the LRA rebel army, with devastating effects on the people of the region, and the creation of ARPLI as a counterforce that eventually succeeded, with the help of others, in restoring peace.

Chapter 7 continues the story of ARLPI peace activism in the present and examines the many challenges that face the Acholi region as it seeks to reestablish normal social and economic life after the end of the civil war. As the attention of global media has moved on to other zones of conflict, and after the international aid community has closed up its distribution centers and closed its offices, ARLPI continues to play a key role in healing the lasting wounds of the civil war and helping communities rebuild. In the final chapter I will offer some reflections and recommendations drawn from the example of ARLPI, suggesting reasons why it has been able to bridge deep religious divisions in ways that provide a model for collaboration and conflict resolution, widely relevant but too little known, for other situations of conflict around the world.

The Perspective of a Philosopher

And why, a reader may well wonder, has a philosopher undertaken to write about a conflict and its aftermath in East Africa? Is this study a philosophical inquiry as well as a historical narrative? Some explanation is in order.

My undergraduate and graduate study of philosophy prepared me to teach a variety of courses in what some would call applied philosophy—political philosophy, philosophy of law, philosophy of the arts, philosophies of war and violence—in addition to courses in topics that are regarded as more central to Western philosophy, such as history of philosophy and logic. My interest in Africa was sparked by opportunities that arose to teach and conduct research in African university settings. Four times in the past decade I have served as director of my college's Study in Ghana program, which offers a full semester of credits in African literature, African politics, and other topics under the guidance of instructors at the University of Ghana, in addition to courses taught by the director. There I developed an interest in African philosophy, leading to the introduction of a course in that area offered both in Ghana and back home at Calvin College in the following years.

To pursue the relationship between politics, religion, and social change more deeply, I arranged to spend a semester as a visiting scholar at the University of Kwazulu-Natal in South Africa, studying the remarkable transition in the 1990s from the racially oppressive apartheid regime to a multiracial democracy. A few years later, I was awarded a Fulbright Teacher/Scholar position at Daystar University in Nairobi, Kenya, where I taught philosophy to undergraduates and assisted in curriculum development. I have thus had the exceptional good fortune to live and work for several months in three countries in three major areas of the continent. Having observed the ways in which Western aid, local traditions, and government interact, for good or for ill, I also began studying the emerging field of development ethics, and an intensive seminar, organized by the National Endowment for the Humanities and offered at Michigan State University, provided essential background in this area of inquiry.

While teaching in Kenya in 2010, I visited Uganda for the first time and met colleagues at several universities there. With their encouragement, and with the assistance of the staff of the international relief organization World Renew, I planned a return trip with a group of students two years later. The students completed a one-month study tour of church-assisted aid initiatives in several regions of the country, visiting communities to talk to residents about their lives and learning of efforts to promote agricultural productivity, local infrastructure, and sustainable economic development.

What my students and I learned was an invaluable supplement to our readings about the purposes and best practices of development aid. In effect, our time in Uganda was an intensive study of applied philosophical ethics. We observed instances where well-intentioned projects initiated by outsiders only diminished the well-being of those affected on the one hand, and projects born out of consultation and collaboration that yielded rich benefits for individuals, families, and communities on the other.

Conformity to sound principles, we observed, is seldom a sufficient reason to adopt a policy or practice. Ethical and sustainable development requires patience, sensitivity to local needs and perceptions, and leadership that comes from within a community, not from outside. One of the most remarkable instances of locally originated community activism first came to our attention as we visited development projects in northern Uganda. This was the work of ARLPI in mitigating the effects of LRA occupation and later, after the LRA's departure from Uganda, in assisting with rebuilding communities and re-integrating those who had been caught up in the conflict.

My first visit with students led to a second, two years later. After my students returned to the United States, I returned to northern Uganda to conduct a series of interviews that had been arranged in advance with the assistance of a colleague at Uganda Martyrs University. I spoke with church leaders and leaders of the Muslim community who had helped launch ARLPI, staff members of several agencies working to assist families and communities, and individuals who had been kidnapped in LRA raids and later escaped, or were released, back to their communities. These interviews have provided much of the material for this study, supplemented by a variety of published and broadcast sources about the history of East Africa and about the LRA.

This is, then, an extended study in applied philosophy—or perhaps it would be better to call it philosophically informed anthropology, or ethically weighted history. I have come to see in the recent history of northern Uganda an unusual sort of laboratory for testing and evaluating political and social structures, a laboratory in which the residents of the region are both the investigators and the subjects. The questions put to the test in this historical experiment include these:

- Can the divisions and power imbalances of colonialism be overcome after independence?
- Can ethnic divisions and the resulting mistrust be overcome to achieve common goals?
- Can competing religious communities find common cause against conflict?
- What do "consent" and "accountability" mean in religious and ethnic communities? What is their meaning under an autocratic regime?

The work of ARLPI since its founding two decades ago shows that religious differences need not impede shared commitment to address the wounds inflicted by war. It demonstrates, too, that ethical action is possible only with insights gained from patient listening to the voices of those whose lives and futures are at risk—not just reflection on goals and principles. In this story of courageous interfaith peace activism in northern Uganda, there is much to be learned—by philosophers, religious leaders, and community activists—about healing and conflict resolution in any community that has been caught up in a destructive conflict.

Acknowledgments

Support for this study of conflict and its aftermath has been generously provided by Calvin College, first by supporting my proposal to plan and direct three January Interim study trips for undergraduate students to East Africa in 2010, 2012, and 2014, and then by providing a sabbatical leave in 2016 during which I was able to complete the writing of this study. I am grateful to the provost, the president, the Faculty Development Committee, and the Board of Trustees for the support and encouragement that I have received.

The interviews on which I have relied to tell the story of the LRA and of ARLPI were made possible by my appointment in 2013–2014 as a Fellow of the Nagel Institute for the Study of World Christianity, which provided financial support for my initial round of interviews in Uganda and for the early stages of writing. I express here my deep gratitude to the Institute, and my personal thanks to its director Joel Carpenter and staff members Donna Romanowski and Nellie Kooistra, for their support and encouragement.

Supplementary travel support enabling me to return to Uganda in 2016 for follow-up interviews was provided by a travel grant from the Calvin Center for Christian Scholarship. I extend my thanks to director Susan Felch and program manager Dale Williams for this valuable assistance.

I have received insightful comments on my work in its preliminary stages from colleagues who attended lectures I was invited to present at Calvin College (by the Nagel Institute), at the Center for Philosophy of Freedom at the University of Arizona, at the National University of Groningen in the Netherlands, and at the Institute for African Studies of the University of Ghana. I have also benefited from comments received from fellow participants in two international conferences of the International Ethics Development Association, at the University of Costa Rica in 2016 and at the University of Bordeaux in 2018.

My invitation to participate in a four-week Summer Institute on "Development Ethics: Questions, Challenges, and Responsibilities" in 2013 provided a comprehensive introduction to this emerging field, through readings and seminars and guest lectures, and a network of colleagues with whom I could share my project as it was taking clearer shape in my mind. I am grateful to the National Endowment for the Humanities for making this intensive period of professional development possible and to seminar directors Fred Gifford of Michigan State University and Eric Palmer of Allegheny College for their capable leadership.

The seeds of this project were planted on a brief visit to Uganda from Kenya, where I was a Teacher/Researcher with the support of the Fulbright Foundation in spring 2010. My wife and I were invited to accompany longtime friend and colleague Father David Burrell, C. S. C., then serving a short-term assignment in philosophy at Uganda Martyrs University, on visits to a number of church-related development sites in central and northern Uganda. It was thanks to Father

David's generosity in sharing his friends and colleagues that I began to work with Margaret Angucia, lecturer in the Institute of Ethics and Development Studies at Uganda Martyrs and author of an important study of post-conflict rehabilitation of child soldiers in northern Uganda.

From Margaret's account, based on having lived in Gulu through some of the worst years of the LRA rebellion, I learned of the courage and the effectiveness of the work of the Acholi Religious Leaders Peace Initiative. When Margaret was unable personally to assist me in arranging interviews with its principals and others, she introduced me in turn to her colleague Sister Lucy Dora Akello, lecturer in education. Sister Lucy has lent indispensable assistance at several stages of my work, helping to refine its topic, sharing her own experiences as a resident of Gulu during the LRA occupation, and, most important, arranging a week of interviews with key participants in the work of the Acholi religious leaders, and with others whose lives had been affected by the conflict, in January 2014. Her resourcefulness, sensitivity to others' perspectives and concerns, practical efficiency, and ready humor made her a delightful collaborator. Thanks to an unexpected convergence of travel plans I was able to be present in June 2018 at her final doctoral examination at the University of Groningen, where we had met for the first time in June 2013. Sister Lucy's lucid account of the benefits of mother-tongue instruction in primary education will help Uganda's teachers and pupils in the years to come.

The staff members of World Renew (formerly Christian Reformed World Relief Committee) in Uganda worked closely with me in the planning and implementation of two study trips for students at Calvin College and in helping me and my students gain a better understanding of the challenges that face church and society in East Africa today. They also provided an inspiring model of development assistance that seeks to assist local communities in attaining objectives that are important in their lives, coming alongside rather than imposing their own plans. Joseph Mutebi, Edward Etanu Okiror, and Carol Musoke both described and exemplified effective development assistance for me and for my students.

Of all the students who accompanied me in two study trips to Uganda, one deserves special recognition for having undertaken the challenging task of transcribing audio recordings of all the interviews I conducted in Gulu in 2014. Seth Hamrick had been so fascinated by what he observed on our brief January 2012 visit that he returned for a semester's study of international development at Uganda Martyrs University in 2013, and his deepened knowledge of the cultural and religious environment in Uganda enhanced the accuracy of his transcriptions. The other students who accompanied me also deserve to be mentioned and thanked for their patience and flexibility when plans went awry (as when frigid Chicago conditions delayed our first flight and stranded us overnight in Istanbul) and their commitment to learning and to service. In the large 2012 group of students, in addition to Seth, were Mikelle Badge, Kristin Brussee, Jake Christiansen, Luke DeJong, Eric Doornbos, Aleida Douma, Alicia Driesenga, Bethany Engel, Eva Kort, Sabrina Narukawa, KyuHyung Park, Anna Slachter, Stephanie Toering, Rachel VanderPloeg, Anneke Walhout, Kayla Westman, and Madalyn Witte. A smaller group made the journey in 2014: Alex Eriksson, Claire Gillen, Ellie Hutchison, Andrea Jehl, Jun Park, Olivia Rozdolsky, Erin Smith, Lydia Song, and Sarah Truax. Several of the students in each group, after completing their studies, are pursuing careers in international development, in the United States or abroad.

My wife, Susan Bosma Hoekema, was able to accompany me to Uganda in January 2012 and on a brief return visit in 2016. Her education and experience in the field of history and in the practice of law helped open my eyes to dimensions of the contemporary situation in Uganda that a philosopher might have overlooked. She has been an unceasing source of encouragement and inspiration, and a helpful reader and editor at every stage, from initial inclinations to try to tell the remarkable story of courageous peace activists in Uganda to the completed book.

David A. Hoekema

July 18, 2018

I

How the World Sees Uganda

Mtesa [the Buganda king, or kabaka] has determined henceforth, until he is better informed, to observe the Christian Sabbath as well as the Moslem Sabbath, and the great captains have unanimously consented to this. He has further caused the Ten Commandments of Moses to be written on a board for his daily perusal—for Mtesa can read Arabic—as well as the Lord's Prayer, and the golden commandment of our Saviour, "Thou shalt love thy neighbour as thyself." This is great progress for the few days that I have remained with him, and, though I am no missionary, I shall begin to think that I might become one if such success is feasible.

But, oh that some pious, practical missionary would come here! What a field and a harvest ripe for the sickle of civilisation! Mtesa would give him everything he desired— houses, lands, cattle, ivory, &c, he might call a province his own in one day. It is not the mere preacher, however, that is wanted here. The Bishops of Great Britain collected, and all the classic youth of Oxford and Cambridge, would effect nothing by mere talk with the intelligent people of Uganda. It is the practical Christian tutor, who can teach people how to become Christians, cure their diseases, construct dwellings, understand and exemplify agriculture, and turn his hand to anything like a sailor—this is the man who is wanted. Such an one, if he can be found, would become the saviour of Africa.

—Letter from Henry Stanley, 1875
(Royal Geographical Society 1876, 152–153)

THREE YEARS AFTER THE *New York Herald* had dispatched him on a quest to find missionary doctor David Livingstone in what is now Tanzania, the renowned explorer and journalist Henry Morton Stanley was back in "the dark continent," a phrase that he had coined. In 1875, in the midst of a two-year expedition to the African interior, he found his way unexpectedly to the royal palace that was the seat of the Buganda kingdom, on Lake Victoria's northern shore.

Two thousand of the *kabaka's* subjects lined up to greet him as he approached, beating drums and blowing on horns. Herds of goats and sheep, dozens of chickens, rice, eggs, and local wine were all sent to Stanley's quarters to sustain him and his porters and companions—those who had survived the journey, at any rate. Only half of the members of the original party of 228 were still alive.

A rather breathless popular history published two decades later observed:

> Many African nations were small tribes of a few hundred or a thousand people, and most so-called African kings were chiefs over a small group of African villages. The kingdom of Uganda was a most notable exception. Here was a country as large as the New England states, with four million people, all ruled by one powerful monarch. Nor did he rule in the fashion of most African chiefs. His House of Lords met daily in his palace for counsel. . . . To the white man, Mtesa seemed like some great Caesar of Africa. (Fahs 1907, 9–10)

Through accounts such as Stanley's, Europeans came to be fascinated by the mysterious lands and peoples of Africa. In it they saw great natural riches, exotic modes of life in primitive and pre-literate societies, and a limitless field for Christian missions. Lands of the interior such as Uganda were so remote and so difficult to reach that very few explorers ventured there. Stanley had set out with three European companions to assist in leading the expedition. All three of the others died of diseases contracted during their travels.

The letter from Stanley to the royal society quoted above was dispatched with a French explorer who was murdered a few weeks later on his journey north. The letter was found concealed in the dead man's boots by passing English soldiers and—according to the same popular history, whose scholarly authenticity may be open to challenge—it was passed on to English authorities in Cairo, then to newspapers in

London. There it was splashed across the front pages, stoking popular interest in the intrepid explorer and the lands through which he was traveling. "Little wonder then that the letter was seven months old when it appeared in the morning newspaper. When one thinks of the way it came, the marvel is that it ever reached England at all" (Fahs 1907, 2–3).

In the 19th century, in the eyes of Europeans and North Americans, Africa was a boundless and impenetrable land of both mystery and opportunity. Explorers returned with fantastic tales of cannibalism and ritual murder. These lurid accounts probably owed more to malarial dreams and fantasies, and to the desire to titillate and scandalize, than to careful scientific observation. From time to time an African chief, bedecked in beads and colorful robes, would pay a ceremonial visit to a European monarch.

Examples of traditional African woodcarving appeared in a few galleries and anthropological museums, as did the extraordinary bronze busts and plaques of the Benin kingdom in what is now Nigeria. The delicacy of these artifacts, dating from several centuries earlier, gave rise to groundless speculation that Renaissance Italian artisans must have traveled to the interior of Africa to teach the craft of lost-wax bronze casting. It was inconceivable to Europeans that indigenous African societies could have arrived at such advanced technology on their own, without the assistance of the more civilized cultures of Europe.

The horrors of the Triangular Trade in slaves were beginning to break through centuries of moral blindness, when European traders had packed enslaved men and women into filthy and overcrowded holds on slave ships, bound for the New World to cultivate cotton and sugar. Priests and pastors had obligingly offered theological assurance that it is the duty of Christians to be compassionate toward their slaves but not to set them free. The products of enslaved plantation labor in turn kept the mills and bakeries of Europe running, manufacturing cloth and spirits that became the currency with which more slaves were obtained. By the late 18th century, however, the moral compass in Europe and North America had begun to swing in a different direction. Abolitionist movements sprang up across Europe and in the northern colonies of the British empire in the New World. In the first decade of the 19th century, the legislatures of Denmark, the United States, and the United Kingdom passed legislation prohibiting all trade in slaves.

The history of East African slavery is a topic to which we will return briefly in Chapter 2, since it set an inescapable backdrop for the purported benevolence of European activity in the colonial period. And indeed the practice of slavery and the export of captured slaves did not come to an end when laws were passed outlawing the practice. West Africa was several days' perilous journey by sea from the centers of European government, after all. Colonial authorities and local chiefs alike could draw a handsome profit illicitly filling the holds of slaving ships. The number of enslaved men and women sent to the New World from East and West Africa actually increased after the abolition of the trade, responding to continuing demand.

But by the late 19th century, when Stanley undertook his journey, European interests had shifted from capturing living human beings for plantation labor to new priorities: hunting and bringing down the trophy animals of the African savannah, extracting mineral wealth to fuel manufacturing back home, and evangelizing all the millions of Africans who were seen as languishing in ignorance and superstition. The African safari became a rite of passage for wealthy industrialists, who brought home stuffed heads and tales of bravado. Prospectors set out in search of legendary gold and diamond mines. Missionaries were dispatched, in wave after wave, to pursue the "pious and practical" work that Stanley recommended.

How did the nations of the North see the peoples and lands of the African continent, from the time of Stanley until the early 20th century? In the eyes of big game hunters, Africa was populated—sparsely—by natives who enjoyed a unique communion with the animals around them, yet were happy to assist in transforming them into trophies for the country houses of European gentlemen. For prospectors and other seekers of wealth, it was a land of thieves and thugs, perpetually double-crossing and cheating their benefactors. In the eyes of the missionaries, on the other hand, Africa was a continent of people living in perpetual childhood, manipulated by witch doctors and oppressed by vengeful deities, who had long been waiting for the liberation that would come with the light of the Christian gospel and the benefits of European culture. Stanley was an explorer and an adventurer, but in the letter quoted above he suggests—not very convincingly—that he is nearly ready to take up the missionaries' role.

The reports of explorers remind us that, then and now, the Africa that is visible from the perspective of Europe and North America may scarcely resemble the Africa in which its residents actually dwell. Communication is vastly improved today over a century ago: text messages and emails, news videos and Facebook posts and tweets, flash back and forth millions of times each day, across and between continents. For Europeans and North Americans, travel to and from Africa takes a matter of hours, not weeks. Europeans and Americans are present in large numbers in every major African city, and Africans in every major city of Europe and North America. And yet a great gulf still stands between Africa as seen from afar and Africa as home (A. Perry 2015).

Stanley's account is representative of one way in which Africa has been seen from the developed world of Europe and North America. (Remember the Ten Commandments inscribed on the *kabaka's* wall— we will hear about them again as a purported foundation for two rebel movements a century later.) News media and politicians have learned to see the continent far more clearly today, acknowledging both its problems and its potential. But stereotypes do not die easily. When I was describing my preparations for spending a semester in Ghana as director of my college's program there, a well-meaning member of my church inquired, "Do you have to take all your food with you, dried or canned?" I fought back the temptation to reply, "Actually, agriculture has been practiced in Africa for quite a long time now." Instead I simply said, "We'll have access to as wide a range of meat and fish and fruits and vegetables there as here, but there they will all be in the markets just a few hours after they have been harvested or caught or slaughtered."

Uganda Featured in a Record-Setting Video

In Stanley's day the principal source of outsiders' knowledge of Africa was the spoken and written word. Explorers sent letters home and eventually—if they were fortunate—returned alive to share their tales. Missionaries submitted reports to their sponsoring churches and went on speaking tours to raise support for their work. Photographs, projected as lantern slides or published in photogravure, sometimes supplemented words, but the challenges of carrying heavy cameras and plates to remote locations and bringing images home limited their usefulness.

In the 21st century, an event that takes place anywhere on the globe can become known instantly over the Internet. A political upheaval, a natural disaster, or a celebrity sighting in the remotest region of the world will show up on the screens of viewers everywhere within minutes. The contemporary equivalent of the visiting explorer addressing a geographical society or a missionary reporting on baptisms in his village to his home church—and therefore the principal basis for contemporary perceptions of Africa in the developed world—can be found in electronic journalism, online video, and film.

It was by means of an extraordinarily popular online video that the region of northern Uganda and the activities of the Lord's Resistance Army (LRA) suddenly broke into worldwide public view in February 2012. The release in that month of the video "Kony 2012," by the organization Invisible Children, set off one of the strangest episodes in the recent history of humanitarian aid, foreign policy, and mass communications. *Los Angeles Times* writer Tony Perry summarized the events of that year in an October 2012 article:

> First came the sensation: an activist video that captivated tens of millions of viewers in just a few days with its plea for the capture of African warlord Joseph Kony and an end to his mass abductions of children for use as soldiers and sex slaves.
>
> Then came the scandal: the video's creative director running naked through the streets of San Diego, talking gibberish, all caught on cellphone video by a bystander and splashed onto TMZ.
>
> Six months later, the San Diego-based group Invisible Children is attempting to recapture the lost momentum of the spring with a new video—explaining the naked escapade and trying to refocus public attention on bringing down the messianic Kony and his Lord's Resistance Army.
>
> The new 30-minute video, "Move," was posted on YouTube on Sunday night.

Invisible Children plans a Nov. 17 rally in Washington to lobby the White House and leaders in Africa and Europe to redouble efforts to catch Kony, who fled Uganda in 2006 and is believed to be hiding in central Africa. (T. Perry 2012)

Perry actually understated the amazingly rapid dissemination of the 30-minute video. It was uploaded and made available on YouTube on March 4, and within one week, according to a Web-tracking news service, it had already been viewed 112 million times, surpassing the previous record for any online posting (Grossman 2012). The follow-up video posted ten months later logged 93 million visitors in its first three weeks online.

"Going viral" has become a media catchphrase, and commentators observe with dismay that cats playing football, country music songs, and dogs on skateboards have become interchangeable units of Internet entertainment, powered by tweets and Facebook "like" ratings into global awareness. But in this instance it was not a celebrity sighting or a silly pet trick that exploded into global distribution, but the plight of a nation long under the oppressive domination of an armed insurgency whose tactics flout all the rules of war and morality.

In a broad critique of aid programs across Africa, journalist Alex Perry highlights the Invisible Children campaign as a telling example of well-intentioned but misguided humanitarianism. He cites an earlier video, titled "Invisible Children" like the organization, that recounts the adventures of three idealistic young men, newly graduated from college, on an expedition to East Africa. Donations collected at showings of the earlier video became the major source of funding for a return visit, when "Kony 2012" was created. Perry comments:

Invisible Children was different from other campaign groups. Young, privileged, and goofy, their DNA was more selfie than selfless. They broke with convention, horrifying old Africa hands by making a film that was as much about themselves as about the war, discarding any notion of neutrality and paying no lip service to concerns about interfering in the sovereign affairs of a foreign country. While military action was anathema to most of the aid world, Invisible Children demanded it.

In an interview, Perry asked Invisible Children founder Jason Russell whether his advocacy of military action meant "giving up the moral high ground." Russell's response was unequivocal:

> "That's really old-school," said Jason. . . . . "What's more humanitarian than stopping a war? I understand the conviction that violence begets violence. But either you just go on pulling people out of the river or you go upstream, find out who is pushing them in and stop them. That's not about Kumbaya concerts for world peace." Jason said he would prefer Kony captured alive and tried, not killed. But he was realistic about how unlikely that was. "This is a war," he said. "We're not hoping for rainbows and butterflies." (A. Perry 2015, 119–120)

With "Kony 2012" we witnessed the unprecedented capacity of social media to disseminate information about a crisis in one corner of the world to concerned citizens everywhere, in a way that could not possibly be achieved through print or even broadcast media. In a torrent of clicks, forwarded links, "likes," and person-to-person recommendations, this online indictment of Joseph Kony's reign of terror in East Africa captured the attention of more than a hundred million viewers. To put this in perspective: a website that tracks the most successful petition drives in history gives first place to a 2015 petition to the United Nations, urging measures to prevent a recurrence of the disastrous stampede in Mecca that had claimed more than two thousand lives. It received just over half a million signatures[1] (Petitions 24 n.d.). The recorded viewings of "Kony 2012" exceeded these responses by a ratio of two hundred to one.

Invisible Children announced that it would carry its campaign forward in the streets of Washington, DC, on November 17, 2012, anticipating a gathering of hundreds of thousands of young people who would demonstrate their passion for global justice. A Web announcement listed those who would address a massive rally that was expected to fill the National Mall: popular entertainers, journalists, and representatives of national and international governments.

In reality the event drew only about 12,000 participants, far below the organizers' predictions and hopes. A few celebrity figures spoke to the small crowd, as did representatives of the government of Uganda, the African Union, and the United Nations. News coverage was limited to a few videos posted on the Invisible Children site and several articles in campus newspapers. National media took no notice of the event.

Evidently one hundred million viewers of the two videos had moved on to other concerns. Social-media international activism had proven to be an extraordinarily effective means of drawing national and international attention to a crisis. Its meteoric popularity did not translate, in this case, into sustained public attention, to say nothing of concerted concrete actions. Nevertheless the episode offers some important lessons for the story of the Acholi Religious Leaders Peace Initiative (ARLPI). A single half-hour video altered international perceptions of Uganda, and indeed made what had been invisible widely visible. But the image of Uganda that it conveyed does not line up at all closely with the realities experienced by the people of the region. Let us look more closely at how they diverge.

The Video and Its Message

Imagine this experiment: present a group of Americans—your family members, perhaps, or colleagues at work—with a map of the continent of Africa, showing all of the national borders but without any country names. Ask them how many country names they can write in with confidence. (First take away their cell phones so they cannot sneak a look at a map online.)

Most could probably point out Republic of South Africa. Several might recognize Nigeria, Egypt, and perhaps Kenya by size and outline. The tiny landlocked nation of Rwanda became the focus of global attention as a result of the genocidal massacres of 1994, and some might remember where to locate it.

Few who have not traveled to the region could identify the country that lies on the northern and northeastern shore of Lake Victoria as the nation of Uganda—unless they are among the 100 million viewers of "Kony 2012," in which case it may be one of the first names they are able to write in. Thanks to one youth-oriented activist group and its two online videos, Uganda received far more attention in news coverage and in daily conversation than ever before.

And what did the video tell its viewers about Uganda and the challenges that it faced? Stripped to its essentials, the message was this: First, a terrible war has raged for decades in this landlocked African nation, and an unspeakably cruel and unprincipled warlord is responsible for its initiation and its continuation to this day. Second, the people and the armed forces of Uganda lack the will or the capacity to bring the conflict to an end. Therefore, third, it is the obligation of the people of the West, particularly the United States, to send in military forces and bring about the arrest or the death of Joseph Kony, releasing the people of Uganda from their oppression. And underlying all of these was a fourth element: the conviction that a massive public demand to "make Kony famous" will compel the United States government to abandon halfway measures, accede to popular pressure, and send in the troops.

Ugandans, I was told, were amazed when the spotlight of global attention turned toward their nation early in 2012. (My first study tour of Uganda preceded its release by just one month.) They affirmed the message that the conflict in the north had caused great suffering during the years of Kony's effective occupation, from 1986 until 2006. But they were disturbed by the video, if they had the opportunity to view it. Its picture of the situation was many years out of date, its depiction of Ugandans as passive victims was demeaning, and its insistence that more troops and more guns would solve Uganda's problems rang false in many ears.

I had the opportunity to visit Uganda four times during the period between 2010 and 2016, each time meeting with university colleagues, church leaders, aid workers, and residents of rural communities in several regions of the country. From Ugandan friends and colleagues I learned about the desperate situation of the Acholi people of the north while the LRA rebellion subjected them to periodic raids. LRA forces had kidnapped young men and women, maimed or killed those they suspected of aiding the government, and seized crops and food stores during nearly a quarter-century of effective rule.

Among Ugandans whom I interviewed in 2014 as part of my research for this study was John Bosco Komanech, director of the Catholic social service organization Caritas in the town of Gulu, which was at the center of the area where the LRA carried out many of its raids during the rebellion. Early in our interview we discussed the content and the effect of the Invisible Children video, and he commented:

> First of all I want to say I appreciate what they did to capture the attention of American youth. I sent it to many people to watch.
>
> But, second, I want to say that many of the clips were outdated and were not relevant to 2012. So those who do not know about northern Uganda today thought that there is still killing, and cutting the lips and the breasts, and all that, still going on today. Around 2002 or 2003 it would have been very relevant, but not in 2012.
>
> Third, the video "Kony 2012" is very provocative—it is trying to tell the people of Acholi that despite the fact that we have been putting dialogue and reconciliation to the front [giving it top priority], what is needed is more military support from the U.S. government.

Already there are 100 U.S. Special Forces in Uganda, he added. But they are based in Kampala, in central Uganda. The small LRA force that still exists today is deep in hiding in a neighboring country, probably the Democratic Republic of the Congo. U.S. soldiers have brought in large quantities of arms and military equipment—"the gadgets are all there"—for their use and for use by the Ugandan military. But the video's urgent plea that more soldiers and more weapons must be provided in order to solve Uganda's problems is simply "not relevant," said Komanech.

Others to whom I spoke about the video's call for a military solution were equally skeptical. American technical assistance, training programs, and arms had been generously provided to the Ugandan armed forces for decades, beginning in the 1990s, but to little effect. Uganda's army achieved no lasting military successes. Nor were the American advisors able to persuade Ugandan commanders to rein in the abuses committed by their troops in the course of several counterinsurgency campaigns.

Komanech went on:

Also, that video was very political, which many of us did not support. They tried to show it in Gulu, and what happened? People became very rowdy, and the police used tear gas—people were protesting in the whole town. People even wanted to stone the visitors who brought that thing to be screened, saying, "Why do you want to remind us of all these things from the past? This is a far-fetched story."

My recommendation to the international world would be that they should continue to advocate for peaceful means of solving our problems, today and for future conflicts that may arise. (Komanech 2014)

From other Ugandans I heard similar stories of towns and villages where "Kony 2012" had been screened and audiences had erupted in boos and catcalls because of its inaccuracies. Especially offensive was its depiction of the people of Uganda as helpless victims who were unable to take any effective action until a courageous band of young Americans arrived to take up their cause. The suffering caused by LRA violence was very real; but in depicting Ugandans as passive victims the video harked back to 19th-century narratives of helpless and ignorant black people waiting for rescue by benevolent white people.

There was considerable skepticism and pushback from Western viewers, too. Within four days of the release of the video, Nigerian-American writer Teju Cole posted a series of caustic Twitter messages about the mentality that he saw behind the Invisible Children campaign, which he labeled "The White Savior Industrial Complex." Some samples:

The white savior supports brutal policies in the morning, founds charities in the afternoon, and receives awards in the evening.

The banality of evil transmutes into the banality of sentimentality. The world is nothing but a problem to be solved by enthusiasm.

This world exists simply to satisfy the needs—including, importantly, the sentimental needs—of white people and Oprah.

The White Savior Industrial Complex is not about justice. It is about having a big emotional experience that validates privilege. (Cole 2012)

Another Narrative of the Conflict

In traveling in the Acholi region and talking with religious leaders and community members, I heard a very different narrative concerning the experience of northern Ugandans during the period of the LRA insurgency. Certainly Joseph Kony had caused irreparable harm to the people of the Acholi region, through abduction of young people, senseless killing and maiming, and destruction of villages. But when he began his campaign he enjoyed a measure of support because of the neglect and hostility that the Museveni government had directed toward a region of the country where it received few votes. As the LRA insurgency turned more violent, government countermeasures returned tit for tat, committing the same crimes of kidnapping, rape, and murder that they claimed to be preventing. The slightest suspicion of having sheltered or aided the rebels was sufficient grounds for government troops to destroy a village. Many Acholi people came to see the government's campaign against the LRA as motivated in part by the desire to punish the Acholi for voting for the opposition party.

The video's depiction of Ugandans as passive victims waiting for foreign soldiers to rescue them was even more starkly at odds with the accounts I heard from local residents. In particular, I learned that the religious and cultural leaders of northern Uganda, far from standing by helplessly as the LRA carried on its reign of terror, had worked persistently and effectively to bring about the withdrawal of the LRA from Uganda. These efforts, which were evidently invisible to the Invisible Children organization, had been an essential catalyst for the complex negotiations that had led the LRA to disband and withdraw from Uganda in 2006, six years before the release of the video.

The most remarkable story I heard, on each of my visits, was that of a group of Christian and Muslim leaders who came together in 1997, at a time of escalating violence when all previous efforts at negotiation had collapsed in failure, in order to advocate for a resolution of the conflict and assist those whose lives had been disrupted by a decade of civil war.

The ARLPI, I learned, had brought together religious communities that had seldom cooperated in any way in the past. Throughout the ensuing years, they had worked to spread awareness of the conflict in the rest of Uganda and abroad, while providing assistance to those most affected by its disruption of family life and livelihood. Even more remarkable, the leaders of the group had arranged to meet—usually in secret in undisclosed locations, putting themselves at great risk—with representatives of the Ugandan armed forces and with LRA representatives. At these meetings the religious leaders had pressed all sides to come to the negotiating table, in order to state their objectives and then arrive at terms on which the war would come to an end and all the combatants would lay down their arms.

My goal in this book is to share the story, far too little known outside Uganda, of this remarkable and courageous venture in interfaith activism in the face of unimaginable disruption and suffering. By describing the work of ARLPI, I hope to show that it is a model that deserves the attention, and the emulation, of peace activists and members of religious communities in the developed world.

An Account of Life During and After LRA Captivity

The vivid but incomplete picture presented in "Kony 2012" needs to be supplemented and corrected by the voices of Ugandans who lived through the conflict and who still bear its scars. I had the opportunity to hear many such voices on my visits to the north. They will be cited in the chapters that follow. In order to set the background I will close this chapter with two first-hand accounts of individuals who were caught up in the conflict. The first is a portion of the transcript of one of the interviews I conducted—a sort of video clip on paper. The second, a story that coincides in part with the first, is drawn from a published account.

In January 2014 I was able to talk at length with "Patience," a young woman who was abducted and forced to be the sexual partner of an LRA officer. Younger herself than some of his children by other wives, she bore him two children in the bush. She agreed to speak with me about her experiences living in a rebel camp and her subsequent life in the town of Gulu. Uniquely among all of those whom I interviewed, she asked that I avoid using her real name, so I have given her the name Patience, a common name in East Africa and a very appropriate one for someone who has endured what she has endured.

Patience met me in the garden outside a church agency, with her two-year-old son on her hip. Appearing to be in her thirties, she was shy in demeanor. She was neatly dressed in an embroidered ivory blouse and a dark skirt that reached to her ankles, over a pair of sandals. The only colorful element in her attire was a bright red embroidered head wrap. After greeting me in English, in a very soft and hesitant voice, she asked that we continue in her language. Sister Lucy Akello translated our conversation in alternating English and Acholi. [2]

Looking at the infant cradled in her arms, I asked whether she has other children. Below is the conversation that followed.

Patience: Yes, I have four. The first two I had while in captivity and their father has remained in the bush. For the last two I am living with their father.

David: Patience, tell me about your experiences. How did you come to be taken into the insurgency? How did you come to be abducted?

Patience: I was abducted from the Catholic Mission. At that time my father used to work for the sisters. There were no camps yet. They could not find many people in the villages and so the rebels moved long distances and came to Pader trading center. They came and entered into the sisters' gate and abducted us from there. They told us that they don't want older girls, because the older girls are not healthy. I was 12 at the time of abduction.

Lucy: How long did you stay in captivity?

Patience: I was in captivity for seven years.

David: Were you forced to marry someone who was an officer?

Patience: Yes. He was one of the bodyguards of Kony.

David: How old was the man you were forced to marry?

Patience: He was an old person. He already had three wives and each one of them had grown-up children. Some of their children were older than me.

Lucy: How old were you then?

Patience: I was 13 years old.

David: Was Kony someone who deserved to be respected?

Patience: Kony has some spirits guiding him, because when he says something it happens exactly the way he has said it.

David: How did the captivity end?

Patience: I escaped.

Lucy: Was it during an attack?

Patience: Yes, there was an attack while we were in Kitgum. It was in 2000.

David: Did you find some of your siblings when you returned home?

Patience: I found one of my brothers had died, but others were there.

David: When you escaped from the rebel group, were you able to take your children with you?

Patience: I escaped with one child. The other child was with another girl who was staying in another house. When that group escaped, she came along with the second child. The child was taken to a World Vision reception center. I was in the GUSCO resettlement center in Gulu.[3] We were informed that some children had returned but their mothers were not known – that is what I kept hearing. Then one day I went to check and I found that one of them was my child.

David: How did you come to meet your current husband?

Patience: I was working in Lacor hospital as a maid, taking care of the child of one of the medical doctors. My husband was working in the hospital's carpentry workshop, and there we met.

David: Do you have all of your children now, living with you and your husband?

Patience: They are with him, and he takes good care of them.

David: Patience, when you were in the bush, did you have confidence that God would still care for you?

Patience: I had hope, because I kept receiving encouragement from other people who had stayed longer in captivity. They told me I should love prayers because God is in charge of every situation. There is nothing beyond Him.

They also told me that if my mother who has remained at home trusts in witchcraft then I would not survive, but I would be killed. But if she also loves prayer, then God would protect me, and one day I would escape and go back home. So I kept on praying while trusting that one day I would be back home. And here I am.

I kept hopeful and kept praying, because my parents married in the church and they are prayerful people. They have been living a good life. That was the best option I could take. I continued to pray because I wanted to continue with the good life my parents were living. If they are praying for me, then I too need to pray for myself.

David: Patience, when I go back, what message would you like me to take to the people of America?

Patience: The message you should take is that they should continue praying. Because when I was in the bush, I know many people prayed for me and for other people I was with in the bush. I know the Catholics prayed so much, not only from here but all over the world. And their prayers have worked. They should continue to pray for us who are back home, but also for those who are still in the bush to find ways to return home.

David: Thank you so much for sharing with us. We know you went through very difficult times but also I know you have been courageous.

Patience: I am grateful that you have come and listened to my stories, and I am grateful to my husband for having accepted those other two children I bore during my captivity. He does not make any difference between them and the two younger ones. I am really grateful because on my own, I could not really manage. He knows they are not his children, but he takes care of them well. Please support me in your prayers. ("Patience" 2014)

As Patience told her story I pondered how important it is to share her story with others around the world, a story that takes us from abduction, through years of sexual slavery, to escape and the start of a new life. In her narrative there was a great deal of sadness—a few times she needed to pause to recover her composure, and so did Sister Lucy and I—but no bitterness. Her determination to move on with her life, and her husband's unconditional support for Patience and her two children, show how much good can come from evil.

A second voice that comes from inside northern Uganda is that of Angelina Atyam, the mother of a 14-year-old girl abducted from her school near Lira in 1996. She became a leading voice for the parents of the abducted, forming a Concerned Parents Association that appealed to LRA leaders to release their captives and negotiate a settlement. On learning that her daughter had been assigned as a "wife" to a rebel commander, she tracked down the commander's mother and pleaded with her to intervene. She recounted in an interview with theologian and peace scholar Emmanuel Katangole the message that she wanted to convey.

> I went to this mother and I told her, "I am here to tell you that I have forgiven your son who is holding my daughter hostage. I have forgiven your clan, because I need to be free inside. I have also forgiven your tribe. And I want you to be free with me." She didn't find it very easy, but in the end we embraced, and we were reconciled. I felt like a very heavy weight was lifted from my soul, from my heart, so that I could go back and pray and call upon God and tell him what I want from him.

Atyam's public demand for the release of LRA abductees, and the attention she received from national and international media, persuaded an LRA commander to offer her a deal, eight months after her daughter's abduction: stop your campaign against the LRA, he said through an intermediary, and then we will release your daughter. She countered with a demand that all the girls from St. Mary's School be freed, but that demand was refused. She told Katangole, several years later:

> Getting my child back would be absolutely wonderful, but if I accepted the offer, I would be turning my back on all the other families. I'd destroy the new community spirit we had created— the hope of getting all the boys and girls back. (Katongole 2011, 157–158)

In this study I will not focus on individual stories from captivity like that of Patience and Angelina, but rather on the historical roots of the northern Uganda conflict and the work of courageous individuals and groups in bringing peace and reconciliation. I hope that by doing so I will be able to convey something of the hope and the faith that sustained the people of the region and at last brought an end to the civil war. But I cannot hope to equal the simple eloquence with which one young mother told me the story of her life.

Notes

1. In second place was a 2014 appeal to Pakistan to release Iraqi border guards who had been taken captive, with nearly 400,000 signatures. In third place: a protest against a referee's call in the 2016 volleyball match between Thailand and Japan.
2. All other interviews were recorded and transcribed by me or by my student assistant Seth Hamrick, but I am very grateful to Sister Lucy Dora Akello for providing translation during the interview and later providing me with an English version of the bilingual interview transcript.
3. Gulu United to Save the Children Organization (GUSCO) is a nongovernmental organization that provided assistance and housing to returning abductees.

2

From Kingdoms to Protectorate to New Nation

The same afternoon I addressed the chief and his followers, discussing the possibility of growing cotton in their district. I pointed out that thus they could provide the people with the means to pay their taxes and to purchase the various articles that were displayed in the little shop. . . . A local man named Arun stood up and stated: "Bwana, we don't like the white man. He brings much trouble to our country, he makes us work, and everyone knows that work is for women, not men. He prevents us, who are strong and powerful, from taking the women and cattle of the Lugbari, our neighbors."

—J. R. P. Postlethwaite, on his visit to Gulu in 1913
(Cisternino 2004, 403)

IN THE OPENING CHAPTER we took note of two divergent perspectives on Africa in the eyes of Europeans: as a continent ripe for hunting, mining, and preaching, in the eyes of European visitors of the late 19th century; and as a battleground between a rebel warlord who is the embodiment of evil, on one side, and American activists and soldiers on the other side uniquely equipped to rescue them, in the early 21st century. The second picture has been deeply instilled in popular awareness by online videos, news accounts, and campaigns by advocacy groups in the United States. Many more Americans today could name the leader of the LRA than would be able to name any of Uganda's presidents, with the possible exception of the infamous Idi Amin.

The purpose of this study is to tell three interlocked stories. The first is that of the rise of the LRA in northern Uganda and its domination of the region for decades; the second is that of the formation of an extraordinary interfaith activist organization to help counter its depredations, hasten its withdrawal, and rebuild communities thereafter. To these two stories we will turn in the chapters that follow.

But first we need tell a third story to set the background for the emergence of the LRA rebel movement—and allowed its conflict with the Ugandan government to drag on unresolved for more than two decades. The circumstances that gave rise to this civil war are embedded in the history of Uganda as a nation, and of the Great Lakes region of East Africa from the time when it was divided among African kingdoms through the colonial period. In this chapter, therefore, we will review the history of northern Uganda against the background of East African history. The story told here will be familiar to students of African history and politics. Still, a brief overview of the decades and the centuries prior to Joseph Kony's rise is an essential corrective to simplistic explanations of the conflict as simply an outgrowth of ethnic rivalry and misguided religious zeal.[1]

The story of modern Uganda is more complex than it appears to most outside observers, and after reviewing some of its principal stages we will also be better able to understand the remarkable joint initiative of Catholic, Protestant, and Muslim leaders and their communities in response to LRA violence. Certainly there is some truth in the widespread view of East Africa as a zone of bitter ethnic conflict and political opportunism. But there are other truths, no less important but far less visible, that need to be set alongside the tales of terror and tragedy.

We have taken note of some European perceptions of Africa in the 19th century in the first chapter. From the period of the first European contact into the 20th century, we find evidence of two diametrically opposed perspectives on the continent, neither of them well grounded in careful observations. Many early explorers brought home dire accounts of the savagery and bloodthirstiness of traditional governance and intertribal warfare. The people of Africa suffered greatly from the cruel oppression of their traditional chiefs, they reported, and they had resigned themselves fatalistically to the vagaries of traditional deities.

They urgently needed the knowledge and the civilized ways that only benevolent missionaries and colonists could provide to them.

In reaction to such self-serving and racist distortions, others in the precolonial period found in Africa an Eden of peaceful harmony with nature, in which the spirit of humanity and the spirits of animals and trees helped and respected each other. Until unprincipled outsiders introduced them to distilled spirits, guns, and foreign diseases, according to this story, Africans lived a life of happy isolation in their idyllic rural villages. This was, of course, a romantic fantasy no more accurate than the falsehoods it sought to counter. Yet, to the present day, both this overly rosy picture and the pessimistic account of a land of savages are echoed in the reports of visitors.

The quotation from an Anglican missionary of the mid-19th century that opened this chapter gives us still another picture of how African peoples and societies appeared to European visitors, one that is utterly blind to the observer's own biases. Writing of his visit to Gulu, later to be at the center of the LRA conflict, the Rev. Postlethwaite informs his friends and supporters that, moved by concern for the welfare of the indigenous people, he urged them to grow cotton. They would benefit from this, he adds—not because they could then produce finished cloth (that was a task for the mills in Manchester) but because they could then pay their taxes from the income. His suggestion received a cool response, however. The natives did not appreciate being taxed by their colonizers, nor were they willing to give up the practice of cattle raids. Moreover—so writes this observer—they were horrified at thought that men as well as women should do productive work each day. The Acholi people, by his account, are not only ignorant and poor but also indolent and prone to thievery. The visitor's proclamation that he seeks only to help the Acholi people rings rather hollow.

In the late 19th century the *khedive* of Egypt, the vice-regent of Turkey, appointed a British governor, Samuel White Baker, to administer its territories in northern Uganda. After his first visit to the region Baker wrote that "human nature in its crudest state as pictured among the African savages is quite on a level with the brute, and not to be compared with the noble character of the dog." His contemporary, explorer John Hanning Speke, bemoaned the "dreadful sloth" of the peoples on the northern shore of Lake Victoria. But Speke dreamed of the day when "a few scores of Europeans" would bring the benefits of an advanced civilization. Then, he hoped, "the present nakedness of the land would have a covering, and industry and commerce would clear the way for civilization and enlightenment" (quoted in Finnström 2008, 30, 58).

Examples could easily be multiplied of European prejudices confirmed by the reports sent home by visitors to East Africa. Both those who saw before them a land of unrelieved darkness and violence and those who found an unspoiled Eden were viewing Africans through the lenses of their preconceptions and fantasies. Leaving these distortions aside, I will offer a brief overview of the history of the region and the ways in which it set the stage for the LRA conflict that arose in the 1980s. To understand that movement we need to review earlier political and ethnic identities as they came into play when the nation of Uganda emerged from British East Africa.

While under British control, Uganda was never designated a colony. It was a protectorate, a territory over which British governors exercised political and economic control more through indigenous proxies than through direct governance. In the protectorate of Buganda, unlike the colony (now the nation of Kenya) to the east, traditional authorities were given a prominent place and an influential role. The *kabaka*, king of the Baganda people who make up the majority of inhabitants of central Uganda, retained his palace, his authority over tribal lands, his public standing, and many of his powers under British rule, even while legislative and judicial authority were transferred to the Crown and its representatives.

An important distinction between colony and protectorate had to do with the rights granted to European expatriates. In Kenya a large settler community was established in the early 20th century, concentrated in the higher elevations around the railroad junction hamlet of Nairobi and on the banks of the Rift Valley to the west. Kenya attracted many Britons seeking either escape from family or financial troubles at home or an opportunity to experience the challenges, and reap the rewards, of living in a distant outpost of the Empire. Amid their tea plantations and vegetable and flower farms, they toasted each other on their spacious verandas while African kitchen and household staff waited on them. Thanks to the mid-century memoirs and novels of

Beryl Markham, Isak Denisen (the pen name of Karen Blixen), and Elspeth Huxley, the "Happy Valley" culture of East African settlements came to represent for many readers back home an idyllic escape from the drabness of English life.

Not all was happy in the Rift Valley, however. British policies granted prime agricultural land to new immigrants, removing Kikuyu farmers to reserves with far poorer soil and few means of transporting crops to market. This policy fueled resentments that exploded in the anti-settler violence of the Mau Mau movement—and the equally brutal British efforts to defeat the rebels. Government records of this dark period in African colonial history were kept hidden from public view for half a century after its end, until scholars were at last permitted an uncensored look at both Kikuyu and British actions. One of the leading historians of the Mau Mau period, David Anderson, has described the conflict as "a story of atrocity and excess on both sides, a dirty war from which no one emerged with much pride, and certainly no glory" (Anderson 2005, 2). An earlier account, fictionalized but revealing of the deep divisions created in the Kikuyu community by this war, has been provided by novelist Ngugi wa'Thiongo in *A Grain of Wheat* (wa'Thiongo 1967).

In the neighboring protectorate, on the other hand, settlers were not welcome. Immigrants from Britain, elsewhere in Europe, and India traveled and traded freely, and some remained and raised families in the protectorate. But British policies prohibited them from buying land. The settler communities of Kenya could not exist in Uganda.

Ethnic conflicts had been a factor in the history of the region long before European contact. Rivalry between traditional kingdoms, and between the ethnic groups that compose them, had waxed and waned for many centuries, here as elsewhere in the continent—and indeed in Europe and North America in comparable periods of their histories. Yet the dawn of independence in Uganda was comparatively peaceful.

There were storms on the horizon, however. Few nations in Africa, or anywhere else, have suffered under as long a succession of brutal autocrats as has Uganda. The most notorious of them, Idi Amin, remains a household name around the world. But he was neither the first nor the last Ugandan president to subordinate the state to his personal ambitions and fantasies. We will review the post-independence history of Uganda later in this chapter.

Before doing so, it will be helpful in understanding the rise of the LRA and the formation of ARLPI to take brief note of two distinctive features of the early history of this region of East Africa that have shaped contemporary political and cultural life: the regional dominance of the Buganda Kingdom and the East African slave trade. Both provide important clues to the challenges that face the nation of Uganda today.

Early Settlements and Kingdoms

Long before European contact, the region that is today the nation of Uganda was divided among several ethnic groups, some of them organized into large royal states. Of special importance to later developments was its location in a zone of transition between two broad population groups: the Bantu-speaking agriculturalists, whose origins lay in West Africa, and the pastoralists and hunters who dominate regions to the north and whose languages are part of the Nilotic family.

Linguistic and cultural evidence indicates that the Bantu peoples of Africa spread outward from West Africa through much of the continent in the late first and early second millennium of the European calendar, reaching all the way to its southern tip. The largest population groups of South Africa—Zulu, Shona, and Xhosa—belong to the Bantu family, though their languages borrowed from the language of the Khoi-San hunter-gatherers whom they displaced. This massive population movement from west to east and south is remembered in many oral tales and poetry, in the absence of written records.

The first Bantu settlement in what is now the nation of Uganda, on the evidence of oral traditions, was the Bacwezi kingdom, under its ruler Ndahura. They occupied the entire region between the Great Lakes and established a pastoralist economy, grazing their cattle on the grasslands. Pottery fragments from archeological sites give evidence of a distinctive material culture, but other sources of information are so scarce that some regard the Bacwezi as fictional rather than historical forebears. Better documented in historical records is the Luo group who appear to have displaced the Bacwezi, moving into Uganda from the north. In the 15th century they established what historians call the Bunyoro-Kitara kingdom. These newcomers too were pastoralists, not agriculturalists. They dominated the region for several centuries before European explorers began to arrive (Posnansky 1963).

Another Bantu kingdom, the Buganda, established settlements on the shores of Lake Victoria, where they carried on subsistence agriculture.[2] A major crop was the banana, first cultivated in Southeast Asia and the South Pacific and soon dispersed to tropical regions around the world. By about 1000 CE the banana, mashed into *matoke,* had become the major staple food of the region—a rare example of a food culture based not on a grain or a tuber but on a fruit.

Baganda society was originally organized loosely into numerous kinship groups, but, as their numbers and their influence grew, this decentralized system gave way to a royal state under the authority of the *kabaka.* Baganda lands now extended into areas formerly controlled by the Bunyoro, and the population of the kingdom had grown to an estimated one million subjects by the early 19th century.

During the period of Bantu migration and settlement, Nilotic-speaking peoples were also migrating southward into the region, probably drawn by a search for pasture and hunting grounds in periods of drought. Down to the present, the population of Uganda can be roughly classified into Bantu groups, mostly in the south, and Nilotic peoples, mostly in the north, although internal migration and intermarriage have made the boundaries loose and porous.

The differences between these two broad groups were physiological and cultural as well as linguistic. Nilotic-speaking peoples were on average taller and darker than their Bantu-speaking neighbors, their economy built on hunting and herding rather than agriculture. Although some groups of Nilotic origin eventually became large kingdoms under a traditional king and his court, most held to a more decentralized and kinship-based mode of social and political organization. Competition and conflict were inevitable between what a historian has called the "centralized kingdoms found primarily in southern and western Uganda," such as Buganda and Bunyoro, and the "decentralized societies" of the north and east (Lambright 2011, 20). The seeds of tension and mistrust between northern and southern population groups—which, as we will see, fueled the rise of the LRA—had already been planted many centuries before European explorers made their first forays from the coast to the interior.[3]

Explorers who brought reports of the region back to Europe often characterized all of the indigenous groups that they encountered as "native kingdoms," but the various groups who competed for territory differed considerably in their mode of political organization. Even among the more centralized groups, marked differences emerged: the Hima state was rigidly hierarchical, with a pastoralist elite dominating an agriculturalist majority, while the Bunyoro were ruled by a hereditary clan, princes succeeding their royal fathers.

Among the Baganda, in their ever-growing territory, a centralized royal state was established, with an unusual system for royal succession that provided more flexibility and was less prone to conflict than most such systems. In many other African traditions, and in most monarchies elsewhere in the world, royal succession proceeds directly from a king to one of his sons, if there is one who is of age. The result may be bitter conflict over who is best qualified—or the coronation of someone unsuited to wear the crown.

In the Buganda kingdom, each newly crowned *kabaka* is selected by a lottery among all the major clans, who are identified by matrilineal links. This practice dates from the rule of Prince Kimera, in the 15th century, who took an unusual step to forestall future succession controversies: he married women from all the major Baganda clans except his own. Since each of the *kabaka's* wives is descended from a different mother in the royal line, all of his sons are princes of royal blood. Each belongs to his mother's clan, none to that of the ruling king. On the death of the king, the elders of all the clans select a successor by lot from among these princes. Thus no clan can retain its leading position for two successive generations, as the clan of the king.

The Baganda kings built a powerful army, and they built roads for access to newly conquered lands from which they collected taxes. By the time Henry M. Stanley reached Buganda in 1875, the kingdom's boundaries encompassed most of what is now Uganda. Stanley witnessed a military expedition to the east, with an army that he estimated at 125,000, and he counted 250 Baganda war canoes in Lake Victoria standing ready to serve as naval support (Library of Congress 1992, 6–10).

Throughout this period the peoples residing north of the Nile—the Victoria Nile, in modern nomenclature—had little contact with the more centralized kingdoms to the south. The Acholi people, hunters and gatherers, lived in local kinship groups, which established alliances and selected regional chiefs. But no central authority rose up to dominate the region, nor were any of the major ethnic groups organized as royal kingdoms. Then as now, the region was more sparsely populated than the south. Then as now, too, the Baganda were the largest and most powerful of the ethnic groups in the region.

Governors, Slavers and a Railroad in the Interior

Early European explorers who ventured into the interior of East Africa brought back colorful reports of their encounters with native authorities. Some kings and paramount chiefs welcomed them warmly and threw week-long celebratory feasts. Others were suspicious and resentful and refused to feed or house the uninvited intruders. In their wake, in the second half of the 19th century, only a few British, French and German merchants followed. They established no permanent European settlements in the interior.

Samuel White Baker, quoted above, arrived in 1869. Already recognized by the Royal Geographical Society and by the queen for his earlier explorations of the African interior, he was dispatched by *Khedive* Ismail of Egypt to drive the slave traders from the region of southern Sudan and northern Uganda, then under Egyptian and British control. Baker established the Province of Equatoria and served as its first governor general. A colorful figure, a renowned big-game hunter and anti-slavery crusader, Sir Samuel relished his life as aristocrat of the bush.

Many years earlier, captivated by the sight of a woman in a market near Bucharest where white slaves were offered for sale by Ottoman merchants, Baker had tried to purchase her. When he was outbid by the Pasha of Vidin, he had a backup plan: he bribed her guards and abducted her, promising to marry her when they reached England. At any rate this is the story he told, with relish, to shocked audiences back home. Florence proved a most unusual governor's wife, joining her husband in his hunting expeditions with pistols strapped to her waist. Because of their scandalous past, Queen Victoria refused to admit

Sir Samuel and Lady Florence to her royal presence when she named Samuel a Knight Commander of the Bath (Wilson 2004).

Much of our information about this period comes from the meticulous reports filed with mission societies, in whose eyes Baker was a baneful influence, a playboy and adventurer who proclaimed himself a freethinker. Nor did he harbor any scruples about enlisting the aid of armed mercenaries to serve British interests. All the same, with the support of the *khedive*, he was determined to destroy the slave trade in Equatoria. Slave traders were arrested, slave camps broken up, and slaves found in captivity released and allowed to return to their communities. "Love cannot exist with slavery," he declared: "the mind becomes brutalized to an extent that freezes all those tender feelings that Nature has implanted in the human heart to separate it from the beasts" (Cisternino 2004, 44). This moral conviction seems to have come to him late in life: Baker's father had amassed great wealth in the slave trade in Jamaica, and Samuel himself had used slave labor on his own farms in Mauritius and Ceylon.

Slavery was by no means a recent development in East Africa. On the contrary, as in traditional societies around the globe, it had been a common practice since earliest times. Men and women might become slaves when their clan or village was defeated in war, when they fell into debt, or when a stain on a family's honor required compensation in the form of a slave boy or girl. Slavery might be a penalty imposed for a limited time or a permanent condition. In traditional slavery, in many regions of Africa, slaves could marry and bear children who did not inherit their parents' status. One historian argues that "Africa has had in its history a wider variety of servile relationships than anywhere else," with some serving as domestic servants, others as dockhands, others as concubines, others as agricultural workers and fishermen (Kollman 2005, 43).

In contrast to the many varieties of indigenous servitude, the commercial slave trade introduced a new system, an extractive form of "chattel slavery," to East Africa, similar to the system of enslaved plantation labor that sustained the triangular trade between Europe, West Africa, and the New World. This form of slavery had begun in East Africa far earlier than the Western trade: it is mentioned, as a practice already long established, in a Greek source from the first century

CE. From the beginning, traveling Arab merchants dominated the slave transport routes, while Turkish traders also played a role in the trade along the Nile (Cisternino 2004, 9).

Arab colonization of the region along the Swahili Coast and in the interior increased the demand for slaves, both for domestic service and as impressed soldiers. Slave armies of captured Africans were maintained in Iraq in the 9th century and in India in the 15th. Two African slave soldiers were even appointed as rulers of the kingdom of Bengal in the late 15th century. African slaves were exported far beyond the Middle East, as far as the East Indies and China. In duration and in scope, the East African slave trade dwarfed the trade with the New World. It is estimated that, during the past twelve centuries, 28 million slaves were captured and sold from East Africa, compared with approximately 11 million caught up in the West African trade (Coupland 1939, in McEwan 1968).

European merchants and their West African agents enslaved and exported far more men than women, consigned to hard agricultural labor on the plantations of North and South America and the Caribbean. Demand in the Middle East, on the other hand, was far greater for women who would serve as enslaved domestic workers and as concubines. Many of the male slaves taken from East Africa to the Middle East were castrated, to make them more tractable and to fetch the higher price that buyers were willing to pay for eunuchs as household slaves. This cruel practice is not documented as a common one in the West African slave trade.

Since there was a far smaller European presence in East Africa than in West Africa, reports of the Arab slave trade seldom came to the attention of Western reformers and abolitionists. Among slaves from the region there was no individual like Olaudah Equiano (the freed West African whose narrative captivated British readers in the late 18th century) to tell the story of East African slavery to a broad reading public. Moreover, the transportation routes for slaves—down the Nile, along the Swahili Coast, and along inland trade routes between Ethiopia and the Arabian region—were little used by outsiders. Traders from the Middle East developed close commercial relationships with the sultan of Zanzibar, and their consortium dominated the coastal trade (Cisternino 2004, 9). Very few Europeans visited East Africa, and even fewer settled there, nor were there established trade routes with the nations that would eventually colonize most of the continent.

Even while Britain's official representatives carried out a highly public campaign in the early 19th century for the eradication of the evils of slavery, others in the service of the Crown were quietly profiting from the trade, buying and selling ivory that was transported to the coast by slaves. Both the ivory and the porters were offered for sale at the ports. On one occasion, too, a "ship full of brigands" trading in ivory and slaves was observed in an Egyptian port under an American flag. Evidently the principled opposition of British and American authorities to the evils of slavery was not always strictly applied in practice (Cisternino 2004, 42).

Mortality among captured slaves was shockingly high in the East African trade. About 90 percent of West African slaves survived the Middle Passage, but only about 20 percent of East African slaves reached the slave markets of the Middle East alive. The highest rate of mortality occurred in the slaves' forced march from the interior to the coast, a journey that often took several months. Contemporary observers, including explorers and missionaries, describe the harrowing sight of bodies littering the main routes to the coast. Some of the captives had been executed for insubordination, others simply left to die when they became ill.

David Livingstone and other travelers estimated that for every slave safely delivered to Zanzibar for transfer by sea to buyers in the Middle East—numbering as many as 35,000 men and women each year—four or five others had died along the way (Shorter 2006, 63). In one of his last diary entries, Livingstone wrote that "the sights I have seen, though common incidents of the traffic, are so nauseous that I always strive to drive them from memory" (Coupland 1939, in McEwan 1968, 204–205).

In the late 19th century in what is now northern Uganda, slave traders began taking enormous numbers of male captives to serve as impressed soldiers for warring factions to the north. Oral histories collected by anthropologists in the West Nile region, adjacent to the center of the LRA conflict, described frequent raids by Sudanese warlords' agents.

The captured slaves were tied together by their necks and taken into the Sudan. To help them identify their run-away slaves, the Arabs

marked their captures' cheeks by making three deep vertical cuts on
each cheek. The slaves walked the whole distance to the Sudan and
were forced to carry heavy loads including ivory. However, children
were allowed to ride cattle as they were too young to walk such a long
distance. Any slave who became too weak to continue the journey
was either left in the wilderness to die a slow death or was shot down.
(Geria 1973, 80–81, cited in Leopold 2006)

In 1900, out of a total population of five million in Sudan, slaves
accounted for as many as one million. Slave soldiers of Nubian
ethnicity—whose three incised facial lines earned them the nickname
"one-elevens"—served in the armies of the independent Sudanese
kingdoms of Darfur, Sennar, and Tegali, and also in the Egyptian army.
Lent to allies throughout the eastern Mediterranean, they fought in regional conflicts in Syria, Greece, Tanganyika, and as far away as Mexico
(Leopold 2006).

Several decades earlier, Sir Samuel Baker had undertaken to drive
all the slave traders out of the regions north of Lake Victoria and put
an end to the practice that—after enjoying its economic benefits in
his early life—he had come to despise. His successor as governor was
another Englishman, Colonel Charles George Gordon. Gordon continued Baker's anti-slavery efforts while also seeking to expand trade
networks and enhance British control in the region. But his efforts had
little effect, and he soon resigned his post and returned home. The
two governors' hopes for the abolition of slavery, economic reform, and
better trade routes fell victim to vested economic interests and regional
conflict. Even when in 1896 Britain at last outlawed owning slaves, as
well as buying and selling them, Protestant traditional chiefs whose authority was recognized by the British under the policy of indirect rule
were permitted to retain their slaves. The capture and export of slaves
did not cease but was simply kept hidden from colonial authorities
(Shorter 2006, 69).

Yet Britain did not abandon its hope of dominating the region. A principal means by which it displaced Egyptian dominance and subjugated
the indigenous kingdoms was the movement of goods, settlers, and
soldiers along a newly constructed railway line from Mombasa on the
coast, through an isolated location that would become the regional

metropolis of Nairobi, and on to the head of the Buganda kingdom at Kampala. Lord Salisbury of Glasgow summed up the urgency of this task in an 1891 address to the British Anti-Slavery Conference:

> We now spend large sums on ships and boats to arrest the accursed slave traffic with considerable success, but also at great cost, not only to the Treasury at home, but also to the lives and health of the sailors, who under that sun have to give themselves to that tremendous labour. If we are able, instead of taking this expensive and difficult precaution, to pursue the evil to its home and kill it at its root, we shall not only have saved mankind from a fearful curse, but we shall have spared the Treasury of our own people and the lives of the gallant sailors. (Dealtry and Bentley 1892, 39)

Construction of the railway, employing large numbers of workers brought in from British-ruled India, began in 1896 and was completed in 1901. Even before its completion the line was used to transport disassembled steamers for use on Lake Victoria. A 110-ton ship, reassembled following the instructions of its Scottish builders, began carrying passengers and goods on the inland lake in 1898. The bold investment achieved its purposes effectively: by the early 20th century British settlers had begun farming on the Kenyan highlands, the colonial authority of the British in the region was undisputed, and slavery had been nearly eliminated, apart from small and secret networks that persisted for decades and, by some accounts, down to the present.

The episodes briefly recounted here—of British explorers and governors, of the history of slavery, and of the building of a rail line— had a profound influence on the communities and people of northern Uganda that can still be discerned when we turn to the events of the 1980s and later. Clashes between rival warlords across the Sudanese border continue to claim thousands of lives, and they frequently spill over into Uganda. Shifting alliances and rivalries between British, French, German, Egyptian, and Sudanese agents persisted for many decades, although Germany's colonies were dealt out to other European powers after its defeat in 1918. Moreover, even as the new railroad secured British control over the region to the north and to the east of Lake Victoria, its route from the coast to the Buganda kingdom, but no farther, entrenched Baganda domination of the new protectorate. The communities farther to the north had less access to trade networks, benefited less from British infrastructure investment, and found themselves in many ways treated as outsiders rather than full participants in the new political and economic order. As we will see, this was one of the factors that contributed to the alienation of the north from the south and helped to facilitate the rise of rebel movements such as the LRA in the 1980s.

"Indirect Rule" in the New British Protectorate

British control over what is now Uganda was initially established through the British East Africa Company in the 1880s, but within a decade the company surrendered its control to a newly established British Protectorate of Uganda, encompassing the territory of the Baganda kingdom north of the lake. Fierce conflicts broke out between Protestant and Catholic communities, aligned respectively with the British and the French governments, as will be described in the brief account of Uganda's religious history in Chapter 4. British victory over the French was secured by an alliance with the Buganda *kabaka,* assisted by Nubian mercenary soldiers.

The designation of Uganda as a protectorate, not a British colony, implied a greater degree of shared governance than in neighboring Kenya, as well as a prohibition on land ownership or permanent settlement by Europeans. The Buganda kingdom was rewarded for its loyalty with expanded territory and a recognition of the royal status of the *kabaka.* Protectorate status remained in place until independence in 1962 (Commonwealth Secretariat 2017).

The policy of "indirect rule" was a key to Britain's success in establishing hegemony across large portions of the African continent, in West Africa and Southern Africa no less than in Kenya and Uganda. Rather than appoint local authorities to replace traditional authorities, Queen Victoria's representatives sought out local chiefs and elders who already enjoyed the respect of their communities and deputized them as agents of British rule. Local customs were permitted to continue, so long as they did not undermine colonial authority or directly contravene what the colonizers regarded as universal and non-negotiable moral imperatives. The *kabaka* could keep as many wives in the royal compound as he wished, for example; but the traditional practice of capturing strangers along the roadside and sacrificing them to hasten the king's recovery from illness would no longer be tolerated.

When conflict erupted into war between British colonizers and African communities, as it did from time to time in most of the regions under British control, the sparks igniting the conflict were often conflicting claims on resources and land. In theory, the policy of indirect rule provided a means of mediating such disputes and arriving at a mutually acceptable resolution. In practice, this frequently broke down. Across the continent in the Gold Coast Colony, now the nation of Ghana, Britain's demands for gold in tribute from the Asante court and its insistence on free passage for British soldiers and traders led to a series of battles in the last decades of the 19th century. They ended in British victory and exile for the Asante king and queen.

In South Africa, during the same period, conflict between the Zulu kingdom, the Dutch settlers who had colonized the coastal regions 200 years earlier, and the newly ascendant British authorities fueled more than a decade of bloody clashes at the end of the 19th century. British military power was brought to bear against the Dutch most decisively, and most destructively, in the Anglo–Boer War of 1899–1902, a war that introduced many features that would become characteristic of later regional conflicts around the world. Knowing they were greatly outgunned in conventional weaponry and troops, the Boers turned to guerrilla tactics, mingling with the civilian population and conducting terror attacks on civilian and military targets. The British responded with scorched-earth policies to drive Boer farmers from their lands. They also established the first modern concentration camps, in which thousands of Boer men, women, and children died from starvation and disease (Pretorius 2013).

The last decade of the 19th century and the first decade of the 20th were times of recurrent conflict in the new protectorate of Uganda and, as in South Africa, the principal antagonists were European representatives. A bloody confrontation between British and local rulers illustrates the proxy elements of colonial disputes. In 1892 Lord Frederick Lugard, a British military officer who served as governor of Hong Kong and Nigeria after his brief term in Uganda, launched a military campaign against *Kabaka* Mwanga, demanding that he declare himself a British subject and expel his Catholic advisors, who were too friendly to French interests. Distributing arms freely to Protestant civilians, Lugard's forces drove the king from his palace and, at the cost of several hundred casualties, forced the *kabaka* into submission.

The Baganda king submitted to Lugard's terms briefly but soon fled into hiding. Joined by the king and the army of the Bunyoro Kingdom, he launched a guerrilla insurrection. This brief alliance among African kings ended in their defeat and exile to the Seychelles Islands, a British territory in the Indian Ocean. Unlike the *asantehene* of the Asante, who returned home and was given some of his former authority in the Gold Coast, the Buganda and Bunyoro kings lived out their lives in exile (Cisternino 2004, 185–197).

Relations between Catholics and Protestants had long been strained, but the incident of the Uganda martyrs, recounted later in Chapter 4, had brought them together. Lugard's campaign against Catholic influence drove them apart again, igniting what one historian has called "the civil war between Catholics and Protestants" that continued well into the 20th century and was still evident in the north when Catholics and Protestants began working together to form ARLPI, over the misgivings of many parishioners and church leaders (Shorter 2006, 9).

Periodic manifestations of African resentment against European domination in the region were put down swiftly and often brutally. In nearby Tanganyika, for example, the Maji-Maji rebellion of 1905–1907 was "an explosion of African hatred towards European rule which spread to more than half the ethnic groups in the country." German colonial authorities responded with a devastating scorched-earth campaign that rendered large areas of the colony uninhabitable for decades (Shorter 2006, 33).

In the protectorate of Uganda, the period from 1910 until independence was comparatively free from large-scale conflict. The policy of indirect rule was implemented mainly through support for the *kabaka* and the Buganda court, a sharp departure from Lugard's attempt to unseat him 20 years earlier. Favoritism toward the Baganda generated resentment and criticism from other ethnic groups in the northern and southwestern regions, but this seldom issued in open defiance or civil war. The economic burdens of colonialism were lighter, too, in Uganda than in Kenya. British demands for export commodities were limited to agricultural products, and the tariffs that were demanded did not place inordinate burdens on the native population.

Cotton soon became a major export from Uganda, as in Kenya, but in the former it was produced not by settlers but by native farmers who began cultivating cash crops in addition to their traditional subsistence farming. The Baganda were especially well situated to make this change, occupying low-lying lands where cotton could flourish. Cotton exports increased exponentially: from £2,200 in 1905 to £21,000 in 1906 and to £211,000 in 1907. By 1915 tariffs from the cotton crop, now valued at nearly £2.5 million, were sufficient to replace British subsidies to the protectorate. Other crops such as sugar cane and coffee also proved profitable, and Uganda became a prosperous agricultural producer for global markets. Large farms controlled by traditional chiefs were broken up, with the assistance of British authorities, and in the decades following the first World War farming came to be dominated by independent African smallholders (Library of Congress 1992, 14).

Britain in Africa After 1945

The Second World War brought fundamental changes to the political climate in colonial Africa. Independence movements became more visible and more assertive, in the colonies and territories of France and Portugal as well as the United Kingdom, as an indirect and unanticipated result of widespread deployment of African troops to assist in the fight against Germany and Japan.

The King's African Rifles were an elite division of British forces deployed across the Pacific theater in the last years of the Second World War. Having fought alongside British and American and Australian troops, suffering casualties for a king they had never seen and a country to which they had only distant ties, the returning soldiers lobbied for an end to colonial status and recognition as independent states. Their example remains an important part of contemporary African history and local cultures. To this day, for example, Ghanaian fighters in South Asia are commemorated in the name of one of Accra's central residential districts, Burma Camp.

By 1949 Baganda residents had had enough of British price controls, British and Asian control of cotton processing, and complacent Baganda chiefs who marched to the beat of colonial drummers. Crowds of protestors burned down the houses of chiefs who cooperated with British authorities, but their rebellion was quickly quashed. Popular movements for independence from the British gained little traction and never erupted in a bloody conflict like the Mau Mau rebellion in Kenya to the east.

In Uganda, initial steps toward eventual independence were initiated by the British authorities, most notably under the oversight of a reformist governor, Sir Andrew Cohen, who was appointed in 1952. Cohen removed price controls on coffee, opened up the cotton processing industry to Africans, and established a fund to support African-initiated businesses. Without abdicating colonial authority, he also introduced direct elections of representatives to parliament from districts across Uganda.

When the governor proposed the creation of a single nation incorporating Kenya and Tanganyika as well as Uganda, however, popular support disappeared rapidly. Ugandans took note of the way in which the newly created Federation of Rhodesia and Nyasaland (now the nations of Zimbabwe, Zambia, and Malawi) had consolidated and entrenched white rule in southern Africa. They observed, too, that in response to armed resistance in neighboring Kenya, British policies had become ever more harsh and racist attitudes more prevalent. The idea of a unified British East African state, one in which Kenya was sure to be the most powerful partner, had no appeal for Ugandans.

Having abandoned the idea of a unified East African state, British governors began laying plans for nationwide elections to what would become the parliament of an independent republic. But the close alliance between Baganda and British leaders sparked fears not only in other ethnic groups but also among Catholics, both European and African, who feared that they would be shut out by the overwhelmingly Protestant British and Baganda power brokers.

Ethnic politics became deeply entwined with colonial politics in the decade before Uganda's eventual independence in 1962. The paramount Baganda chief, *kabaka* Freddie, had been viewed as a British collaborator and held in low esteem by his own people, but when he took a firm stance against unifying the three colonies he regained their respect—and the enmity of the British governor, who exiled him immediately (but only temporarily) to London.

Protracted negotiations between the Buganda kingdom and the British in the early 20th century had yielded an outcome that appeared favorable to British interests, granting control over half of the traditional territory of the kingdom. But in fact the negotiating tables were tilted strongly toward African interests: all the best agricultural land had been reserved for Baganda, while the assigned "Crown lands" consisted mostly of swamp and scrub. Negotiations undertaken in the 1950s similarly yielded provisions that appeared favorable to the British side but that actually served Baganda interests, both with respect to the colonizers and in relation to neighboring ethnic groups such as the Bunyoro and Toro. The effect was to enhance the power of the *kabaka* in shaping the politics and policies of the new nation that was on the horizon. In these instances, we see the natives playing tricks on the colonizers, not the reverse.

Baganda influence provoked pushback from other groups in the years before independence. A Lango leader from the north, Milton Obote, for example, formed a new political party, the United People's Congress (UPC), which drew support from his Lango people and other non-Baganda who feared that the *kabaka* was ready to step into the shoes of the British and exercise complete domination. Roman Catholic leaders formed another party, the Democratic Party (DP), similarly motivated by opposition to Baganda domination and also by the concern to prevent Protestant hegemony.

In March 1961, the British conducted a nationwide election in the Protectorate of Uganda to elect representatives to a provisional parliament, with the intent of cultivating leaders whose experience in governance would serve them well in a new nation. When the *kabaka* received no assurance of future Baganda autonomy, his party called for an election boycott, resulting in an upset victory for the Democratic Party. The DP convened a provisional interim government, but in the legislature it was outmaneuvered by a newly formed Baganda party, Kabaka Yekka (KY), which soundly defeated the DP in April 1962 elections immediately preceding independence (Library of Congress 1992, 19).

When the new nation's legislature convened, therefore, Baganda representatives once again held the upper hand. On being elected prime minister, the UPC's Obote fulfilled his campaign promise and rewarded the *kabaka* with the title of head of state. This post was largely ceremonial, but it served as a symbol of Baganda support for the new government.

Before turning to the first decades of independence, let us pause to take note of some significant features of Uganda's recent history that shaped its life as a nation. In the first place, Uganda's location on the interior of East Africa, with no direct access to coastal ports, provided a measure of insulation against the conflict over trade and economic control that broke out frequently in coastal areas. The Arab slave trade was a source of longstanding disruption to communities in the interior as well as along the Swahili Coast. But British efforts to drive the traders out of the territory they came to control were eventually successful. Uganda's comparative isolation thus provided some advantages in the period preceding independence.

Second, the reliable rainfall and moderate elevations of many regions of Uganda are well suited to agriculture, both for traditional crops that had been cultivated for many centuries, such as bananas and maize, and for the new cash crops such as cotton and sugar that became major sources of income to the protectorate. Where the lands to the north are far more arid, and those near the coast to the east are subject to extremes of heat and seasonal rainfall, Uganda enjoys a moderate climate. In many areas, considerable reserves of rich volcanic and alluvial soil support farming as the backbone of the Ugandan economy, down to the present day. Ugandan farmers produced more than enough to feed the local population and supplemented food crops with export crops that generated significant income for colonial masters.

Third, we can identify in the complex relationships between British colonizers and indigenous populations many of the alliances and conflicts that have surfaced in the decades since independence. The Baganda people and their *kabaka*, we have noted, gained a great deal of power and influence, at the expense of their neighbors to the north and west, under British colonial rule. The Bunyoro saw their influence diminish as their neighbors achieved domination. When the Baganda king was appointed head of state, his counterpart among the Bunyoro was shut out of power, and large tracts of Bunyoro land were seized and given to others. The peoples of northern Uganda, the Acholi and Lango to the east of the Nile and the Alur and Kakwa to the west, were largely ignored by British colonists, who seldom traveled to their homelands and saw little potential for development so far from the capital with such inadequate means of transport.

Uganda's comparative isolation and distance from potential trading partners, its favorable climate and self-sufficiency in agriculture, and its complex relationships among ethnic groups all had an effect on its history in the last decades of British rule. Uganda was less attractive than its neighbor Kenya to traders seeking quick profits from African minerals and crops, and it was off-limits to settlers. Until very late in the period of British rule it had comparatively little of value to export. Favoritism toward southern groups and neglect of northern regions were already entrenched under the British, and although this had not caused major conflicts like those that erupted in Kenya, it shaped the reception extended to Uganda's first few rulers after independence in different regions, as will be described below. Both the attitudes and the actions of the Museveni regime that came to power in 1986 in the regions north of the Nile contributed in significant ways to the rise of northern rebel movements.

Independence and Autocracy: The First Obote Regime

In 1962 the complex religious, cultural, and political gamesmanship of the late colonial period culminated in the birth of the new nation of Uganda. A long disputed British–German–Egyptian territory adjoining East Africa's Great Lakes, dominated by Great Britain from the middle 19th century and established as a British protectorate at the dawn of the 20th century, would now be self-governing, not ruled from Whitehall. The name assigned to the new country is the Swahili form of the name of its dominant ethnic group.

This was the era of liberation across the continent. The first of the newborn nations, the former Gold Coast Colony, became the nation of Ghana in 1957. Twenty-two other new nations were created in the few years preceding Ugandan independence in 1962. Kenya followed one year later, and then 11 other new nations achieved independence by 1970 (Mazrui 1993).

A striking fact about the liberation of African colonies is the persistence of boundaries drawn in faraway Berlin during the "scramble for Africa" in the 1880s, even where those lines bisected the major settlement regions of a single ethnic group. In a few instances the newly independent states realigned or consolidated. Zanzibar joined Tanganyika to form Tanzania, for example. Other nations changed their names without changing their borders. The Malagasy Republic became Madagascar, the Republic of Dahomey became the Republic of Benin, and the Republic of the Congo became Zaire and then the Democratic Republic of Congo. But the borders between them remained almost precisely where they had been drawn on crude maps of the continent in a Berlin conference room 80 years earlier.

European colonial powers remained critical trading partners and sources of support for their former colonies. Moreover, nearly all of the new nations adopted the language of their former colonial masters for use in government and public education. A noteworthy exception to this pattern occurred in East Africa in the new nation of Tanzania, where founding president Julius Nyerere sought to instill a sense of national unity by adopting the dominant African language of the coastal region, Swahili, as the sole national language.

In neighboring Kenya, the Mau Mau rebellion had ended at last, and the dawn of independence brought comparative peace and stability, if not responsible or transparent government. In Uganda the succession of events was almost reversed. The protectorate had enjoyed decades of British rule that were only occasionally interrupted by protests, never by large-scale anti-colonial rebellion. But the early decades of the new nation of Uganda were marked by recurring cycles of ethnic violence and struggles for power. Its governments were autocratic and corrupt at best, murderous and repressive at worst.

It was against this background that the Lord's Resistance Army emerged as a potent force in the 1980s, as will be described in the following chapter. The rebel movements of the 1980s in northern Uganda, we will see, reflected local grievances and particular circumstances, but their roots can be found in the tumultuous postwar governance of Uganda—and also in the benefits that some other nations derived from promoting conflict in Uganda.

In Uganda, unlike many other new nations in Africa, no dominant anti-colonialist party waited in the wings to assume control after independence. Instead, several parties, reflecting longstanding ethnic and religious divisions, each sought to gain the upper hand. Achieving dominance was difficult, maintaining it even more so. Milton Obote's Uganda People's Congress and the Baganda party Kabaka Yekka succeeded in shutting out the Democratic Party, which just one year earlier had held a parliamentary majority. This "fragile alliance of two fragile parties" proved sturdy enough to be the foundation for Obote to build a highly centralized and autocratic state (Library of Congress 1992, 21).

President Obote's path from precarious leadership of a fractious coalition to autocratic and nearly unlimited power was complex and required delicate balancing of the demands of various supporting factions. To satisfy the KY allies of the *kabaka,* we have noted, Obote named him head of state, an illustrious-sounding but largely ceremonial post. That led to demands from the Bunyoro and Iteso groups to bestow a high political office on their respective kings as well—even though the latter had never previously had a king.

Obote offered limited concessions to these centrifugal political forces when it was politically necessary, but his primary goal was enhancing UPC domination. He created no more heads of state, but he won Bunyoro support by restoring their control over the "lost counties" that the British had ceded to the Baganda many decades earlier. Himself a Northerner, Obote consolidated and extended his control by expanding the Ugandan military, recruiting mainly from northern groups such as the Acholi, Lango, Kakwa and Lugbara. Favors and promotions given to officers from these groups helped solidify northern support for the UPC. The divisions that were exploited in this policy have colonial roots, writes Margaret Angucia:

> The divide and rule policy of the British pitted the economically and politically powerful southerners, the Baganda, against

the northerners, who then found consolation in joining the military. . . Obote capitalized on these differences and consolidated his government on the strength of an army whose personnel mainly came from the northern ethnic groups. (Angucia 2010, 13)

By 1966, the composition of Parliament had tilted dramatically in Obote's direction: his party now held 74 seats, compared to just eight each for DP and KY. Among the Prime Minister's closest associates, one rose to a position of considerable influence—and later notoriety. This was Ida Amin Dada, a member of the Kakwa ethnic group in the West Nile region, who had distinguished himself while serving in the King's African Rifles in both Kenya and Uganda.

As a colonel in the Ugandan army, Amin unintentionally placed himself at the center of a bitter controversy over Obote foreign policy in 1966 when he presented a gold bar worth £217,000, bearing the stamp of the Belgian Congo, to a bank manager in Kampala and asked to exchange it for cash. The unusual request was honored, but the incident became widely known. Leaders of opposition parties looked for evidence that Obote was using Ugandan forces to meddle in the volatile politics of his neighbor to the west. What they found was circumstantial but convincing: despite public declarations of neutrality in the conflict between the newly installed pro-American government of the Republic of Congo and an insurgent group led by Patrice Lumumba, the Ugandan army was assisting Lumumba's forces in importing weapons, arranging for illegal export of ivory, and moving gold abroad secretly without payment of duties.

The parliamentary delegates of Obote's UPC were so angry with their leader that—while he was away from Kampala on a visit to northern Uganda—they passed a vote of no confidence, expecting that he would resign as prime minister. Instead Obote rebuffed the deposition attempt and tightened his personal control over the government. He suspended the constitution and wrote a new one, without consulting parliament. Ministers from his own cabinet who had supported his ouster were thrown into prison.

Uganda was now largely governed by Obote's military advisor Colonel (soon to be General) Idi Amin. The Ugandan army, not

Parliament, issued regulations and enforced them. Obote had carried out what one observer called "a coup d'état against his own government in order to stay in power" (Library of Congress 1992, 24).

The *kabaka* and the leaders of the KY party objected to Obote's power grab, particularly the provisions in the new constitution that revoked the federal structure of the central government and deprived regional authorities of local control. They demanded that the prime minister step down and began legal proceedings to remove him from office. Obote was not interested in arguing his case in the courts but sent the army, led by Amin, to attack the Buganda royal palace. The *kabaka* managed to escape capture by climbing over the wall of the palace compound during a cloudburst, and he fled into exile. The honeymoon between the northern upstart Obote and the formerly dominant Baganda ruler was over.

Obote declared martial law and assumed direct control over all of the Buganda kingdom, canceling all of the powers of limited autonomy that he had promised. His betrayal alienated the *kabaka* but was welcomed by others in the coalition that had brought him to power four years earlier. Amin, newly promoted to major general and given command over all of the Ugandan armed forces, implemented the new policies with a firm hand.

From this point forward Obote faced little domestic opposition, and he gave it no soil in which to grow. He outlawed all political parties except the ruling UPC, making use of newly created internal security forces and a strengthened paramilitary police force to enforce his policies and silence critics. Even while he continued to rely on Amin as chief military advisor, tensions developed between them. The army was suspected of complicity with an assassination attempt on Obote in 1969, and Amin himself appeared to have approved the murder of one of his military rivals. Worried that Amin was consolidating his own power base in the military, and faced with evidence that he was seeking allies abroad in Sudan and in Israel, Obote built up a large internal security force independent of the Army, recruiting heavily from the Acholi and Lango regions and not from Amin's West Nile region. By 1970 it was evident that the former allies no longer trusted each other (Library of Congress 1992, 23–25).

Field Marshal Al Hadji Doctor Idi Amin Dada Seizes Power

In January 1971, Prime Minister Obote decided it was time to clip the wings of his overweening military chief. Departing for a Singapore gathering of British Commonwealth nations, he left orders with trusted Lango military officers to arrest Amin and his highest-ranking associates. Amin got wind of this order, and before it could be carried out he took forceful action of his own. Troops loyal to Amin, in heavily armored units, opened fire on government buildings in Kampala and on the airport at Entebbe. As the nation's army drove the nation's elected representatives and administrators from the corridors of power, General Idi Amin Dada declared himself president of the Republic of Uganda.

Early assessments by non-African allies were mostly positive. The new military regime was quickly recognized by Great Britain, the United States, and Israel. Hope was expressed that Uganda would now align itself with Western powers rather than insisting on its neutrality, which in the Cold War era was construed as refusal to aid the global struggle against communism.

Officially the Obote regime was non-aligned, supporting neither communist nor anti-communist global efforts. But in reality the Ugandan head of state had assisted whichever side in a regional conflict would maximize the flow of cash from illicit arms, ivory, and gold. In Western eyes, Obote was a treacherous and duplicitous autocrat, one who had risen to power through a democratic process but had then used the apparatus of the state to entrench his control. Diplomats in London and Washington were happy to see him deposed. And Amin appeared to be well positioned to serve as a transitional leader until democracy could be restored. Both Ugandans and outsiders blamed Obote more than Amin for their mutual animosity.

African leaders were more skeptical. President Julius Nyerere of Tanzania offered hospitality to exiled prime minister Obote. Neither he nor Presidents Kenneth Kaunda of Zambia and Jomo Kenyatta of Kenya would recognize the legitimacy of the Amin government. Amin's subsequent behavior showed their skepticism to be far more realistic than the optimism of the British and the Americans.

Having dissolved Parliament, Amin reorganized the government and administration of Uganda along military lines. He created an advisory council of senior military officers, elevated military tribunals over civil courts, and administered local affairs through military outposts. Soldiers who showed unswerving loyalty—a more important qualification than professional training or demonstrated competence—were appointed to head government agencies and parastate organizations. Even civilian members of the president's cabinet were required to adhere to strict military discipline. Officers and soldiers whose loyalty was doubtful were ruthlessly rooted out. One of Amin's first actions as president was to order mass executions of Acholi and Lango in the armed forces, taken by surprise in their barracks by loyalist Kakwa and Lugbara troops.

Within this reorganized government, personal feuds and professional rivalries came to frequent and violent expression. There were purges in the military, with summary execution of commanders suspected of disloyalty or malfeasance. The ensuing disorder opened unimaginable—and implausible—opportunities to soldiers from lower ranks. The officer promoted to commander of the Ugandan air force, for example, was a new recruit, trained as a telephone technician. Military units judged sufficiently loyal to the president were generously supplied with weapons and ammunition, but other units received no bullets for their guns. Mutinies and murders in the ranks were frequent. Two American journalists attempted to investigate a barracks rebellion in 1972, but they disappeared and were never seen again (Library of Congress 1992, 26–27).

Like many of his advisors, President Amin was functionally illiterate, and he governed the nation through verbal orders on the basis of advice from trusted officers. The initial optimism of British and American observers faded quickly as Amin's policies became ever more idiosyncratic and arbitrary.

In a country that was, and remains, overwhelmingly Christian, Amin had spent his childhood in a largely Muslim area of the north. As president he reaffirmed his Muslim identity, which helped attract generous financial and military aid from Libya's leader, Muammar Gaddafi, and from the Saudi royal family. When Amin's reliance on Israeli advisors did not sit well with the Islamic states from which he sought assistance, he expelled the Israelis summarily from Uganda. In Kampala, Amin claimed an expansive site in a prominent location, on a hilltop with commanding views in all directions, and ordered the construction of a gigantic mosque, able to accommodate nearly 18,000 at Friday prayers. Gaddafi paid the construction bills.

Uganda's large Indian population was his next target. From the first decades of colonial rule, Asian immigrants had worked in the sugar cane fields and built the railroads, and their descendants had risen to significant positions as Uganda's merchants and bankers. Their growing wealth elicited the envy and resentment of many Ugandans. President Amin decided that they had become a parasitic force sapping the economic health of the nation, and in 1972 he ordered the expulsion of Uganda's 50,000 Asian residents and the confiscation of all of their property, with just a few weeks' notice. Their lands and businesses, said Amin, would be distributed to ordinary Ugandans, but they went instead to favored military officers.

In an economy already in decline, the result was catastrophic. The new owners of confiscated businesses had no clue how to run them, and many collapsed. Newly appointed authorities in Uganda's ports were unable to keep equipment in working order, and imports and exports were blocked or delayed. Production of agricultural export goods such as sugar and cotton ground to a halt, as did the supply of essential industrial supplies such as concrete. Revenues from Ugandan products that managed to reach foreign markets were diverted to army officials.

As an officer of the King's African Rifles and of the Ugandan armed forces, Amin had been recognized and promoted for outstanding service. He had earned the highest rank open to Africans serving in British forces, and in the nation of Uganda he was promoted through the ranks from lieutenant to colonel to general and then, still serving under Obote, Commander of the Armed Forces. Many more honors and decorations were added—by his own order—after he became president: "His Excellency, President for Life, Field Marshal Al Hadji Doctor Idi Amin Dada, VC, DSO, MC, Lord of All the Beasts of the Earth and Fishes of the Seas and Conqueror of the British Empire in Africa in General and Uganda in Particular." The DSO and MC titles, Distinguished Service Order and Military Cross, are genuine British honors, but they were never given to Amin. "VC" was a decoration invented by Amin, the Victorious Cross, intended to mimic the Victoria Cross bestowed on outstanding British officers (Gates and Appiah 2005, s.v. "Amin").

Yet another self-bestowed title that caught outsiders' attention became the title of a popular book, *The Last King of Scotland,* and a film based on the book. Author Giles Foden told the story of the Amin regime through the eyes of Amin's personal physician, a Scot who was amazed and amused by his patient's claim of Scottish ancestry and royal descent. The character of the physician was invented, possibly based on an actual advisor to Amin. But the story that unfolds in the book, and is powerfully reenacted by Forest Whitaker in the 2006 film, is faithful to historical facts, implausible as they frequently are (Foden 1999, MacDonald 2006).

What explains Amin's rise to power and his ability to deflect or defeat any attempts to depose him for more than eight years? How could such an idiosyncratic figure occupy the presidency of a nation for so long, handing lavish favors to his cronies while issuing arbitrary decrees that made the people of Uganda far worse off than under the previous regime? His rise was facilitated by widespread dissatisfaction with the favoritism and corruption of the Obote government. Although some aspects of Amin's character had been evident in his years as military commander—ruthlessness against those he saw as enemies of the regime, for instance, and reliance on a close circle of advisors to compensate for his own illiteracy and lack of education—many Ugandans were ready, as were many foreign representatives, to take at face value his assurance that he would call elections very soon. Instead he abolished parliament and ruled by personal decree.

Always alert to real and perceived threats to his authority, Amin did not hesitate to eliminate enemies and potential enemies, even those who held high public office. A former head of government in the brief period of DP control of parliament, High Court Judge Benedicto Kiwanuka, was seized from his courtroom by armed men, taken away in the trunk of a car, and never seen again. Undercover informants brought frequent reports of citizens plotting against the Amin government, and the accused soon disappeared. News of alleged plots was disseminated on government radio stations. Those who criticized Amin's policies, or who had simply made remarks that others interpreted as signs of disloyalty, would sometimes hear their own names announced on the radio as traitors to Uganda who must be held to account. If they were fortunate, they still had time to go into hiding.

If Amin's rise to power was facilitated by the abuses and excesses of the Obote regime, he retained his position by unstinting and unhesitating means of domestic terror. Factional conflict within his own government led to internecine bloodletting, frequently fueled by longstanding ethnic divisions and resentments. Observers estimate that during Amin's eight years in power as many as 300,000 Ugandans were killed by military and paramilitary forces. Sometimes the killers were acting on the orders of the president, but at other times they were simply securing their own positions of influence by eliminating potential rivals. Little of this was known to a wider public, however, in Uganda or abroad. The government retained complete control over domestic media, and foreign observers were either refused entry or prevented from gathering accurate information. Few journalists were brave or foolish enough to investigate incidents that, the government insisted, had never occurred but were only malicious fictions concocted by its enemies. Some who persisted in their investigations, as we have already mentioned, simply disappeared and were never seen again.

After Amin, Obote Returns to Power

By 1978 the Amin regime was rotting from within. Many of the president's closest associates were no longer part of his government. Of those who had not been executed, many had fled into exile. General Mustafa Adrisi learned how dangerous it could be to become a close and trusted advisor to the president: he was reported to have been killed in an auto accident, but troops under his command understood that the accident had been no accident. They began to defy the president's orders and talk of deposing him, and with some other military units they made clandestine plans for mutiny.

Given the breadth and depth of Amin's system of informers, such plans could not be kept secret for long. The president called on troops who remained loyal to him to chase down and capture the mutineers in October of 1978. The attempt to put down this internal rebellion set in motion a chain of events that led to Amin's overthrow six months later.

The rebellious troops, pursued by Ugandan army loyalists, moved south and sought refuge in Tanzania. Amin pursued them there, accusing Tanzanian president Julius Nyerere of having assisted the mutiny.

Nyerere and his small army, augmented by Ugandans in exile, launched a counterattack. With his blessing, these exiles had formed the Uganda National Liberation Army (UNLA) and were awaiting the opportunity to unseat the dictator at home.

Despite the assistance of Libyan reinforcements dispatched by Amin's ally Gaddafi, the Ugandan army withered under the counterattack and retreated toward Kampala, looting the communities through which it passed. In April 1979, UNLA and Tanzanian forces occupied Kampala and took control of the national government. Amin fled by air, initially to Libya. A year later he moved on to Jiddah, Saudi Arabia, where the Saudi royal family provided him with a generous living stipend and lavish quarters, on the condition that he stay out of local and international politics. And he did stay out, but not for lack of trying to meddle. In 1980 he attempted to recruit a liberation army in the Congo, then renamed Zaire, but President Mobuto Sese Seko sent him straight back to Saudi Arabia. He remained in exile there until his death in 2003, never voicing regret for the suffering that he had inflicted on the people of Uganda but frequently telling interviewers that his people were longing for his return (Bronner 2003).

Unfortunately, the deposition of a ruthless dictator did not usher in an era of peace or tranquility. Nyerere had convened a gathering of Ugandan military and civilian groups in Tanzania shortly before the fall of Kampala in hopes of creating a government of national unity, to be organized politically as the Ugandan National Liberation Front. But the first UNLF head of government, former Makerere University vice-chancellor Yusef Lule, was ineffective and unpopular, and his party deposed him and sent him into exile after few months. His successor, Godfrey Binaisa, had been an official of Obote's UPC. He too was unable to persuade the interim parliament to work together. National unity was soon buried under factional squabbling.

In this period the Ugandan army—purged of Amin's cronies, built around the small UNLA army in exile—numbered no more than 1,000 troops. Many of Amin's soldiers had fled into exile in Sudan rather than be held to account for their actions in Uganda. Some of the principal figures in the post-Amin era now seized the opportunity to augment their political influence by building up military forces under their personal command. The most important of these was Yoweri Kaguta

Museveni, who had helped to train the rebel army in exile. In the months after Amin's ouster his private army, the National Resistance Army (NRA), grew from 80 to more than 8,000 soldiers. His ally Major General David Oyite Ojok built a small force of 600 into an army of 24,000. These independent militias, former rebels now nominally allied with the new Ugandan government, continued to live in Tanzania, as did former president Obote.

When Museveni and Ojok began sending their soldiers to harass political opponents, President Binaisa tried to reassert the Ugandan government's control over all military operations. The effort failed completely. Instead, Museveni and Ojok led a military coup that overthrew Banaisa.

A former Obote associate, Paulo Muwanga, was installed as head of state, and his first priority was to build up the national army. Ojok's militia became in effect a unit of that army, but Museveni kept his distance. In the disorder and conflict that attended preparations for the first national elections in 18 years, Muwanga's "government of national unity" fragmented into several squabbling factions. The stage was set to go forward by going back—to a second Obote regime.

Former president Obote, newly returned from exile, set out to ensure electoral victory for his UPC party. Seventeen candidates for parliament were assured of election when their opponents' names were kept from appearing on ballots. Fourteen district election officials were removed and replaced by UPC loyalists. Even the chief justice of the Ugandan Supreme Court, who would be called on to resolve complaints about election fraud, was replaced by an Obote loyalist. Opposition candidates who managed to get their names on the ballots were arrested and jailed, and one was killed.

On election day, independent observers reported that despite all of these efforts to manipulate the outcome, the Democratic Party appeared to be heading for a solid parliamentary majority over the ruling UPC. Both BBC and Voice of America duly reported on this development, and DP supporters filled the streets of Kampala to celebrate their historic victory. In response Muwanga took over control of the Electoral Commission, giving him the power to count the ballots. A day later he announced that the earlier tallies had been incorrect, and the UPC had won in 82 of 126 legislative districts, gaining a substantial parliamentary majority. Rebuffing any challenges, Obote resumed the reins of power, in effect taking up the task of securing his own autocratic rule where he had left off a decade earlier when Amin had deposed him.

The second Obote regime was probably the most brutal and destructive in Uganda's troubled history. Outraged by Obote's machinations, Yoweri Museveni and his National Resistance Army began staging guerrilla raids in areas where Obote had little support. Obote's armed forces responded with great brutality, and there followed the "war in the bush" that engulfed much of central and western Uganda from 1981 to 1985. The destruction of homes and farms during these four years exceeded the devastation of eight years under Idi Amin, and the number killed in the conflict is estimated at 500,000. In the "Luwero Triangle," a region to the north of Kampala that Obote regarded as an NRA stronghold, 750,000 residents were forced to abandon their homes and relocate to internment camps, where they were handled roughly by military guards. Civilians who did not move to the camps were presumed to be sympathizers with Museveni, and many were detained, tortured, and killed (Library of Congress 1992, 34–35).

Ethnic animosities were exploited once again in the service of political ends, or simply to settle scores. Soldiers from Amin's home region, the West Nile district, had been responsible for terrible atrocities against Acholi and Lango residents of northern Uganda under Amin's rule, for example. Now that the Acholi and Lango dominated the ranks of the national army, they took their revenge, killing and burning the homes of anyone they suspected of having supported Amin. On one occasion soldiers from the national army attacked a Catholic mission and killed the civilians who had sought refuge there. When the International Red Cross reported on these abuses, the Obote government expelled all Red Cross staff from Uganda.

Despite its advantage in weaponry, troop strength, and funding, Obote's armed forces were unable to achieve a decisive victory over Museveni's NRA insurgency. Obote set one faction in the army against another, recruiting spies to disclose signs of disloyalty—and thus he set in motion the same sorts of military resistance that had led to his overthrow by Amin. Repeating history detail for detail, Obote left Kampala in July 1985 after giving orders for the arrest of an Acholi military officer whom he regarded as especially dangerous, Lieutenant Basilio

Olara-Okello. As Obote fled into exile in Zambia—this time, reportedly, taking much of the nation's wealth with him—Okello and troops
that he mustered took control of Kampala. Uganda's brief period of
nominally democratic rule, riven by unprecedented levels of violence,
gave way yet again to military rule (United Press International 1985).

Installed as head of the new government was another member of
the Acholi group, General Tito Lutwa Okello (unrelated to the lieutenant). He sought to defeat Museveni with the help of Amin's exiled
soldiers, invited back from their camps in Sudan. They were effective
in the field—Amin had trained them well—but were so rapacious and
avaricious in their conduct that their deployment only increased popular support for Museveni's rebel force. Within six months the Okello
government was losing control of its own armed forces, to say nothing
of the country as a whole. A ceasefire agreement worked out in Kenya
brought a brief respite—and gave Museveni a chance to gather forces
for his imminent assault on Kampala. When NRA forces occupied
the capital, Okello fled north with the Ugandan army into his Acholi
homeland.

Yoweri Museveni declared himself the president of Uganda on
January 29, 1986. Despite years of vilification and military attack on
his militia by the national government, he was welcomed by many as
a figure who could bring unity and peace to a land deeply scarred by
war after war.

Museveni has now been president of Uganda for considerably more
than half of Uganda's history as a nation, and he has put his stamp on
the country in many ways, as will be noted in the following chapter.
Before turning to these later developments, let us pause to take note of
some of the ways in which the first decades of the Republic of Uganda
affect its political life down to the present.

In many situations, we have already observed, the porousness of national boundaries has affected life in Uganda. Before the era of colonial
rule, daily life in the Great Lakes region revolved around agriculture,
hunting, and regional trade. Allegiances were to the village and to
larger or smaller chiefdoms and kingdoms, whose shifting boundaries
were largely ignored when the British asserted their claim to the upper
portions of the Nile watershed against Egypt, France, and Germany. In
the British protectorate, new political boundaries frequently separated

previously united ethnic communities, particularly in the northern regions. Yet the colonial boundaries were reaffirmed at the time of independence, and they remain essentially unchanged to the present day—not just in Uganda but across the continent.

In each of the conflicts and civil wars that bedeviled the first decades of Uganda's life as a nation, the ease of movement across borders and the lack of effective border controls played a central role. Idi Amin's power base was essentially internal, centered on the Kakwa and Lugbara areas of the West Nile region. But when he was driven from power, the troops who remained loyal to him were able to slip across the northern border of Uganda into Sudan. Ten years later, they returned in force to lend assistance to the short-lived Okello government in its campaign to destroy Museveni's National Resistance Army. Far from ensuring victory, their return, and their brutal tactics of looting and pillaging, turned public opinion against Okello and helped prepare the way for Museveni's triumph.

Museveni, for his part, lived for many years in exile in Tanzania, where he built and trained a small rebel army with the knowledge and approval of Tanzanian president Nyerere. When Amin pursued his domestic enemies into Tanzania, this was just the sort of provocation that the exiles had been waiting for. Amin's attempt to consolidate his power by a forceful cross-border attack led instead to a far more effective counterattack, driving him from power and into lifelong exile.

This pattern of internal divisions leading to movement back and forth across Uganda's borders is a familiar one across much of Africa, facilitated by the remoteness of many border areas and the arbitrariness of borders. It was also an important element in the ascendancy of the Lord's Resistance Army. When conditions in Uganda became too dangerous for LRA soldiers, nearly all of them drawn from the Acholi and Lango people of northern Uganda, they could move temporarily into Sudan, whose government was hostile to the Museveni regime and ready to assist its enemies. LRA forces also moved freely in and out of the Democratic Republic of Congo and Central African Republic—not because their governments were openly friendly, but simply because there was no effective central government in the regions where they established their camps.

It is a mistake, then, to visualize Uganda as a nation with well-marked and well-respected boundaries. Its governments have held a high level of control over the regions nearest the capital, much less in more distant areas. The proximity and the porousness of national borders have contributed to the rise of counter-government movements in the provinces, especially those of the distant and often neglected northern regions.

Another element of the history recounted in the present chapter may also have contributed to the failure of the Museveni government to prevent or to resolve internal rebellion—a factor that can be traced back to the attitudes and assumptions of the Europeans who held local authorities in check for nearly a century. The policy of indirect rule, we have observed, was a keystone of British policy in Africa. Under this policy the British remained at a distance from the daily affairs of local communities and delegated oversight in many areas to local chiefs and elders, rather than replace them with Europeans at every level.

An implicit foundation of this policy, more evident to us today than to those who put it in place, was a judgment that local governance structures and customs were not only categorically different from, but also essentially inferior to, the centralized and rationalized system of European rule. From one viewpoint, indirect rule was a more benevolent form of control than direct colonial administration, as in British colonies such as India. Yet its moral foundation was the supposedly objective characterization of African peoples and societies as having attained only a primitive level of development, from which their European masters could help them to emerge.

Todd Whitmore, a theologian at the University of Notre Dame who has done extensive ethnographic fieldwork in Uganda and South Sudan, goes so far as to identify "social Manichaeism" as "the sin embedded in development." He explains:

Colonialism ... whatever the claims of its practitioners to be Christian, superimposes a Manichaean worldview onto society, supplementing the terms *light* and *dark*—fortuitously allied with skin color—with those of *civilized* versus *primitive* and *modern* versus *backward*. Colonialist thought drew on—and distorted—Darwinism to undergird those dichotomies in a theory of unilinear evolutionism. The theory mapped the differences between sub-Saharan and colonial cultures onto a single timeline that had humanity evolving through pre-specified stages. Given the assumption that European culture was at the most advanced stage, the colonizers identified the cultures of Africa as belonging to earlier stages. (Whitmore 2010, 172)

The Manichaean assumptions underlying indirect rule, Whitmore argues, can still be detected in the language of post-independence leaders of the independent nation of Uganda. Now it is not the European authorities who are bringing light into darkness, offering the benefits of civilization to those still mired in backwardness, but indigenous representatives of the African population. President Museveni declared in 1987 that the conflict between his government and the prophetess Alice Lakwena, whose story we will recount in the next chapter, was "a conflict between modernity and primitivity" (New Vision 1987). He has described his predecessors Obote and Amin as "hyenas mauling Uganda" (New Vision 2001). He is reported to have used the same term to refer to the Acholi, and also to have described them as grasshoppers in a bottle, who will devour each other before they find their way out through the neck of the bottle (Finnström 2008, 106,114). I have not been able to find documented confirmation of the last comments in other sources, but they are by no means out of character. Indeed, a government newspaper has quoted a similarly disparaging remark: on the eve of the 2006 agreement that led at last to the withdrawal of LRA troops from northern Uganda, Museveni made the bold claim: "We shall transform the people of the North from material and spiritual backwardness to modernity" (New Vision 2006).

In invoking the colonialist dichotomy between modernity and primitivity, the president of the Republic of Uganda was reading from the same script as the governors dispatched from Whitehall to bring the benefits of British rule to the backward African natives. The Ugandan president's language is strikingly similar to that of the 19th-century explorer John Hanning Speke, who described the residents of the region as "both morally and physically, little better than brutes," in dire need of "a strong protecting government." Speke added that only "white or wise men" were capable of providing such guidance. The racial criterion has been renounced, but the supposition that only a strong ruler can tame the unruly natives remains all too much in evidence. When it remains grounded in such assumptions, local and democratically elected government can be no less destructive and oppressive than colonial rule by the representatives of a distant monarch (Finnström 2008, 58).

Museveni's accession to power in 1986 proved to be the beginning of a highly successful and long-enduring regime—extended long past constitutional limits by a compliant parliament. In the next chapter we will review the events of the second quarter-century of the nation of Uganda, in which Museveni consolidated his power, while two charismatic figures in the northern part of the country launched rebel campaigns in hopes of unseating him. One of these movements arose very quickly and was just as quickly defeated. The other proved far more resilient, and before it was at last expelled from the country it subjected the people of the Acholi region to brutality and arbitrary violence that recalled that of the Amin and Obote regimes.

Notes

1. In sketching the history of the Great Lakes region in this chapter, I have drawn on a variety of sources, which will be identified only when quoted or directly cited. Let me note here the sources that I have found most useful in recounting the overall narrative of Uganda's history and prehistory. The history and prehistory, back to the earliest human settlements, are described in a very thorough Library of Congress country profile, dating from the early years of the Museveni regime (Library of Congress 1992). The Museveni years—the *Pax Musevenica,* in the author's coinage—are analyzed in a monograph by Joshua Rubongoya (2007). Sverker Finnström's study, focused primarily focused on the conflict in the north, devotes three opening chapters to precolonial and colonial history (Finnström 2008). The history of East African missions and of early colonization initiatives are recounted by Mario Cisternino (2004). On the East African slave trade, Mark Leopold's account is helpful (Leopold 2006). The study of Uganda's "hybrid regime" by Aili Marie Tripp (2010) includes valuable historical background to contemporary Ugandan political life. A concise review of historical roots of the northern Uganda conflict is provided in chapter 2 of Margaret Angucia's study of the reintegration of the formerly abducted (Angucia 2010).
2. I will follow established usage in using three terms: Buganda is a kingdom, composed of members of the Baganda (sometimes simply Ganda) ethnic group, speaking Luganda.
3. One of the newly arrived groups, the Hima, moved beyond Uganda into what is now Rwanda and Burundi, where they adopted Bantu languages

and came to dominate the Hutu population, whom they placed in a lower agricultural caste. They acquired a new identity there as Tutsi, sharing a language but not an ethnic identity with the Hutu majority. The massacre of 700,000 Tutsi residents of Rwanda in 1994 was a sobering reminder that longstanding ethnic conflicts, with origins related to population movements half a millennium ago, can have devastating consequences in the present.

3

Politicians and Prophets

*Nowhere has the Museveni government failed its own people as much as in the
north and northeast from 1986 to present. The lack of serious effort to resolve
the crisis in the north despite ample opportunities—not to mention the active
sabotage of some of the peace talks—left the northerners feeling that they were
being punished for the actions of previous governments, armies, and armed
groups. . . .*

*Betty Bigombe explained to me: "The international community only wanted
to focus on success stories; nobody wanted to talk about the problems in the
north. Until recently, the perception was that the economy in Uganda was
picking up, tourism was increasing, [and] HIV/AIDS was down." The World
Bank was reluctant to get involved in a region embroiled in war, yet the lack
of development was adding fuel to the conflict.*

*Caught in a proxy war between Uganda and Sudan, northerners felt
ignored by the rest of the country, the government, donors, and the international community. They were not treated as full citizens of Uganda and many
in the Acholi diaspora, rightly or wrongly, felt that the continuation of the war
between government troops and the LRA was part of an effort to . . . eliminate
them as a people.*

—Aili Marie Tripp,
Museveni's Uganda (Tripp 2010, 159)

THE HISTORY OF UGANDA from Museveni's accession to power in the
1980s to the turn of the 21st century is a story of political consolidation, as the president won support abroad and crushed opposition internally. Rebel movements in the north were fueled by the national

government's neglect and mistreatment, by the charismatic appeal of two individuals, and by covert intervention from outside the country's borders by parties who stood to gain from the conflicts. It is a complex story, and one in which there are many villains and few heroes. In this chapter I will recount that story briefly. Against this background the emergence of a courageous group of religious leaders determined to end the protracted civil war, the narrative to which we will return in Chapter 5, is all the more remarkable.

As has been noted in the preceding chapter, the years following the overthrow of Idi Amin were marked by political upheavals, military coups, and a five-year-long civil war that claimed half a million lives. Animosities and resentments simmered, frequently along ethnic lines, in ways that reflected the politics of colonial rule as well as the contest among factions in the post-independence period.

Northern ethnic groups had long dominated the armed forces, in part because the British regarded them as less intelligent but more obedient than southerners. Under Amin's rule, as southerners were forced out of positions of power, northerners held the upper hand in politics as well. But Amin's West Nile supporters from the Kakwa and Alur ethnic groups had treated the Acholi and Lango to their east very harshly, and after Amin's ouster many sought to settle scores. It was conflict between these two factions that led to Obote's overthrow and the appointment of General Tito Okello—a victory for the Acholi over their neighbors the Lango, but one that brought little benefit. "Far from resolving the political crisis that had engulfed the country," writes one observer, "Obote's overthrow generated greater instability, because it created a power vacuum, which the triumphant Acholi faction was too weak to fill by itself" (Kyaga-Nsubuga 1999, 17).

When Museveni's National Resistance Army in turn overthrew the Okello regime in 1986, the nation was already in a state of political and economic crisis. Museveni set out both to rebuild a functioning political order and to strengthen the control of his National Resistance Movement (NRM) over national politics through a systematic policy of inclusion, reaching out and offering important government appointments to representatives of all the factions that had played a role in the chaos of the post-Amin years. (The National Resistance Army had lent its name to the ruling party, now the NRM.) These groups included all of the parties mentioned in the previous chapter—Democratic Party, Uganda People's Congress, and two smaller parties—as well as five independent armed forces that had been built up and deployed during the period of conflict. In a 1998 interview, President Museveni told a journalist, "The groups which were threatening me would bring me a list of twenty bad people, and to preserve peace I would have to choose two or three of the least bad of them" (April 29, 1988 interview, cited in Kyaga-Nsubuga 1999).

This policy of inclusiveness, with room in the new government for those allied with previous regimes and opposition movements, endured for the first decade of Museveni's rule and helped him secure reelection. But as the president prepared to serve for a third five-year term, and beyond—terms that were not possible until the constitution had been amended—he implemented new policies that appeared to expand political freedom but in reality strengthened his autocratic control. Opposition political parties were permitted, but under such restrictive laws that they could not gain a foothold in Parliament, to say nothing of mounting a serious challenge to the president. In what was now nominally a multiparty system, the NRM was more firmly in control than ever (Rubongaya 2007, 10–11).

The new constitution of 1995 authorizing opposition parties had been drawn up following an extended process of review. In advancing the rule of law, this was an important step forward. The nation's first constitution, after all, had been written in London by British colonial authorities before independence, without the involvement of Ugandans. President Obote had pushed a new constitution into effect in 1966, with advice from a few of his allies but little input from Parliament. Amin ruled by edict, rewriting the constitution as he pleased, ignoring it when it got in his way. But Museveni insisted on lengthy review, by Ugandans at home and abroad, as successive drafts were circulated over a period of five years.

The new constitution's provisions for democratic governance were not quite as generous as they appeared at first glance, however. Opposition parties would be free to formulate platforms and discuss strategies, but their candidates would be listed on ballots only by their names, without their party affiliation. Ruling party candidates, far better known and frequently endorsed on state-controlled media, would still be assured of large majorities. The effect was to block any hopes of forming a coherent or effective opposition bloc in Parliament.

The Museveni regime had already created a system of local and regional "Resistance Councils," which were entrusted with the responsibility of settling local disputes, addressing grievances, and reporting to the central government on needs and priorities. This system—"unprecedented in Africa," writes one political historian—was created in rebel-controlled regions of Uganda before Museveni came to power, and it created a form of grassroots democracy that was extended to the entire nation after 1986, with the basic structure of the Resistance Councils carried forward into a system of Local Councils (Rubongaya 2007, 65).

In theory these groups could serve as vehicles to strengthen democracy and as watchdogs on government activities. But the reality was different. Each council reported to a local commissioner, an appointee of the NRM administration. Local council members elected in each district were nominally responsible for local governance, but all decisions on hiring and finances were made by their politically appointed regional supervisors.

The grassroots democracy of the councils, then, was largely illusory. As recently as 2011, a study of Ugandan local government found that "contradictions within the current legislation and features of the political context still enable the central government to undermine the powers of local governments today" (Lambright 2011, 25).

Nevertheless, the NRM regime did implement some important steps toward broader participation. Women were encouraged to stand for election to Parliament, and an affirmative action initiative permitted each district to nominate a woman in addition to the others, always mostly male, who had been elected by popular vote. As a result, the number of female representatives leaped from just 1 of 152 under Obote's second regime to 38 of 263 in the first legislature under NRM rule (Kyaga-Nsubuga 1999, 21–22).

Yoweri Museveni was a young man of 41 years when he became Uganda's president and transformed his National Resistance Army into the NRM, Uganda's dominant political party. Despite constitutional provisions limiting him to two five-year terms, Museveni decided that the job suited him and his country needed him, and Parliament was compliant with his requests. In June 2016, at the age of 71, he was inaugurated for his seventh five-year term as president. He has been Uganda's president for a longer period than all of his predecessors since 1962, added together.

Throughout his three decades of rule, Museveni has shown himself a skillful negotiator with foreign governments and international agencies, ensuring massive inflows of foreign aid assistance. In the decade from 1970–1979, mostly under the Amin regime, Uganda received only about $143 million in aid from donor countries in Europe and North America (in 2012 dollars), less than that allocated to far smaller countries like Togo and Benin. In the 1980s, under Obote and Okello and Museveni, this increased to half a billion dollars; in the 1990s, to more than one billion dollars each year. Each year since 2000, aid has totaled more than $1.5 billion. Uganda has consistently been among the top ten aid recipients among the 54 nations of the continent (World Bank 2016).

Museveni has also implemented economic policies that have won favor with international financial institutions. A 2016 World Bank summary notes, with evident approval:

> Starting in the late 1980s, the Uganda government has pursued a series of impactful liberalization policies. The resultant macroeconomic stability, post-conflict rebound, and investment response to the pro-market reforms generated a sustained period of high growth during 1987–2010. Real gross domestic product (GDP) growth averaged 7% per year in the 1990s and the 2000s, making it one of the fastest growing African countries. However, over the past decade, the country witnessed more economic volatility and gross domestic product (GDP) growth slowed to an average of just about 5%. (World Bank 2016)

Donor nations can only dream of annual GDP growth as high as 5 percent, but this was a decline for Uganda.

The report goes on to add some qualifications to this rosy picture. There are several reasons for caution in assessing Uganda's future, including political tensions related to the lack of a viable opposition party; uncertainties related to future oil production; "inappropriate urban development; the slow development of infrastructure; and the limited availability of credit." These make a return to the robust growth of earlier years unlikely, in the opinion of World Bank economists.

Most Ugandans, in my experience, agree with the World Bank that Museveni has served the country well in many respects. There were questions about ballot manipulation in the north and in the major cities in the 2016 election, where NRM support is weakest. Yet critics acknowledge that overwhelming rural support would have ensured a win for the ruling party even in an unblemished election (Kron 2016).

In September 2017 Museveni's party introduced a bill in Parliament that would remove constitutional age limits in order to clear the way for an eighth term, beginning in 2021 when the president will be 78. Vigorous opposition erupted in Parliament. The debate degenerated into a brawl when plainclothes security officers moved in to eject 27 members of the opposition party from the legislative chambers—a spectacle that was seen around the world but not in Uganda, thanks to an edict from the government's media office forbidding any live coverage. Just a few weeks later a legislative rebellion against another of Africa's longest-standing liberators-turned-autocrats resulted in the ouster of Zimbabwe's Joseph Mugabe, and some anticipated a similar outcome in Uganda. The media debacle proved to have no lasting consequences, however. The ruling party and its president made no concessions and yielded none of their control over Ugandan politics (Economist 2017, BBC 2018).

Criticism of the Museveni regime from Western governments has been muted, given the complex economic networks from which foreign investors draw significant benefits. NGOs have been more forthright. The coordinator of Uganda programs for the United States Institute of Peace, Elizabeth Murray, has commented on the irregularities of the 2016 election, for example, including missing ballots and lack of transparency in counting votes. She has also asked U.S. allies to press the Museveni regime to cease harassment of political opponents, revoke laws that restrict freedom of speech and assembly, and allow an appeal of the announced election results. Yet the president did not need to steal the election: he had made certain that most Ugandans believed it already belonged to him (USIP 2016).

Alice Lakwena's Holy Spirit Movement

Returning to the first decade of the Museveni regime, we turn now to the origins and the predecessors of the Lord's Resistance Army occupation of northern Uganda. Popular accounts of that movement attribute its rise to the restless thirst for power of its founder, Joseph Kony, and the tactics of kidnapping and subsequent indoctrination that enabled Kony to build a large private army and seize control of most of the Acholi and Lango areas north of the Victoria Nile from the late 1980s until the mid 2000s. That is the story told in the "Kony 2012" video distributed by Invisible Children, as has been noted above. But the history of the movement is in reality much more complex. The rise of the LRA insurgency resulted not just from one demogogue's dreams but also from a history of exclusion, exploitation, and repression on the part of the Ugandan government and its armed forces. And the most important figure in that history—a model and mentor for Joseph Kony, the leader of a religious and military movement that set out to restore both moral and political order to the people of Uganda—was the prophetess and military commander who called herself Alice Lakwena.

Alice Auma, to use her family name, was a resident of Gulu who had been married twice but had borne no children. Returning to her father's household, she supported herself as a market vendor during the last years of the civil war of the 1980s. She had been raised in a family that maintained traditional African beliefs and practices, but she had converted to Christianity when she married a Christian man.

In 1985, at the age of 29, she suffered a major psychological breakdown, rendering her unable to hear or speak for a time. When she recovered, she informed her family that a Christian spirit named Lakwena had taken possession of her, and she began calling herself Alice Lakwena. ("Lakwena" means "messenger" or "apostle" in Acholi.) The spirit that spoke through her identified himself as an Italian captain who had died near Murchison Falls during the Second World War. Alice's father visited several practitioners of traditional medicine in hopes of freeing her from the spirit, without success (Behrend 1999, 134).

In a month-long retreat in Paraa, a remote location in the heart of Murchison Falls National Park, Alice reported that she received messages from several different spirits and from the resident animals. She told her family and associates that she convened all the animals and asked them whether they had caused the wars that afflicted her country. No, they replied: we are without blame and free from sin, but the evil human beings who have brought suffering on your people must be held to account. Sacrifices must also be made to placate the angry spirits of those whose lives have been taken unjustly.

Several miraculous events, it was reported, underscored the authenticity of the messages given to Alice by the spirits: a waterfall ceased to flow, a mountain exploded three times, and voices came from the mountain. Alice was instructed to stop the misuse of witchcraft by the Acholi people, and she was given the power to heal disease. This story became the founding myth of the movement she founded, which sought to purify the nation of immorality—and to drive out the repressive Museveni regime.

The site of these revelations has important historical associations. A regional shrine in Paraa had been the center of a traditional cult for centuries, long before the arrival of explorers and colonizers. For many generations, the Acholi and Lango people had made pilgrimages there. But when Amin's soldiers fled from the Ugandan and Tanzanian troops who drove them out of southern Uganda, they hid in the forests of Paraa and slaughtered the resident animals with automatic weapons. During the civil war of the 1980s the forests continued to be the site of indiscriminate killing of both animals and people, and the traditional shrine was neglected. Thus when Alice Lakwena was instructed to go to Paraa and there received her mandate from the spirits to purify the land, she established a continuity between traditional religious practices and the Christian warrior-spirit Lakwena who spoke and acted through her as a medium.

Returning from the forest to her home in Gulu, Alice Lakwena set out to combat evil and restore obedience to God in Uganda, as she had been directed. She began forming a military force, the Holy Spirit Mobile Force (HSMF). Saying that she was conveying the instructions of the spirit Lakwena, she called for war against the persecutors of the Acholi people, and she promised that all who purified themselves would be immune from bullets. Supporters described an occasion when bullets fired at Lakwena bounced off her body harmlessly.

Lakwena began recruiting her band of Christian soldiers during the brief tenure of Tito Okello, the only Ugandan president to come from the Acholi region. When Okello's national army was ousted by Museveni's militia, many Acholi joined the fight against the new government. Armed confrontations between Museveni's NRA and northern rebel forces were frequent, and in revenge for setbacks in the field each side resorted to kidnapping and torture. A truce was negotiated between the two sides in 1985—and then immediately broken.

A new rebel movement, better organized for guerrilla warfare in the north, adopted the name Uganda People's Democratic Army (UPDA).[1] Many demobilized soldiers in the Okello government army joined its ranks. In response to this provocation the NRA, now reporting to Museveni not as rebel commander but as head of state, ordered all Acholi to give up their weapons. This order evoked two painful precedents for the Acholi. In 1913, an order by the British colonial administration to surrender all arms to regional administrators had provoked an Acholi rebellion, quickly suppressed. Much later, in 1971 and 1972, President Amin had ordered thousands of Acholi troops to return to their barracks. While they awaited further orders, he sent loyalist soldiers from other northern groups to murder them en masse. So an order from Kampala to turn in arms was not going to be widely obeyed.

At the time when Alice was reportedly visited by the spirit Lakwena and given a mandate to gather the Acholi into a new spiritual and military movement, she called on them to renounce violence, forsake evil practices such as witchcraft, purify themselves, and deliver the nation of Uganda from its suffering. The renunciation of violence did not last long: in August 1986 Alice announced that evil must be defeated by military means. But the Holy Spirit Mobile Force would operate under highly restrictive rules, absurdly inappropriate for a conventional army but necessary, she insisted, in spiritual warfare.

Preparation began with ritual destruction of small models of enemy weapons, followed by anointing the soldiers' bodies with shea butter oil and ochre to ensure that bullets could not harm them. A limited number of soldiers from each company were sent into battle, following the instructions of the spirits. Leading them were intelligence officers and "stone commanders," whose role is described below:

The Holy Spirit soldiers took up positions and, as ordered by the spirit, began to sing pious songs for 10, 15, or 20 minutes. Then the time-keeper blew a whistle. On this sign, the troops began marching forward in a long line shouting at the tops of their voices, "James Bond! James Bond! James Bond!" Lakwena's chief technician was named James and called himself James Bond. The stone commanders led them and the line commanders ensured that the front line was maintained. Each stone commander carried a stone wrapped in cloth, which he threw at the enemy, at the same time calling to each company and leading spirit, "Cheng Poh, Franko, or Wrong Element, take up your position, command your people!" This stone marked the limit past which the enemy bullets could not penetrate, thus creating a protective zone (Behrend 1999, 59)

In addition to leading a highly unconventional military force, Alice provided physical and spiritual help to dispirited northerners, performing healing rituals and comforting them when they had suffered defeat or believed they were suffering from *cen,* an evil spirit of pollution that can emanate from those one has killed. She assured the Acholi people that "war is a form of healing," and "the healing is on both sides, as those that die are like the rotten flesh cut out by a surgeon. The pure, on the other hand, could not be killed" (Allen and Vlassenroot 2010, 8).

From her shrine and headquarters at Okot, outside Gulu, Alice trained an initial cadre of 80 HSMF soldiers, mostly former members of other rebel groups. An attack on Gulu late in 1986 was swiftly defeated, but afterward the ranks of her military organization swelled rapidly with defectors from other anti-NRA militias. In failing to address any of the grievances of the Acholi people or make amends for the excesses of its forces in northern Uganda, the Museveni regime and its national army in effect helped enlarge the rebel force (Rubongaya 2007, 82).

Remember the prominent display of the Ten Commandments in the palace of the Baganda *kabaka* who received Henry Morton Stanley in 1875. They reappear again and again in the history of Acholi rebel movements. For the Holy Spirit Movement, they were augmented by ten more rules, all of them promulgated by Alice as essential for a life of purity. Each rule was accompanied by a list of Biblical references, most of them from the Old Testament. But the list recalled by her former adherents begins with provisions utterly foreign to the Levitical code. Here are the first few "Holy Spirit Safety Precautions":

1. Thou shalt not have any kind of charms or remains of small sticks in your pocket, including also the small piece used as a toothbrush.

The texts cited in support of this injunction include general prohibitions against keeping idols (Lev. 19:4, Lev. 19:31, Isaiah 3:18–20) and a directly relevant word from the prophet Ezekiel: "Therefore this is what the Sovereign Lord says: I am against your magic charms with which you ensnare people like birds and I will tear them from your arms" (Ezekiel 13:20).

2. Thou shalt not smoke cigarettes.
3. Thou shalt not drink alcohol.
4. Thou shalt not commit adultery or fornication.
5. Thou shalt not quarrel or fight with anybody.

Among the other rules is this one:

9. You will execute the orders and only the orders of the Lakwena.

Cited in support of this command is Deut. 5:7: "You shall have no other gods before me." The rationale does not quite fit the character of the movement: Alice never claimed divine status, only that of a medium through whom God and his representatives could speak.

Some rules for conduct in battle follow:

10. Thou shalt not carry any walking stick in the battlefield.
11. Thou shalt not take cover on the ground, in the grass, behind trees, ant-hill, or any other obstacle there found.

Several passages from the Pentateuch are cited here in support, among them Exodus 23:27: "I will send my terror ahead of you and throw into confusion every nation you encounter. I will make all your enemies turn their backs and run."

Two more examples underscore the idiosyncratic character of this code of conduct:

15. You shall love one another as you love yourselves.
16. Thou shalt not kill snakes of any kind. (Behrend 1999, 47)

In this odd and arbitrary set of twice-ten commandments we can discern some important features of Alice Lakwena's movement and of its successor, Kony's Lord's Resistance Army. From the beginning each called for spiritual cleansing, renewed obedience, and holy living. Along with major elements of Christian teaching, Alice and her guiding spirit Lakwena—a Christian spirit, she said—incorporate traditional folklore and practice. So long as the soldiers adhered strictly to these injunctions, they were assured, victory would be theirs regardless of the forces arrayed against them, because God would come to their aid.

Lakwena's army was organized in a conventional military way, with one supreme commander set over several large companies. But the commanders of these companies were not individual men or women but designated spirits. Lakwena himself was Commander of the Forces. Another high-ranking officer named Wrong Element, a rather hot-headed and tactless American, spoke through Alice, in a pronounced American accent. Then there were Ching Poh, a Korean or Japanese spirit, Franco or "Mzee" (a Swahili term of respect for an old man), and several more, each assigned to a particular area of logistics or combat. There were spirits able to heal the wounded, and spirits who took control in some battles, and many more.

One or more of these spirits usually spoke through Alice at morning and evening gatherings, while she sat in the central temple complex in a white robe. When Lakwena or other spirits spoke, through Alice, a secretary recorded their instructions. It was said that the spirits did not need to identify themselves, because their distinctive voices set them apart. Adherents regarded all of these messages as coming not from, but only through, their leader Alice. Following their directives, they believed, would hasten the purification of the nation from violence and evil (Behrend 1999, 134–135). A report published many years later noted that "for Alice, the roles of healer and military leader were inextricably bound together" (Human Rights Watch 1997).

The most important practical goal of the HSMF was to seize control of Kampala and drive out Museveni and his NRA forces. After that, Alice's spirits prophesied, all the peoples of Africa, Europe, and North America would answer the call to repentance and purification, violence would cease, and all people would live together in harmony and Christian love. But the spiritual struggle was soon transmuted into a bloody and destructive war waged with conventional weapons.

In 1986 and 1987 the Holy Spirit forces launched a series of attacks on Lira and other nearby towns, with mixed results—some victories and some resounding defeats. But they proceeded all the same with a new battle plan: they would march to the south, gathering defectors from other militias along the way, and then defeat the NRA in the capital. Along the way conflict between the various former militias flared up, and the murder of commanders of an allied group led to reprisal killing of HSMF officers. Members of the movement reported later that, in several of these episodes, the spirit Lakwena demanded to know who had given authorization for the soldiers' actions, and his medium Alice admitted that she was responsible. The spirit reprimanded her severely for overstepping her authority: only the spirits could give commands to her army (Behrend 1999, 80–81, 89).

The rebel army moved steadily south—not directly toward Kampala, where government soldiers controlled the route, but along a more easterly path toward Lake Victoria, then westward toward the capital. In the first stages of this campaign the Holy Spirit forces grew from several hundred to several thousand. But the regions through which they were now moving were less and less sympathetic to their cause, and the NRA had strengthened its forces in the area. Several times the NRA staged deadly ambushes. After each setback hundreds of Holy Spirit soldiers deserted and returned home.

On September 30, 1987, NRA forces surrounded the HSMF encampment and rained down mortar shells on their trapped opponents. Some managed to break through the NRA line, but their losses were staggering. A much reduced HSMF army pushed on westward, aiming to cross the Nile on its exit from the lake at Jinja and continue to Kampala.

The soldiers need not worry if bridges were defended, or destroyed, they were told: Jesus would give them the power to walk across the

Nile. But just a few miles short of Jinja a series of battles in and around Magamaga brought an end to the HSMF campaign, and those who survived devastating NRA attacks scattered and fled.

The spirit Lakwena made a last address to the soldiers on November 2, attributing their losses to laxness in following the 20 commandments, particularly the prohibition against unjustified killing. Speaking through Alice, as usual, he announced that he would resume his efforts to deliver Uganda from evil one day. Then he pronounced a blessing on the wounded and allowed the few hundred faithful troops still waiting for his orders to return home to the north.

As for his chosen medium: Alice eluded capture by NRA soldiers and escaped across the border to Kenya, together with a few followers. The account given by Heike Behrend, whose informative study of the Holy Spirit Movement has been quoted and cited frequently above, summarizes what is known of her life across the border:

> After her defeat, Alice fled to Kenya with a few loyal followers. There, lacking identification papers, she was arrested and held in jail for four months before being granted early release for good behavior. She requested, and was granted, asylum with the UN High Commissioner for Refugees. She is said to live in Kenya today. She was last seen in a small bar, wearing a white blouse and a blue skirt and drinking Pepsi-Cola. The spirits had left her (Behrend 1999, 146).

She submitted a request to return to Uganda, but the conditions she set, including repayment of debts owed to her movement by the Ugandan army, were absurd, and the Ugandan government did not bother to respond. In January 2007, she died in a Kenyan refugee camp at the age of 50, reportedly as a result of AIDS (Economist 2007, Encyclopedia Britannica n. d.)

Other Rebel Movements in Northern Uganda

The resounding defeat of Alice Lakwena's Holy Spirit Mobile Force was not the end of the Holy Spirit Movement in northern Uganda. Two other leaders rose up in the aftermath of the ill-fated march to Kampala, each claiming the authority of several powerful spirits, each issuing a call for spiritual renewal and for the expulsion of the NRA from northern Uganda. One of these two achieved very little, and his faction of the movement soon dissolved. The other took the struggle for purification, and the translation of spiritual power into military power, to heights seldom achieved by any movement in any region of the world, disrupting every aspect of northern Ugandan society. Its reign of terror eventually drove nearly the entire population of the region into camps for internally displaced persons, where many remained for a decade or more. The first of these leaders was Severino Lukoya, Alice Lakwena's father. The second, a young officer loosely allied with Lakwena's forces who claimed to be her cousin, was Joseph Kony.

Before offering a brief account of the rise of these successor movements, we should take stock of the circumstances in which they both arose. The complex relationships among different Ugandan ethnic groups and their treatment under several regimes in Kampala have already been described. The Acholi and Lango of the northern regions had been the victims of neglect at best, systematic violence at worst, during Obote's and Amin's rule. Under Museveni, relations with the north were strained from the beginning and rapidly became much worse in response to Lakwena's movement and its successors.

Even while the National Resistance Army was recruiting soldiers from among the Acholi and Lango residents of the north, it was also waging a military campaign against the rebellious armies of the Holy Spirit Movement. This campaign became a nightmare of reprisals and rapacity. The armed forces of the government charged with protecting citizens instead became hated and feared oppressors.

Lakwena's and, later, Kony's Holy Spirit armies were not the only military forces contesting for control of the region. Many soldiers from the Uganda People's Defence Army had changed their allegiance to the HSMF and accompanied Lakwena on her drive to the south, then scattered and fled at its defeat. Others remained in the north to carry on their struggle against the NRA.

An initial effort by the Museveni government to pacify the northern region involved an offer of amnesty to soldiers from the HSMF and other regional armies if they gave up their arms. Several thousand rebel soldiers accepted the offer. Some were integrated into NRA units or assigned to local defense forces, joining in the battle against their former comrades. Others, finding that promises made to them on their surrender had been forgotten, soon rejoined their former rebel armies.

In 1988 a peace agreement was drafted between the NRA and the UPDA, but it had little effect. As many as 20,000 rebels lay down arms and requested amnesty, but rather than observe a ceasefire, government forces took advantage of their opponent's weakness to intensify their attacks. Behrend observes of this period:

> When, following the 1988 peace treaty, the NRA carried out major operations in Acholi to wipe out the rest of the "rebels," many saw their mistrust vindicated. The NRA's brutal methods of waging war also drove a number of people to seek protection with the resistance movements that still existed. Since the NRA behaved worse than the "rebels," it continually lost support among the populace. This, in turn, led the NRA soldiers to consider the people of Acholi in general sympathetic to the "rebels," and they treated them with corresponding violence. The commission installed by the government to prosecute violations of human rights had little effect, because, with a few exceptions, neither women nor men dared give public testimony for fear of the revenge of the NRA troops. (Behrend 1999, 173)

The campaign of pacification was in practice anything but a peaceful initiative. Observers reported that NRA troops killed indiscriminately in their raids on villages suspected of harboring rebels, raped and kidnapped women and girls, and seemed to be held to no discernible standards of behavior by their commanders. But their atrocities were overlooked, or excused as necessary countermeasures against rebel violence, by the Museveni government.

In effect, the Acholi people were being punished severely for the Lakwena rebellion, in hopes of exterminating any sympathizers with anti-government movements. The result was just the reverse: support for the Uganda government was severely eroded, and the people were more than ready to listen to the arguments of self-proclaimed prophets to whom Alice Lakwena's mantle as leader of anti-government resistance had been passed.

The first such prophet, as was mentioned above, was Alice's father Severino Lukoya. Severino told his daughter's followers that, long before his marriage and the birth of his children, God had spoken to him, shining a bright light on a passage from Isaiah that he was reading. God had promised that Severino would enjoy a special covenant relationship with God and would receive instructions on how to fulfill his unique role among the nations of the world.

Ten years later, after having married and begotten several children, Severino reported that he was given another divine vision, this time a conversation with Jesus, Abraham, Moses, and David. They told him that one of his children would be God's special agent in the world. He did not know at the time which of his children would play this role, he said. It was not until twenty years later, when Alice began preaching and prophesying, that he recognized her as the chosen one. He accompanied her on her journey to consult the animals and trees at Paraa and assisted her in gathering followers for the Holy Spirit Movement—frequently claiming to have been the original source of her spiritual vision, a claim that Alice honored in some of her pronouncements but few others took seriously (Behrend 1999, 129–133).

After Alice's flight to Kenya for refuge, her father attempted to re-organize the Holy Spirit Movement under his own leadership, with a mission that would be focused less on fighting against the NRA than on healing and renewal. He established a spiritual center, where various potions were prepared. One was credited with the power to heal wounds, another to ease menstrual discomfort, another to cure headaches, yet another to drive out evil spirits. His guide in these matters, he claimed, was the same Lakwena who had spoken through his daughter until the spirits left her following her defeat in the south. Many other spirits also spoke through him, most of them identified with individuals who had died recently: a military officer reportedly executed by Obote, an officer of the UPDA shot by cattle thieves, an Italian physician who died while serving in Uganda, an American monk who also died while living in Uganda. With the help and advice of all these spirits, he was able to gather a group of about 2,000 followers.

In August 1988 Severino informed Joseph Kony that he was now residing in Gulu District once again, where Kony had been recruiting followers and training soldiers for his own successor movement to the HSMF. In response to this news, Kony took decisive action in support of his claim to be Alice's true successor: he sent a detachment of his own forces to capture Severino, whom he declared to be a false prophet and a sinner.

On Kony's orders, all of Severino's potions, talismans, and relics were destroyed, and his Bible was burned. Kony visited his captive and forbade him to claim to speak for the spirits. Whenever Severino claimed to have a message from the other world, Kony's soldiers beat him. He managed to escape from his captors after a year of such treatment and went into the wilderness to fast and pray. But NRA soldiers found him, and he was held in a government prison for three more years. His movement had been completely destroyed, and the path was open now for Kony's rise (Behrend 1999, 177–178).

Origins of the Lord's Resistance Army

And what sort of movement was it that Joseph Kony launched? Initially it was very similar to that of his claimed aunt Alice: a gathering of the faithful, following the instructions of spirits who spoke through their leader in order to root out the evil that had infected the land. He called on the people of northern Uganda to embrace their true identity as disciples of the Holy Spirit. They would purify their lives by scrupulous obedience to—here they are again—the Ten Commandments, supplemented by other rules the spirits would formulate. And they would take up arms to drive the rapacious NRA army out of their land.

Who were these spirits who would command the movement? Kony claimed to be the spokesman for seven of them, in some accounts, a dozen or more in others. He identified the "Chief Spirit and Chairman" as Juma Oris, a good spirit sent from God. Unlike nearly all other spirit guides claimed by northern Uganda prophets, Juma Oris had not yet departed from his earthly life. He was a former Amin military commander living in southern Sudan, one of the organizers of the UPDA rebel army. Juma Oris the inhabiting spirit announced through Kony that God needed a powerful movement to rid the world of suffering and disease, but since many who receive healing would nevertheless be killed in armed conflict, it would be necessary to kill all those who kill. He had no desire to topple any government, he announced, but sought only to root out evil, end the use of magical potions and charms, and put an end to witchcraft and sorcery (Behrend 1999, 179).

Members of Kony's movement identified many other spirits, each of whom spoke through Kony in a distinct voice or accent. Silli Sillindi, a female Sudanese spirit, had command of Kony's female soldiers: she spoke in a high, thin voice in English. Ing Chu was Asian—Chinese or Korean—and ensured that enemy bullets would hit only Holy Spirit soldiers who had failed to follow the prescribed rules of conduct. El wel Best, another Chinese or Korean, was a military strategist. Silver Koni, a spirit from Zaïre, also helped deflect enemy bullets. King Bruce, an American, gave stone grenades the power to explode when thrown toward enemy lines. Another American spirit, Major Bianca, was a female military commander or intelligence officer. Still another American soldier, a black intelligence officer named Jim Brickey, would help NRA soldiers to punish Kony's troops when they disobeyed orders. He was also given the enigmatic name "Who are you?" (Behrend 1999, 185).

Two members of the Peace and Justice Commission of the archdiocese of Gulu whom I interviewed described the way in which Kony combined Christian practices with invocations of his special spirits in order to strengthen the allegiance of his followers, as described by former LRA soldiers whom they had interviewed after they escaped or were released.

> Some of the returnees said that they used to pray before they would go on an attack. They would see that Kony had the rosary, and they thought that he was Catholic because he would recite the prayers that people recite with the rosary, relating to the cross of Jesus Christ and the beads. They would always recite this before going for an attack. (Aeko 2014)

> Some people say that Kony was once an altar boy. And they say that at one time he became possessed by the Holy Spirit. But it is hard to tell now—it is all mixed up. When he joined the bush, he was having so many spirits, according to those who were with him there. Some spirits were in charge of specific things, such as war, or prayers. Sometimes the war spirits will say, "Don't go," and then they will stay. Then they will say, "Now you go," and that means that when they go they will be successful in the war.

But it was very difficult to identify what religion he followed. It was a mixed religion. Sometimes he would use things from the Catholics, sometimes from the born-agains, sometimes from the Anglicans, so you see it was very difficult. It was generally believed that he was possessed by the spirit. But the question of the Holy Spirit, or what spirit, was hard to answer. (Ogaba 2014)

What are we to make of this bewildering array of supposedly distinct individual spirit commanders, all of them guiding the movement through their chosen medium, Joseph Kony? The spirits were unquestionably real in the eyes of Kony's followers. Those named above spoke only through Kony, at designated times when he dressed in a white gown and awaited their visitations. As in Alice's movement, their pronouncements were recorded by a secretary, with the identity of each spirit speaker duly noted.

Unlike Alice, Kony also allowed others to channel spirits. One of his commanders, for example, became a spokesman for a spirit who called himself Gabriel and enabled him to heal the wounded, predict NRA attacks, and deflect bombs away from Kony's camp. But no one except Kony was permitted to speak on behalf of his special spirits.

It is evident that the Holy Spirit Movement had by this point become anything but a movement for authentically Christian renewal, even though the Ten Commandments remained a central part of the movement's rules of conduct. Already in Alice Lakwena's time the initial prohibition against any direct killing had been quickly abandoned. For both of these leaders, spiritual war had become armed rebellion.

The rule that Lakwena's recruits reportedly found most objectionable, and most difficult to observe, was the prohibition of adultery and fornication. Raping and kidnapping civilian women as spoils of war were common practices for all of the many competing armies of East Africa. On some occasions, soldiers in Lakwena's army were executed for violating this rule.

Under Kony this form of holiness was no longer demanded. There were still strict rules regulating marriage and sexual relations, and some soldiers were punished severely for their violation. But Kony said he had received instructions that captured women should be assigned to keep house and bear children to officers in his army, to reward the officers for their bravery and faithful service. Greater accomplishments warranted the assignment of more women. Kony himself had several dozen wives, according to members of the movement—by some accounts as many as 70.

Until now I have referred generically to the Holy Spirit Movement, of which Kony claimed to be the leader after Alice Lakwena's defeat and flight. The name under which Kony organized his reign of terror on northern Uganda, the Lord's Resistance Army, was not yet used in the first years of his movement. Kony's movement absorbed many former members of the HSMF, as well as defectors from the Uganda People's Defence Army. According to some sources he was once allied with the former, while others identify him as a onetime officer in the Ugandan national army. A rival formed a new army and named it the United Uganda Godly Movement, but shortly afterward he merged his organization into Kony's. In 1988, Kony introduced yet another name when he announced to a group of journalists—kidnapped in order to give them a news briefing and later released—that he was the leader of the Uganda People's Democratic Christian Army.

By the following year, the movement had adopted the familiar title of the Lord's Resistance Army. As a military organization, it was organized into three divisions, plus a mobile reserve unit, and in each division were three sections, the Father, Son, and Holy Ghost companies. Soldiers who joined the movement were first required to undergo an initiation ceremony in which shea butter oil and ochre were painted onto their bodies in the form of a cross, holy water was sprinkled over them, and they recited a pledge to give their souls to God's service. They were told that angels now dwelt within them, and after three days of isolation the new recruits were declared ready for service.

In the first years of the movement Kony's forces followed rituals similar to those of the HSMF, involving periods of singing, sprinkling holy water to confuse enemy soldiers, lobbing stone grenades, and destroying small models of enemy weapons. Kony claimed that bees and snakes fought with them against their enemies, and his soldiers were forbidden to kill any wild animals. The persistence of this regulation may be a lingering reaction to the wholesale slaughter of wildlife by fleeing soldiers of Amin's regime. Recall that the surviving animals at

Paraa had reportedly spoken to Alice Lakwena about the suffering they had endured at the hands of evil men.

Kony's Appeal and His Changing Tactics

What has been related above concerning the protracted conflict between north and south, between Museveni's National Resistance Army and the Amin armed forces they displaced, and between the NRA on its punitive campaigns and the numerous militias of northern Uganda, provides essential background for understanding the rapid rise of the LRA. From its origin as a spinoff from the Holy Spirit Movement, Kony's movement enjoyed widespread support in the Acholi region because it promised to restore the status and privileges that had been snatched away after Museveni's rise to power.

The NRA campaign to root out the vestiges of Alice Lakwena's rebel army in the north proved to be no less brutal and rapacious than the tactics of the rebel armies, and it received little local support. Those who aided government forces in locating the strongholds of the rebels feared for their lives, and many were tracked down and executed for their betrayal. It was safer to cooperate with the various rebel forces, who waged war on NRA soldiers but—at least in the 1980s—left the civilian population alone to carry on as normal a life as they could while bullets flew around them.

American political scientist Aili Marie Tripp, whose bleak assessment of Uganda's ineffectual response to LRA violence was quoted at the beginning of this chapter, has characterized the Museveni government as a "hybrid regime," a "pseudodemocracy" in which regular elections are held but there is little political freedom. On the basis of ratings by the international NGO Freedom House, which assess citizens' political rights and civil liberties, she has classified the 47 nations of sub-Saharan Africa into four categories: democratic, "semidemocratic" hybrid regimes, "semiauthoritarian" hybrid regimes, and fully authoritarian governments. Uganda falls into the third category, as do its neighbors Kenya, Ethiopia, the DRC and Rwanda. This analysis is helpful in understanding why the Ugandan government's efforts to crush northern rebels achieved so little.

The lack of effective democracy, despite its superficial features such as parliamentary and presidential elections, made the southern-dominated government deaf to the appeals of northerners for more effective protection. And in the north, where the NRM party wins very few votes, government denials of army misconduct and assurances that victory over the LRA was imminent had no credibility. Thus the political divisions of the country and the lack of effective accountability for the behavior of its army helped indirectly to build Kony's movement (Tripp 2010, 11–22).

It is difficult for an outside observer to get an accurate sense of whether Kony's calls for spiritual renewal and his invocations of guiding spirits enhanced his appeal to the Acholi people. The individuals whom I interviewed in Gulu in January 2014 who had been part of the LRA movement all gave the reports of spiritual communication a great deal of credibility. The spirits' pronouncements were genuine messages, they said, not fictions invented to serve Kony's purposes, even if the medium might have shaped their content in ways that suited his purposes. Yet no one whom I interviewed seemed to regard Kony's claimed access to an entire Olympian parliament of spirits as an important influence on potential followers. Nor was his claim to be a prophet speaking in a Biblical vein, calling on people to follow the Scriptural commandments more faithfully, regarded as either credible or influential as his movement grew.

Why, then, did Kony draw so many enthusiastic and dedicated volunteer followers in the first years of his movement? The people of the region had been worn down by unrelenting violence and counterviolence, in which all the warring factions played a part. Government troops, heavily armed but poorly disciplined, had oppressed their communities for many years. One of the church workers whom I interviewed commented:

When Museveni came into power, because of fear that they might be killed by the government, many Acholi joined Alice Lakwena. When Alice tried and failed, many of the former soldiers thought they would find a safe haven by joining Kony. . . . And this fear was increased because of some killings by government soldiers. So people thought that if they joined Kony they would at least have somewhere to hide. (Okot 2014)

One of the most perceptive accounts of Kony's movement is that of Swedish anthropologist Sverker Finnström, informed by several extended periods of residency among the Acholi during the time of LRA domination. Without dismissing or in any way justifying LRA tactics, Finnström refutes Western perceptions of Kony as an unprincipled terrorist seeking the death and destruction of any who oppose him. His informants recount the many ways in which they have been oppressed by the Museveni government, whose spokesmen—once more reverting to racial stereotypes from the colonial era—have described the Acholi people as "very violent—it's genetic" (Finnström 2008, 114).

Acholi society grants a high degree of deference to the elders, advisors to the traditional chiefs. Kony's relationship to these traditions was complex, Finnström shows. Although he claimed to be acting to preserve both the people and the traditions of the Acholi community, he never met the criteria that tradition requires for elders' review and approval of any resort to war. According to Acholi tradition, declaration of war requires that clan elders reach consensus in support of this recommendation and seal their approval by giving a pair of sacred fire-making sticks to the clan's warriors. Kony claimed to have received the blessing of Acholi clan elders for his struggle to drive out the NRA and restore respect for his people. There was no credible testimony that any elders had given him the fire sticks, however. For this reason, his claim to be acting on behalf of the Acholi people was disputed.

Moreover, the actions and words of Acholi elders in the early years of the conflict provoked further controversy. Many of Finnström's informants looked to their clan elders for wisdom and guidance, but what they saw instead were signs of opportunism and weakness. The elders who were expected to help address Acholi grievances, and to take forceful action to restrain Kony's excesses in his campaign of liberation, were indecisive and inconsistent. Initially they spoke in support of Kony's movement and encouraged young people to join, but later they denounced those who had joined. Worse yet, many of the elders themselves fled to the safety of Europe or North America rather than stay to relieve the suffering of their people. Young people told Finnström that they had lost their respect for "veranda elders," respected leaders who are hypocritical and cowardly in their words and actions (Finnström 2008, 211–218).

Just what was the key to Kony's early appeal is difficult to discern, even if we consider only the period before its most brutal practices were adopted. Kony's claims to speak for powerful spirits, and his invocation of Old Testament laws, seem to have had relatively little appeal to new followers. His unrelenting opposition to witchcraft and to the use of potions and amulets may have been a more important element in attracting followers and winning support. In this respect Kony could be seen as a source of liberation from traditional practices that caused a great deal of anxiety and suffering in northern Uganda, and indeed across the continent of Africa. Like the Protestant and Catholic missionaries of the 19th century, Kony promised deliverance from sickness caused by spells, potions, and curses. But where the missionaries discounted any claims of harm resulting from witchcraft or spirit possession, Kony took these phenomena seriously. His response was not to deny that such supernatural mischief could occur, but rather to offer a more powerful array of spirits who could defeat the spirits who sought to do his followers ill. Followers of the LRA were strictly forbidden to resort to witchcraft of any sort, but they were also assured that when it was used against them it would not prevail.

Before long the character of the LRA and the tactics that it used changed dramatically. What had been a small and idiosyncratic spiritual renewal movement, linked to grandiose but unattainable military goals, became one of the most cruel and repressive rebel movements that the world has ever seen and that its people have ever endured. By the middle 1990s, the LRA was enlarging its ranks by staging raids on villages, killing and maiming at will, and kidnapping young men and women. Where LRA troops had once emerged from the bush, weapons at their sides, primarily to steal grain and livestock, they turned increasingly to campaigns that left villages leveled and burned, littered by the bodies of any who resisted their demands or who were simply judged too old or too young to be useful to the movement.

Raiding parties preferred to seize children no older than 16, leaving behind the adults and younger children who had not been killed. Boys were trained as soldiers, using intense psychological pressure and inhumane tactics to overcome their resistance to killing on command. Abducted girls were assigned as wives to LRA commanders, most of whom already had one or more wives in their compound. Some reported being treated with respect and even affection. Others were beaten and deprived of food, living as domestic slaves. Along with the training of the abductees came an unceasing diet of propaganda extolling the wisdom of Kony and the wickedness of his enemies.

Even as the tactics of the movement became more violent, and destruction of villages and disruption of families more common, LRA leaders continued to circulate statements of their political goals for Uganda, which centered on an end to the repressive one-party rule of the NRM.

Among all those who have written about the conflict, Finnström is the only observer who highlights the content and the purpose of LRA political statements, circulated from hand to hand in the region or posted on the Internet. Copies of the manifestos in written form were sometimes given to travelers when they stopped at LRA roadblocks, along with an impromptu lecture on the justice of the LRA cause.

In 1997, during fieldwork, I was given one such manifesto. The one-page document promotes, first, the immediate restoration of multiparty politics and, second, the introduction of constitutional federalism. The next items express the need for free and fair forthcoming elections, the establishment of good relations with neighboring countries, improvements in the judicial system, and demands that the military organization be separated from the judicial and executive. A subsequent and much longer manifesto also promotes human rights, as well as "national unity" and the restoration of "political pluralism." (Finnström 2008, 122)

Most observers of the movement dismiss these and similar documents as fabrications written by Acholi living abroad—a position in line with that of the Ugandan government. Finnström found, however, that they were frequently mentioned, and taken as serious political statements, by residents of Acholi towns and villages. The government not only refused to respond to these demands but actively suppressed any information concerning LRA political goals. Some activists were arrested, and at least one died in government custody, simply because they had spoken publicly about the content of the manifesto statements.

The government's categorical denial that there was a political dimension to the LRA movement probably increased the credibility of Kony's claim to be the champion of the Acholi. It may even have contributed to the increasing brutality of LRA tactics, Finnström suggests: many of his informants believe that government denunciations of his terrorist tactics served only to encourage their intensification.

> As one informant put it in 2002, when he imagined Joseph Kony's way of thinking, "They say I am a terrorist. Well, let it be so, and let me then give them terrorism." (Finnström 2008, 128)

The political demands of the LRA movement cannot be taken at face value, needless to say. Calls for multiparty democracy and proclamations of respect for human rights ring hollow when their authors wage a campaign of kidnapping, abduction and rape. Rather than lend assistance to local government representatives who sought peace, LRA commanders condemned them, and sometimes murdered them, as suspected collaborators with the Uganda People's Defence Force (UPDF, known until 1995 as the NRA). All the same, it is important to recognize that the official account of the LRA that was disseminated worldwide by the Museveni government—that it was nothing more than the private army of a rapacious and power-hungry warlord seeking to subjugate and dominate the region—was far from the whole truth.

Life Under the LRA

Just as the film adaptation of "The Last King of Scotland" had brought home to global audiences the brutality and instability of Idi Amin, the Invisible Children video "Kony 2012" conveyed to more than a hundred million viewers worldwide the ferocity of LRA tactics. As we have discussed in Chapter 1, the video was inaccurate or misleading in many ways, most notably in implying that the LRA was still active in northern Uganda, six years after it had withdrawn and released most of its abductees, and in depicting the people of the region as passive victims of violence. The depiction of the brutality with which the LRA had once dominated the Acholi region, however, was all too accurate, as numerous sources have documented.

Several of the individuals I interviewed who had been LRA captives described how incidents of unspeakable cruelty that would once have shocked and horrified them came to seem normal. After he had spent about two months in the bush, Moses Okello related:

> We saw an officer who had been beaten with 600 strokes because he had violated the rules [by having unauthorized sexual relations with an abducted girl]. Then the order came from Kony that he should be killed. They don't want anyone to go ahead and have sex with recruits. So he was killed with a bayonet. Being killed with a bayonet is very painful. (Okello 2014)

Lucy Okwarmoi described an induction ritual from which, thankfully, she was spared, thanks to her successful deception.

> They say that when you are abducted, all of you must kill someone. Each time they captured someone who had been abducted and who tried to run away, they would kill him. And they would say, there are those of you who have not yet killed a person—you must come and kill. They would give you a stick and make you beat the person until he was dead. But I would tell them, me, I have already killed. And then they would not disturb me. So that is why I came out without having any blood on my hands. . . .
>
> Sometimes these people would clash with the UPDF soldiers and they would fire guns everywhere. I have a wound just here on my back—the bullet came through like this and then it came out here. If it had gone straight I would be dead. I was running away and praying. I was very young, I did not know how to pray very well, and I was only saying, "God, protect me—I have faith." (Okwarmoi 2014)

One of the most revealing published accounts of the devastating effects of LRA violence is a work of fiction, not journalism: American writer Susan Minot's 2014 novel *Thirty Girls,* which retells the story of a 1996 raid on St. Mary's School in Aboke, near Lira in the Acholi region. There, 139 girls were rounded up and marched into the forest under armed guard, pursued by a courageous nun who confronted the LRA commander and demanded their release. The commander agreed to release most of the girls after selecting 30 who would be taken on to LRA camps, there to be distributed to the most loyal and effective officers as sexual partners. Five of the girls died in captivity, at least two of them after brutal beatings for minor infractions of the movement's rules. Minot's novel follows one of the girls through her ordeal, and while accurately conveying what is known about the treatment of abductees she also enriches her narrative with poems that convey the search for meaning and the inner suffering that the girls endured. (A more extensive discussion of the strengths and the shortcomings of *Thirty Girls* can be found at Hoekema 2015.)

Children who had been abducted and later escaped provided vivid accounts of what they had witnessed and endured. A girl of sixteen named Susan, for example, told volunteers from Human Rights Watch:

> One boy tried to escape, but he was caught. They made him eat a mouthful of red pepper, and five people were beating him. His hands were tied, and then they made us, the other new captives, kill him with a stick. I felt sick. I knew this boy from before. We were from the same village. I refused to kill him and they told me they would shoot me. They pointed a gun at me, so I had to do it. The boy was asking me, "Why are you doing this?" I said I had no choice. After we killed him, they made us smear his blood on our arms. I felt dizzy. There was another dead body nearby, and I could smell the body. I felt so sick. They said we had to do this so we would not fear death and so we would not try to escape (Human Rights Watch 1997).

A boy of fourteen named Timothy described his experiences as a child soldier in combat:

> I was good at shooting. I went for several battles in Sudan. The soldiers on the other side would be squatting, but we would stand in a straight line. The commanders were behind us. They would tell us to run straight into gunfire. The commanders would stay behind and would beat those of us who would not run forward. You would

just run forward shooting your gun. I don't know if I actually killed any people, because you really can't tell if you're shooting people or not. I might have killed people in the course of the fighting . . . . I remember the first time I was in the front line. The other side started firing, and the commander ordered us to run towards the bullets. I panicked. I saw others falling down dead around me. The commanders were beating us for not running, for trying to crouch down. They said if we fall down, we would be shot and killed by the soldiers.

In Sudan we were fighting the Dinkas, and other Sudanese civilians. I don't know why we were fighting them. We were just ordered to fight. (Human Rights Watch 1997)

One of the women who was abducted from her home village and assigned as a wife to Joseph Kony himself has described her experiences in extraordinary detail. The individual is Evelyn Amony, now working as a human rights advocate in Gulu, and her book is entitled *I am Evelyn Amony: Reclaiming My Life from the Lord's Resistance Army*. She set out to write about her experience, she writes, because "I want my family to know what I went through, but I cannot just tell them, for they would begin to weep." The family to which she refers includes the two children whom she bore as Kony's wife, set free with her when the NRA overran the camp where they were living.

It is easier for my children to read and learn about how I was abducted and all that I went through, how I conceived and gave birth to my daughters. They can then ask me for clarification. If I were to narrate this verbally to my daughters, it would be too heartbreaking. These are difficult stories. (Amony 2015, xii-xiii)

The "difficult stories" are often unimaginably brutal. On one occasion, when a village was not being sufficiently cooperative, an LRA captain ordered his men to come back to him with the private parts of fifty men they had killed and the unborn fetuses they had ripped out of the wombs of five pregnant women (Amony 2015, 94). Yet Amony insists that the horrible acts of LRA forces were no more cruel or more frequent than those committed by NRA troops. "The truth has to be brought out that both sides committed atrocities in this war," she insists: "the government did certain things, and the LRA did certain things" (Amony 2015, xiii).

Conducting research for his book on the LRA conflict, Polish journalist Wojciech Jagielski found in the files of a Gulu orphanage the story of a boy named Samuel who had been kidnapped from his village and trained as an LRA soldier. Based on Samuel's account, Jagielski provides a heartrending description of the cruelty of LRA forces when attacking a village that they regarded as harboring government informants. The attack occurred at night and took all the villagers by surprise. Gathering all the residents in a central square, some of the LRA guerrillas questioned the adults about the movements of government soldiers, while others looted their huts, then set them on fire.

> The flames shooting into the sky made the square as bright as day. When they had finished their interrogation, the older guerrillas started killing the villagers. The commanders forbade them from shooting unnecessarily, to save bullets, and also because the noise of shots could alert the army. The peasants were tied up and made to lie on the ground, as the guerrillas unhurriedly murdered them one by one—men, women, old people, and also small children who weren't fit to be prisoners. They killed them with machetes, hoes, and large knives, usually used as agricultural tools. None of the villagers put up resistance or fought for their lives. Terror and a sense of doom had taken away their capacity for any kind of action.
>
> As they left the brightly burning village, they cut down the mango trees growing on its edges. They always did that, to prevent the trees from bearing any more fruit, which could have saved the inhabitants from dying of hunger.

According to the boy's account, the guerrillas stayed away from army posts but only raided Acholi villages—those that were seen as unsympathetic to Kony's movement.

> So, on the order of their superiors, the guerrillas killed the villagers in extremely cruel ways. They butchered and burned them alive,

forced the prisoners to commit cannibalism and infanticide. They raped and tortured, cut off people's lips, gouged out their eyes, and chopped off their hands and feet. They left behind bloodied corpses and gutted houses. And also the wrappers from cookies and candy they stole from the village stores, which instantly changed them back into children unable to resist sweets. With every murder the more senior guerrillas kept telling the younger ones, "Now you have nowhere to go home to. There's no way back for you." (Jagielski 2012, 120–121)

The brutality of life in rural areas of northern Uganda was unknown to outsiders for decades. Escapees related their sufferings to family members, pastors, and imams, but because the region was unsafe for journalists these stories were seldom relayed to a broader audience. Moreover, many of those who escaped said little about their experiences for fear of being ostracized by their families—or captured and killed by government forces, as Kony's propaganda had led them to expect. Only in the years after the LRA disbanded in Uganda, and travel became safe once more in and out of the region, did these horrors become more widely known.

International Forces that Sustained Kony's Movement

Why, we may well wonder, was Kony's movement able to hold so much of northern Uganda in the grip of terror for nearly a quarter-century? How could a small rebel group sustain itself against unrelenting pressure from well-armed government troops, and how could it meet its own demands for food, supplies, and arms from a country already mired in poverty?

The answer is that the LRA did not long remain solely a domestic insurgency. It became an element of a regional power struggle between the governments of two nations—Uganda and Sudan—each of which was fighting against several private militias that moved back and forth across the porous borders of East Africa. And this in turn was a small piece of a larger contest between the major international powers, each of whom backed one of the combatants in Uganda for its own strategic purposes.

In a well-documented journalistic account of Kony's movement and its place in regional and global politics, Matthew Green writes that

> Following Kony's fortunes from reports that filtered into the Nairobi newsroom, it was easy to assume that the war was driven mainly by the prophetic voices in his head. Viewed from Khartoum, the picture looked rather different. The more I talked to people in Sudan, the more I began to realize that Kony was a bit player in a much bigger drama. (Green 2009, 205)

An important development of the 1990s that made it possible for the LRA to draw on Sudanese sources for funds, supplies, and weapons was the establishment of an Islamist regime in Khartoum, which enlisted the help of a number of internal militias to suppress any resistance in rural areas. The Arab Baggar militia was sent out to loot, rape, and capture slaves in areas that opposed the new government. Another armed group, the Equatoria Defence Force, was commanded by Sudanese warlords but included many Acholi soldiers from the Sudanese side of the border.

Museveni was seen as a principal adversary of the new Sudanese regime, and there were frequent clashes between NRA soldiers and Sudanese militias. For the Islamist regime in Khartoum, the temptation to enlist the LRA as an ally of the pro-Islamist and anti-Museveni cause was irresistible, even though the LRA was supposedly a Christian movement. Kony and his army were richly rewarded with funds and weapons for their assistance in protecting Sudan's southern flank against the NRA. They were also allowed free movement across the border, providing a place of refuge whenever the Ugandan military drew too close for comfort.

Green draws attention to the way this regional conflict came to be part of a larger conflict:

> Alex de Waal [in *Islamism and its Enemies in the Horn of Africa*] writes that by late 1996 an "undeclared regional war" had broken out between Sudan and a short-lived alliance of Uganda, Rwanda, Ethiopia, and Eritrea. By this time, Kony was just one counter in a

battle entangling myriad militias, rebel groups, and armies, all divided roughly along pro- and anti-Khartoum lines. Uganda played
a pivotal role, sending troops into Sudan to fight the Sudanese
army alongside the SPLA, with support from Ethiopia and
Eritrea. Some even argued that Museveni was happy for the war in
northern Uganda to continue because it served as a smokescreen
for the weapons and troops being shipped into the Sudan border
region. Behind the scenes, the United States was the biggest player
of all. Washington financed its allies in the so-called "frontline
states" in their efforts to contain Khartoum, with Museveni at
center stage. During a visit to Kampala, US Secretary of State
Madeleine Albright called him a "beacon of hope," prompting
one frustrated opposition politician to say, "She's a witch." (Green
2009, 207–208)

In his historic visit to Africa in 1998, visiting more countries and
extending his stay longer than any predecessor, President Clinton hailed
the "new breed" of democratically elected African leaders, singling out
Museveni for his commitment to economic growth and to a purportedly multiparty democracy. In a widely publicized speech in Ghana he
expressed the hope that "100 years from now, your grandchildren and
mine will look back and say this was the beginning of a new African
renaissance."

On his arrival in Uganda President Clinton joined six African presidents in signing a wide-ranging commitment to human rights, press
freedom, democratic governance, and international collaboration.
Their joint statement affirmed "a shared commitment to respect for
human rights, as articulated in the UN Declaration of Human Rights
and the African Charter on Human and People's Rights." All the signatory parties pledged to uphold humanitarian principles, including the
right of civilians to assistance in situations of conflict and the protection of refugees and noncombatants (Clinton 1998). Not long after this
trip, Clinton welcomed the Ugandan president to the White House for
an official visit, an uncommon honor seldom given to an African head
of state.

Green adds his observations concerning America's blinkered view of the conflict.

> Washington even dispensed some praise for Museveni's conduct of the war in the north. The then Assistant Secretary of State for African Affairs Susan Rice told Congress in July 1998 that she believed the Ugandan government was trying to respect the human rights of noncombatants and deal "as humanely as possible" with abductees in the rebel ranks, though she said more had to be done on those fronts. Looking back, I wondered if she might not have been a tad harder on the army, who tended to list captured rebels as "rescued children" while the abducted youngsters they sometimes shot were added to the body count as "terrorists." (Green 2009, 208)

Subsequent events bore out the concerns of the skeptics. Within a year after the proclamation, several of the leaders had launched or lent their support to cross-border wars on each other. Uganda and Rwanda were supporting a rebellion in the Congo, then clashing with each other. Ethiopia launched a border war with Kenya. The African renaissance welcomed by the American president was looking rather threadbare already (Onitsi, 1979).

While Western governments lauded Museveni's achievements and asked few questions about the tactics employed by his army, there was also, Green discovered, a network of Ugandans in exile in Europe, Britain, and North America who were helping the LRA, sending donations and helping recruit external support. Some were motivated by the suffering that their family members had endured at the hands of the national army. Others were angling for a position of influence if the LRA should succeed in driving Museveni out. The president had promised to protect the Acholi people against civil unrest and build up the economy, but in fact he had allowed them to sink deeper into poverty and left them living in constant fear. Why, then, should they place their allegiance with the Ugandan government?

From the perspective of Western governments and donors, however, the LRA was scarcely visible. The limited information that trickled out of Uganda seemed to support the government's claims that it was a small band of rebels that would soon be defeated. Green comments dryly:

It was hard to think of two more contrasting public personas than the soldier-scholar who was welcomed at the White House [Museveni, by Clinton] and the dreadlocked clairvoyant who spoke to angels, but they shared one thing in common. Both seemed oblivious to the suffering their strategies were causing. Casting Kony as the arch villain of the piece made it easier for Museveni's powerful backers in London and Washington to turn a blind eye, not only to his failure in dealing with the conflict, but to their complicity in tacitly endorsing his strategy. . . .

Vacillating between futile jingoism and demanding the surrender of men he had branded "terrorists" or "hyenas" when the time came to talk, Museveni never really seemed to acknowledge the genuine grievances nursed by the Acholi, let alone come up with a convincing plan. But he was a useful ally, so few questions were asked. (Green 2009, 311–312)

Back on the ground in northern Uganda, LRA tactics of terrorism, kidnapping, maiming, and rape continued through the 1990s, but the world took little notice. Even residents and visitors in the more populated southern regions of Uganda were scarcely aware of events just a few hundred miles to the north. Journalists and the public relied on government reports of periodic clashes, and they had no access to more accurate information that would contradict the government's repeated assurances that the LRA army had suffered devastating losses and would soon collapse and disband. Visitors to Kampala in the late 1990s and early 2000s reported hearing only that the national army was involved in a clean-up operation in remote regions of the north. An exhaustive study commissioned by the World Bank and published in 2001, co-authored by the eminent development economist Paul Collier, lauded "the recovery of peace in Uganda during 1986-99," making no reference to the LRA and other internal rebel groups except to note that they had been "unable to escalate their operations to become a serious threat" (Collier and Reinikka 2001, 22).

Outside Uganda, the conflict was scarcely visible to anyone except Ugandans abroad, owing to the scarcity of any information sources not directed and controlled by the Museveni government. Journalists who ventured north of the Victoria Nile were risking their lives, and very few did so. Reports trickled out of the region from time to time, from pastors and development workers who had seen the horrors of the LRA's campaigns at first hand. But they attracted little attention and were given little credibility. When both the national government and leading international agencies discounted the LRA movement— "not a serious threat" to peace, according to the World Bank authors in 2001—it was easy to dismiss the reports of atrocities.

In contrast with the absence of information conveyed to the outside world, in the Acholi region information about the tactics and goals of both sides was quickly carried by word of mouth—including information that was completely false but difficult to refute. Much of the misinformation reinforced fears of the national government and its allies. Relief agencies, arm in arm with the Kampala government, were trying to poison the people, informants told Finnström. Their evidence: the death of eight rebel soldiers after they ate bags of seed that had come from NGO trucks. The seed was intended only for planting, not human consumption, and may have been coated with hazardous pesticides, but accusations of intentional poisoning—or witchcraft—seemed plausible. When HIV/AIDS and Ebola outbreaks occurred in the northern regions, rumors circulated that the Ugandan government was deliberately sending infected soldiers into the north. Whatever atrocities LRA soldiers were committing, many believed, the tactics of the government army were just as cruel—and intended, so it appeared, to wipe out not just the LRA movement but the Acholi people (Finnström 2008, 158, 188–190).

A resident of the Gulu region recalled, ten years later, events that had occurred at a time when most of the world believed peace had been all but restored to the northern regions:

> The LRA like to attack at this time of day [at dusk]. They can see you, but you cannot see them well enough to recognize who they are. It was at this time of day that they came to my hut. They asked for food; I gave them that. They asked for money; I gave them that. Then they tied my hands behind my back. They were going to abduct me. When they turned to get the money I ran away. My brother and I lived on Mount Lalak for two days on soda and crackers until they left Lokung.

This occurred in early January, 1997, his companion added. In the Lokung subcounty, in three days' time, LRA raids killed 550 Acholi residents. The retaliatory bombing raids of the Ugandan army, raining down on villages as well as rebel outposts, killed 417 more (Whitmore 2010, 158).

For nearly two decades, from 1986 until the early 2000s, Joseph Kony's guerrilla army maintained control of large areas of northern Uganda and staged frequent raids on villages of the region, killing or maiming anyone who resisted the seizure of crops and other goods, kidnapping adolescent boys and girls, and inflicting severe reprisals on anyone who gave information to NRA forces. The Ugandan army in turn wreaked vengeance on villages they suspected of harboring or aiding Kony's troops, killing and raping and kidnapping at will. Several of those whom I interviewed quoted an Acholi proverb: "When elephants fight, it is the grass that suffers."

The Museveni government eventually acknowledged its inability to offer effective protection against LRA raids to the people of northern Uganda, even after several major military campaigns had led to massive casualties but ended in a continuing stalemate. As rural residents fled for safety to nearby towns, the government assisted them in resettling, and soon this small-scale movement was transformed into a massive network of temporary camps for internally displaced persons. Voluntary transfers gave way to a policy of forced removal from rural areas, and by the late 1990s 90 percent of the people of the Acholi region had left their home villages for the new resettlement camps for internally displaced persons (IDP camps). The situation of camp residents was depicted vividly in a 2007 documentary film, "War Dance," recounting the decision of school pupils from an IDP camp in Patongo to compete in a national music and dance competition in 2005, bringing home several awards. It is in the end an uplifting documentary film despite the horrors endured by the children (Fine and Nix 2007).

Only hinted at in the film are the squalid conditions of poverty and inactivity in which most of the people of northern Uganda were forced to live for a decade or more. We will look more closely at life in the camps later, in chapter 5. By the late 1990s, it is clear, the people of northern Uganda had descended to a level of poverty and inactivity that had seldom been endured by any large population in Africa or elsewhere. Culture was disrupted as well, as traditional celebrations and festivals were abandoned. The complex relationships between parents and children, between old and young, between farmers and traders and teachers and pupils, were all thrown into disarray by the crowded conditions and insecurities of life in the camps.

Yet profound changes for the better were in store. How these changes came about will be the subject of another chapter, in which we will take note of the "night commuters" whose daily journey heightened awareness of the conflict, the formation of the Acholi Religious Leaders Peace Initiative, and the intervention of several other parties including NGO organizations and neighboring governments in bringing the LRA nightmare to an end at last.

Before recounting these developments, however, we will pause to fill in some background concerning the history of relations among various religious communities in Uganda. In order to grasp how difficult a task the leaders of ARLPI faced when they sought to bring together their respective communities for mutual assistance, we need to understand a little more about how Protestant and Catholic missionaries were received in the 19th century by adherents of traditional African religion, and by the small but long-standing Muslim communities of East Africa. It to these topics that we turn briefly in Chapter 4.

Note

1. This group existed only from 1986–1988, and it had long been dissolved when the Ugandan army, the National Resistance Army, was renamed the Uganda People's Defence Force in 1995, as described below.

4

Religion and Culture in Uganda

The way religion came to Uganda, and maybe all of Africa, the religions came differently with different motives. So people have grown up thinking that an Anglican person has nothing to do with a Catholic person and a Catholic person has nothing in common with a Muslim person. The Catholics had their own churches, their own structures, their own schools, and Catholics would provide these things for Catholics. And it is the same with the Muslims. That kind of arrangement, we still see it up to now. Traditional people still think in that traditional way, remembering how religion came to Uganda.

When a Catholic bishop sits with an Anglican bishop and a Muslim imam, people look at this and think, this is weird! But we organize our events and activities in a neutral way that brings all different groups together so that all of the congregations can see how these people are living in harmony.

You are a Christian and I am a Muslim; we are different people with different beliefs. But really we are the same people, believing in one God. We are just taking different directions, but we have the same destinations. Even some of our holy books are the same, but we have different ways to pray—which way we face. That is why we always advocate using many different media that we are one people taking different roads to the same goal. And that is why ARLPI is unique.

—Abdalla Latif Nasur,
ARLPI project officer (Nasur 2014)

AS I BEGIN WRITING THIS chapter, the annual fast of Ramadan has just begun. This 28-day dawn-to-dusk fast commemorates the time when Prophet Mohammed reported that the angel Jibril (Gabriel) dictated the text of the Qur'an. Observant Muslims began fasting today, eating a light pre-dawn breakfast and then taking no food or water until evening. The fast is held during the ninth month of the Islamic lunar calendar, which does not track the Western solar calendar, so it can occur in any season.

For Muslims in Europe and North America, a Ramadan fast in midsummer is especially difficult, since the period of fasting is longer than in other seasons. Here in Western Michigan the sun rose at 6 am today and will set at 9:20 pm. That means more than 15 hours of fasting. (Those who are very young, very old, or ill are exempt from the fast.) In London this week the period of daylight is an hour longer, in Oslo three hours longer. Muslims in the tropical latitudes are fortunate in this regard: no matter what the solar season, their Ramadan fast lasts exactly 12 hours. (Some Islamic authorities, it should be noted, caution that the fast should never extend longer than 18 hours, and others recommend that those in extreme latitudes simply schedule their fast in accord with sunrise and sunset times in Mecca.)

When the next new moon first becomes visible in 28 days, Ugandans will honor the feast of Eid al-Fitr with a national holiday, as will their neighbors in Kenya, Ethiopia, and Rwanda. Many other countries in Africa—not just those with Muslim majorities, such as those of North Africa and former French West Africa, but also Ghana, which is overwhelmingly Christian—will celebrate a national holiday to mark the festival. But in Europe and North America, the day will be an ordinary business day.

What are the historical and cultural factors that explain the public acknowledgment of the Muslim religious year in many parts of Africa, even where Christians are a large majority of the population? Western democracies see the right to free exercise of religion as an inalienable right, one that is enshrined in national constitutions and in United Nations documents, and yet their national holidays continue to favor Christians. Federal holidays declared by Congressional action in the United States include Thanksgiving Day and Christmas, but no religious holidays celebrated by Muslim or Jewish citizens. The United Kingdom adds Good Friday and Easter Monday to the list. A petition drive in 2015 seeking to add Eid al-Fitr to the federal holiday list in the United States gathered more than 100,000 endorsements but achieved no success (Chan 2015). But the Muslim minorities in many African countries—no larger proportionally than in some European countries—are given special recognition.

This seemingly small difference in the designation of national holidays offers some clues to the complex relationships between religion, ethnicity, and politics in East Africa. As a supplement to the history of Ugandan political life from pre-colonial times to the present, which has been provided in earlier chapters, we turn aside for a moment from the depredations of the LRA and the increasingly important work of ARLPI in order to provide a brief sketch of the religious history out of which both of these movements emerged in the late 20th century.

We will understand the significance of the interfaith activism of ARLPI better if we take note, in this chapter, of several factors that have shaped its environment. These include the history of Christian and Muslim propagation in the Great Lakes region; a shocking historical event that has shaped contemporary expressions and perceptions of Christianity in particular; and the highly public role that religion plays in African life, in contrast with its more private function in the developed world. A brief account of these factors in this chapter will help us assess the contributions of ARLPI more accurately in the remaining chapters of this study.

Muslims and Christians Across Africa

The religious history of the continent of Africa could be characterized, in broad strokes, as having three stages. First, from the time of the earliest organized human settlements, indigenous traditions have arisen, differing from one ethnic group to the next, even from one village to the next, yet sharing some common elements as pre-literate or "primal" religious traditions. Among their common elements, argue religious historians such as Andrew Walls, are seamless integration of natural and spiritual worlds and respect for ancestors. Features such as these are found not only across Africa but in other regions of the world as well, linked to traditions and rituals handed down orally from generation to generation (Walls 1987).

Second, beginning in the 8th century CE, Islam spread in Africa along with traders from the Middle East, both along the Swahili Coast and along interior trans-Saharan caravan routes, and in a few centuries it had become a dominant religious tradition alongside traditional religions in much of sub-Saharan Africa, as well as on the Mediterranean coast.

The third stage was the period when Christians from Europe began to travel along the coast of West Africa and around the Cape of Good Hope in the 15th and 16th centuries CE. Small coastal outposts were settled by European traders in the 16th and 17th centuries. Missionaries soon followed, initially in very small numbers, then in larger regional missions in the 18th and 19th centuries. Church membership increased steadily in the 19th century and continued at an even more rapid pace in the 20th.[1]

The Catholic presence in the Great Lakes region began with the arrival of the Spiritan Fathers (members of the Congregation of the Holy Ghost), who established missions at Zanzibar and on the nearby coast in the 1860s. The missionaries sent by Rome to the interior, in the decades that followed, were predominantly White Fathers (Society of Missionaries to Africa). Protestant missions to Buganda had begun decades earlier with the earliest British explorers, nearly all representing the Anglican communion—indeed, in Uganda "Anglican" often serves as a synonym for "Protestant."

None of these movements displaced the earlier ones. Traditional beliefs and practices remain widespread and important, not just in remote rural areas but in Africa's cities as well, and they often coexist today with Muslim or Christian affiliation. But there has been very rapid growth in the Christian churches of Africa, and substantial growth also in adherence to Islam.

The relationship between these two missionary faiths in Africa, Christianity and Islam, is probably more complex, and more variable from region to region, than in any other part of the world. A few examples from West Africa will illustrate this complexity. In Nigeria, the northeastern regions have witnessed wave after wave of violence committed by Christians against Muslims and by Muslims against Christians. A group that claims to be an indigenous branch of the radical Islamist movement, Boko Haram, has carried on a campaign of kidnapping, murder, and destruction of homes in dozens of Christian villages. Nigerians from other regions of the country, however, look on in horror and disbelief at this departure from generally amicable relations between the two major religious communities. In much of Nigeria cooperation and mutual respect are far more prevalent than mistrust and recrimination.

In nearby Ghana, where I have had the opportunity to live on four occasions and to interact with members of both Muslim and Christian communities, relations have been cordial and mutually supportive, for the most part. Christian secondary schools regularly enroll Muslim students whose parents appreciate the high quality of instruction that they provide. In many Muslim families, especially those from the northern regions where Islam has a greater presence, some children have converted to Christianity while others hold to Islam. It is somewhat less common, but not unheard-of, for children of Christian families to embrace Islam. Parents may try to persuade their children not to leave their family's religious community, but even when such departures do occur they seldom lead to lasting divisions in families.

Among my friends and associates in Ghana were Christian pastors whose families have been Muslim for several generations but who found, when they converted to Christianity and pursued theological study, that relatives with the financial means stepped forward readily to finance their seminary education. Stories such as this tend to provoke disbelief from Americans, who cannot imagine that religious differences could be so graciously overcome. To Ghanaians, on the other hand, and to many East Africans too, this seems an entirely normal and expected way of helping one's relatives.

On the campus of the University of Ghana, where I directed a semester-long study program for American students on four occasions, religious life is vibrant and varied. On weekday mornings—as early as 5:00 am—Christian students gather for prayer meetings in their residence halls. Others congregate on the university's athletic fields for evening charismatic gatherings, their multilingual prayers a joyful cacophony audible from a considerable distance. On Friday afternoons, Muslim students, faculty, and staff come together for prayers at the mosque located on the university campus. On Sunday mornings, their Christian counterparts congregate in large numbers at the Catholic and Protestant churches nearby, also on university grounds.

In Ghana it is common for Christian students to present the Gospel message to their Muslim classmates, hoping to win them over to Christian faith. Muslim students counter with arguments against what they regard as Christian distortions of the message of the great prophets, which was given its full and final expression in the Qur'an. The same patterns are evident in university life in Uganda and Kenya, so far as I have been able to observe. Yet by many measures—playing together on football teams, collaborating on school projects, sharing lodgings—differences of religion are readily accommodated, without conflict. Many of the international students visiting the University of Ghana from the United States and Europe, of whom there are several hundred each semester, are taken aback by the mutual respect that is shown by each group to the other, even while each holds firmly to its theological convictions.

Interfaith dialogue in Europe and North American sometimes begins by setting aside conflicting religious truth claims, on the ground that they are not truth claims at all but expressions of individual values and attitudes. If you and I affirm different creeds, it is said, the key to bridging our differences is to regard religious faith as a private matter, a personal preference. Religion is about personal values, not truth or falsity, and mutual toleration should displace argument.

Few Africans, whether Christian or Muslim, would affirm this construal of religious belief. Adherents of each faith affirm their traditions' theological positions forthrightly and unambiguously. They recognize that there are fundamental and irreconcilable differences between the religion of submission to Allah as conveyed by the Prophet Muhammed and the religion of salvation through Jesus Christ as God's Son. Yet this does not prevent them from collaborating whenever they can, nor does it lead either group to seek to exclude the other from participating in public life.

Mutual respect and cooperation are by no means universal traits across the continent, of course. Only a few hundred miles separate the regions of West Africa where Muslims and Christians live side by side in an atmosphere of mutual respect and ready cooperation from those where professedly Christian mobs burn down mosques and purportedly Muslim terrorists kidnap Christian children. If we shift the focus 3,000 miles to the east to Uganda and its near neighbors, we find that relationships between Christians and Muslims in recent history have usually fallen between these extremes. Muslim–Christian violence is by no means absent from the region. The self-proclaimed Islamist group el-Shabaab launched two bomb attacks in Kampala in 2011, after all. And a purportedly Christian militia, the anti-Baraka group, has recently increased its attacks on Muslims in the neighboring Central African Republic (Reuters 2017, CBS 2017).

But these have been isolated and infrequent incidents, often emanating from countries where there is effectively no central government and rival military forces flourish. Among Christian and Muslim communities in Uganda and in Kenya, lack of understanding and mistrust have been more prevalent than cooperation, but open violence has been rare.

To understand why, we need to return to the history sketched above and look more closely at religion in East Africa. During the centuries preceding European contact, as was mentioned, Arab merchants traded primarily with residents of settlements along the coast of the Indian Ocean, the region called the Swahili Coast. Before long they had established their own settlements along the coast, whose peoples and languages were different from those who lived father inland. In the colonial era, Arab influence remained especially strong in this area. The island of Zanzibar and most of the Swahili Coast came under the control of Muslim sultanates, with the seat of government located first in Mombasa (now part of Kenya), later in distant Oman, and then from the mid-18th century in Stone Town, Zanzibar (Library of Congress 1992).

From the 18th to the 20th century, conflicts between Arab settlers on the coast and European colonial authorities were frequent. When plans were made for the governors of British East Africa to move aside and pass the responsibilities of government to the new nation of Kenya, difficult and protracted negotiations with the sultan eventually yielded a compromise in which the territory of Kenya would include the portion of the Swahili Coast adjacent to British territories inland. It was agreed, however, that in the coastal region Islamic identity would be preserved and Islamic laws applied.

Disputes over political and religious divisions continue to flare up today in Kenya. In 2010, for example, many politicians and church leaders called on Christians to reject a proposed new constitution because it would recognize the legitimacy of Islamic courts not only in the coastal region but everywhere in the country. These courts would be authorized to adjudicate matters of marriage, divorce, and inheritance, if all parties agreed to allow their dispute to be resolved in that forum rather than in the civil courts.

This provision simply continued one of the key agreements that had persuaded the residents of the coastal region to join the new nation in 1962, a compromise without which there would have been no unified nation of Kenya extending to the coast. The extension to the entire nation was motivated by recognition that all the major cities of Kenya now have significant Muslim populations. But many Christian pastors and politicians campaigned vehemently against this change, characterizing it as a Muslim power grab and an infringement of religious liberty. Their opposition—unsuccessful, in the end, in blocking the adoption of the new constitution—was an unfortunate indication of how little communication and mutual understanding there is between Christian and Muslim communities in Kenya, even in the present (Hoekema 2010).

Uganda's history includes many episodes of violent religious conflict, including small-scale battles between Catholic and Protestant mission communities in the 19th century. These might more accurately be regarded not as religious disputes but rather as proxy conflicts among Britain, France, and Germany for domination of the region's natural resources. The "civil war between Catholics and Protestants" instigated by British governor Lugard, a military campaign against the *kabaka* that also sought to drive out the Catholic missionaries, has been described in Chapter 2. Historical accounts from that period recount many tales of Protestant missionaries "snatching" young Catholic catechumens from their mission compounds, and vice versa.

One noteworthy event of the late 19th century has shaped relations between Catholic and Protestant Christians in profound ways and has helped them overcome their previous mistrust. This was the episode in which 45 young men, half Catholic and half Protestant, were executed by a capricious and cruel traditional ruler. The story of the Uganda martyrs remains such an important part of Uganda's religious history that it deserves to be recounted in some detail.

The Christian Martyrs of Uganda

The story of the young men put to death in 1886 at the order of the *kabaka* is familiar to every Ugandan but relatively little known elsewhere. To understand what happened, and why, we need to turn our attention back to the Buganda court in the period that preceded the declaration of a British protectorate.

The authority of the *kabaka,* the Buganda king, was nominally exercised with the advice and consent of the elders of all the royal clans. In practical terms, however, many selected for that office saw themselves as absolute monarchs and did not hesitate to rule with an iron fist. In 1886, the man who had just been crowned Mwanda II was locked in a bitter conflict with both Catholic and Protestant missionaries, who he feared were in league with European powers in a conspiracy to depose him and strip him of his authority. He decided that preserving his own rule necessitated striking out cruelly against those in his own royal court who were in league with the missionaries.

Mwanda had been selected from the eligible princes by Buganda elders on the death of his father Mutesa in 1884. He was installed, with elaborate ceremony, at the age of just 16. The young king was inexperienced, inconstant, and more than a little paranoid, seeing conspiracies all around him. Many of his advisors, moreover, were angling to eliminate their own rivals at court. An Anglican missionary described Mwanda as "nervous, suspicious, fickle, passionate," to which a colleague added: "and, I fear, revengeful." These qualities took a disastrous toll on the community of Ugandan converts to Christianity (Faupel 1962).

To the bewilderment and disgust of the missionaries, but with the collusion of his inner circle of advisors and elders, Mwanda had sought out young boys as sexual partners even before his elevation to the throne. As *kabaka,* he took advantage of his many young pages, most of them ready to serve their master in whatever way would please him. But those who had converted to Christianity reportedly resisted. A former page gave this testimony decades later, when the Catholic church conducted an intensive investigation as part of the process of canonization:

> At that time the *Kabaka* practiced the works of Sodom. Muslims and
> pagans were prepared to do these things for him, but the Catholics
> absolutely refused. For that reason the *Kabaka* began to detest us,
> and deliberated with the pagans and Muslims about putting us to
> death, us the Catholics. With my own ears I heard him utter words
> of anger because the young Catholics refused to sin. I, for one, was
> often importuned by him, but refused. (Faupel 1962, 83)

It should be noted immediately that the commonly held view that the
execution of royal pages was motivated primarily by anger over their
refusal to grant sexual favors is probably a blend of fact and fiction.
I heard this explanation repeated many times by Ugandans, and it
features in many histories of the period. But some historians regard it as
a moralistic fiction intended to ennoble the victims—victims who were
sacrificed to royal whim, without question, but perhaps for reasons
other than their resistance to the king's sexual predations.

The testimony of eyewitnesses such as that just quoted should therefore not be taken at face value. Homosexual practice was no less categorically condemned by faithful Muslims than by faithful Christians of
the late 19th century, after all, so the page's testimony that "Muslims and
pagans" were ready to comply with the king's demands is not very credible. Nor can we determine whether there were some Christians among
those who engaged in sexual activities with the king, willingly or not.
Political factors and personal grievances undoubtedly also contributed
to the king's acts of wanton violence (Hoad 2007, Ssemakula n.d.).

The king's predilection for young boys was noted, all the same, by
a number of contemporaries, both Ugandan and European, and it
was undoubtedly one of the factors that fueled his opposition to the
missionaries and led to the killing of the pages. Many other acts of equal
cruelty against Christians preceded the mass killings. In 1885 the *kabaka* had ordered the killing of an Anglican bishop, James Hannington,
together with his English companion and fifty African porters and
servants, as they made their way toward Buganda from the north. Over
strenuous objections from both Protestant and Catholic leaders who
were frequently received at court, he issued this order on the basis of
implausible and wholly unfounded suspicions that Hannington was
complicit in a German plan to win control of the Great Lakes region

and make the *kabaka* a German vassal (Faupel 1962, 94–107). Shortly afterward, the *kabaka* ordered the execution of his most trusted advisor, Joseph Ballikudende Mukasa, a Catholic convert who had angered the king by his advocacy for the missionaries and their young converts (Faupel 1962).

It is safe to say, then, that several factors converged to motivate the *kabaka* to target his pages for punishment: anger over sexual favors refused, suspicions of Christians' support for European interests, and not least a vengeful delight in flexing his own unlimited powers of life and death. As a result, 45 of the royal pages were arrested, bound, and led on a forced march to a ceremonial site of execution ten miles from the palace. They were invited to renounce their Christian beliefs and gain their release but refused to do so. Instead, observers reported, they encouraged each other with assurances that they would soon be welcomed into God's presence for their faithfulness.

On June 3, 1886, 22 Catholics and 23 Protestants, most of them in their twenties but some as young as 14, were bound, wrapped in palm-frond shrouds, and piled onto a gigantic stack of dry wood. Another of the pages, spared at the last minute and later released, testified to church authorities in Rome many years later:

> When Mukajunga [a royal executioner] saw that all was ready, he signaled to his men to station themselves all round the pyre, and then gave the order, "Light it at every point." The flames blazed up like a burning house and, as they rose, I heard coming from the pyre the murmur of the Christians' voices as they died praising God. From the moment of our arrest, I never saw any one of them show any sign of lack of courage. (Faupel 1962, 197)

The number of those reportedly executed together on Namugongo hill varies somewhat in different accounts. The canonization process for the 22 Catholic victims provided extensive documentation of their names, ages, and clans, but some sources list fewer than 23 Protestant pages. Some sources also identify some of the victims as Muslim, others as adherents of traditional religion, individuals who had been accused of various offenses at court and added to the party by the king's officers. In any case, these were by no means the only victims of the whims and suspicions of the *kabaka*. On many other occasions Christians and others who displeased the king were sent off to summary execution.

This horrific tale of the abuse of royal authority, fueled by personal animosity and paranoia, and the human conflagration that resulted remains an important symbol today for all Ugandans of the abuses to which unlimited power can be put. Equally important, in the century that followed, the unity and the courage of Catholic and Protestant victims of the *kabaka's* rage helped to overcome the longstanding rivalry between the two Christian missions. Earlier in the 19th century, Catholic and Protestant missionaries had themselves resorted to kidnapping young men and women to populate their pews, and communication between the two communities was rare, to say nothing of cooperation. After 1886 they joined in mourning the massacre and honoring its victims, and a spirit of collaboration and mutual respect was planted that paved the way for initiatives such as ARLPI a century later. Even Lord Lugard's misperception that the Catholic presence in Buganda was a cover for French dreams of conquest, which made him view priests as allies of the *kabaka* and enemies of the Crown a decade later, did not lead to lasting hostility between Protestant and Catholic communities in the period of British rule. But the two communities remained relatively distant from each other.

Varieties of Religion in African Life

During most of the history of the British protectorate of Buganda, and during the history of Uganda since independence, churches and mosques have stood side by side in cities and towns. At the level of villages, on the other hand, the most common pattern remains that of religiously unified villages—some predominantly Catholic, others Church of Uganda, others Seventh-Day Adventist. There has been relatively little conflict, but also relatively little cooperation.

Different religious communities are concentrated to some extent in geographical clusters, and the Muslim population is larger in the northern and northwestern regions of Uganda than its central and southwestern regions. In neighboring Kenya and Tanzania, a large concentration of Muslim residents remains in place along the Swahili Coast, the area where Arab trading settlements have been present for more than a thousand years, even while others have moved inland. And in all of Uganda's major cities today are significant numbers of Catholics, Anglicans, "born-agains," and Muslims alike.

Uganda's recent history has included several recent episodes that heightened the division between religious communities. As has been noted earlier, after Idi Amin came to power in the early 1970s he identified more and more closely with Muslims, in Uganda and abroad. The highest posts in his military and his administration were given to his West Nile compatriots, nearly all of them Muslim. When Amin was overthrown in 1979, retaliatory massacres against Muslims in the northern regions of the country ensued.

Episodes such as this arose from the special circumstances of a brutal dictator's overthrow, not from a sudden explosion of simmering antipathy between Uganda's Christians and Muslims. All the same, even if their differences have erupted into violence only rarely, communication and cooperation between the two religious communities has not been the prevailing pattern. Religious differences have been compounded by ethnic mistrust, not just during Amin's rule but in other periods of recent history as well.

An aspect of the religious life of African societies that many European and North American visitors find surprising and unexpected is the place of religion in public and private life. Religion is regarded as a matter for public exercise and profession, in the public square and the government office no less than in the home and the place of worship, in contemporary societies across the continent. A particularly striking example of the intertwining of religion with national life came with the March 2018 announcement that a new National Cathedral has been commissioned for Accra, the capital of Ghana. It will be built, on a 14-acre site, in the center of the government ministries area of the capital, near State House and Black Star Square, where Ghana's independence was proclaimed in 1957. Renowned Ghanaian-British architect David Adjaye's design incorporates elements of Ghanaian traditional carving and construction in a huge complex including a two-level 5000-seat auditorium, choral rehearsal and art gallery spaces, and "Africa's first bible museum and documentation center, dedicated to Christianity and nation-building in Ghana." Adjacent to the entrance will be a towering campanile surmounted by a cross (Designboom 2018). A statement accompanying the announcement emphasized that the building "will be an inter-denominational house of worship and prayer, as well as serve as the venue for formal state occasions of a religious nature, such as presidential inaugurations, state funerals and national thanksgiving services." The author of these words was not a Catholic or Protestant church leader but Nana Addo Dankwa Akufo-Addo, President of Ghana (Adjaye Associates 2018).

Religious life for North Americans, by contrast, is above all a matter of personal choice, protected by laws that guarantee freedom of belief and practice. Its role in public discourse is limited. Political candidates are expected to speak from time to time about their religious convictions, but explicit appeals to religious teachings in political debate are rare—and they are likely to provoke unfavorable commentary from opponents and journalists. In Europe, levels of religious affiliation are lower, and the visibility of religious language in public debate is correspondingly lower as well. The same assumption that religion is a private matter of voluntary choice prevails across Europe, and many other regions of the world, as in North America.

A European or North American visitor to any of the major capitals of Africa will notice immediately how prevalent religious language is in daily discourse and in political life. Even more obvious is its place in the realm of commerce and transport. The shared taxis and minibuses that are the veins and arteries of city life across the continent are often emblazoned with religious mottoes reflecting the Christian or Muslim beliefs of their drivers. Shop signs advertising "Holy Spirit Diesel Engine Repair" and "Allah is Great Electrical Service" are common in West Africa.[2] Public meetings usually open with prayers, frequently offered alternately by Christian and Muslim religious leaders. Politicians' speeches are liberally seeded with quotations from Scripture or from the Qur'an, alongside proverbs and folk tales.

Traditional religious beliefs and practices dating to the time prior to European contact also continue to play an important role in African societies and cultures, particularly in rural communities, to different degrees in different regions of the continent. Even residents of major cities, and Africans living abroad, return to their ancestral villages for festivals and other traditional celebrations. Rituals associated with birth, attainment of adulthood, marriage, and death continue to be observed, with modifications and adaptations, even by Africans whose parents or grandparents left the village long ago. Even as African societies embrace many aspects of the secular and the modern, ceremonies that have been practiced for a thousand years continue to mark important life transitions.

Traditional rituals and beliefs were once resolutely condemned by missionaries as manifestations of paganism and idolatry. Attitudes today have become far more tolerant, in practice and even in formally articulated theology. This change has resulted from a reassessment of the place of traditional beliefs in Christian theology, and from practical and political developments as well. Taking note of these will help us see more clearly the significance of the interfaith collaboration that has had such a powerful effect on post-war Uganda.

Scholars such as Placide Tempels in what was then the Belgian Congo, John Mbiti in Kenya, and Kwame Bediako in Ghana have identified elements of African traditions that constitute a distinctive philosophical and theological approach to the nature of the self, the community, and the divine. Tempels and Mbiti have been widely criticized for oversimplifying and overgeneralizing African worldviews, conflating hundreds of distinct cultural traditions into a pan-African consensus. This criticism has some merit; and yet common elements such as an emphasis on the seamless continuity between physical and spiritual realms, and on the inextricable links between individual identity and community membership, can be traced across widely separated traditions and cultures. Bediako, a Protestant theologian, called attention to the close resemblance of traditional African conceptions of the world to those that dominated the world of the early church (Tempels 1945, Mbiti 1969, Mbiti 1986, Bediako 2004). These features, we have already noted, are characteristic of what some scholars label the primal religion of societies in which traditions remain more oral than written (Walls 1987).

The influence of the theologians just cited has led to a reassessment of the continuing value of traditional rituals, including those that acknowledge the role of ancestors in establishing cultural continuity. Pouring a libation to named and unnamed ancestors on the occasion of a birth or a marriage would once have led to a stern rebuke if not a formal disciplinary sanction for anyone affiliated with a Christian church. But today it is a common occurrence at both civic and family gatherings. Both in the Catholic church and in major Protestant denominations, pastors and priests view such practices as a legitimate way of acknowledging spiritual realities that are very different from, but not in direct conflict with, Western Christian doctrines. A Protestant theologian at a North American seminary, Ross Kane, has urged Western Christians to expand their conception of the communion of saints to encompass ancestors as well, citing Bediako and other African theologians on the importance of this openness to African churches (Kane 2017).

Acceptance of such practices is much less prevalent in evangelical Christian churches and among the more conservative communities of Islam. But official condemnation is sometimes tempered by practical toleration.

Another important factor leading to a philosophical and theological reappraisal of African traditions, in addition to the theological shift just mentioned, was the wave of political independence that swept across the African continent in the 1960s. New African nations sought to understand their respective African traditions more fully and to preserve them for the future. The transition from colony to independent nation that began with Ghana in 1957 and swept across the continent in the following decade brought with it an affirmation of the continuing place of tradition in contemporary African life.[3]

This has not resulted in a significant turn away from Christianity, or from Islam, as one might have expected. Affirming African identity and achieving nationhood did not imply renouncing the colonists' religion in favor of its indigenous predecessors.

The two major religious movements of Islam and Christianity, imported from abroad over many centuries, are today the most pervasive and most potent religious influences on the continent. The percentage of Christians across Africa grew steadily but slowly during a century of colonization and evangelization by Europeans, then increased at a far quicker pace after independence. But churches today are less likely to demand that their followers renounce all of their traditional practices when they convert to a new faith.

A few statistics will underscore this reality. The Pew Charitable Trusts have conducted exhaustive studies of religious affiliation in Africa and elsewhere in the world. Their reports document both the dramatic changes in African religious life in the past century and the current pattern of Christian and Muslim dominance. Summarizing data from all the countries of the sub-Saharan region, a Pew report observes that the number of adherents to Islam has increased more than twenty-fold from 1900 until 2010, from 11 million to 240 million. During the same period, the number of Christians increased almost seventy-fold, from 7 million to 470 million (Pew Research Center 2010).

These numbers need to be set in the context of global population growth, from fewer than 2 billion to nearly 7 billion in the same timespan. All the same, the shift in religious affiliation represents a dramatic global redistribution. In 1910, for example, two-thirds of the world's Christians resided in Europe, and another quarter in the Americas, North and South. Only 1.4 percent of Christians were African, while 5 percent were residents of Asia and the Pacific. By 2010, the percentage of Christians living in Europe had declined to about 27 percent, offset in part by growth in the Americas, to 36 percent. At the same time the proportion of Christians in the Asian-Pacific region had nearly tripled, to 13 percent, while the percentage living in Africa had increased nearly twenty times to 24 percent. A century after Africans had accounted for one in 70 Christians worldwide, they now accounted for one in four (Pew Research Center 2011).

Shifts in the global Muslim population have been less dramatic. The most populous centers of Islam in Indonesia, the Indian subcontinent, and the Middle East have continued to hold this place through the past century. The countries of the Maghreb—Morocco, Algeria, Tunisia, and Egypt, along the southern coast of the Mediterranean—are all 90 percent or more Muslim. These patterns remain much as they were a century ago. South of the Sahara, however, Islam has seen dramatic growth.

Reviewing population data for nations across Africa, we can identify several in the sub-Saharan region that, like those of North Africa, are predominantly Islamic. They include Mali, Senegal, and Niger in the Sahel region. Moving farther south in the continent, religious affiliations are more divided. Burkina Faso, Côte d'Ivoire, and Nigeria, in West Africa, all have approximately equal numbers of Christians and Muslims. Chad's population is about 40 percent Christian, while

Ethiopia, historically a major center of Christianity, is about 40 percent Muslim (Pew Research Center 2012).

As we move still farther south in the continent, the proportion of Christians increases: more than 90 percent in Rwanda and Burundi and Namibia and Zambia, more than 85 percent in Kenya and Zimbabwe. Eighty-one percent of South Africans identify as Christians, but—uniquely in the continent—that nation also has a significant number with no stated religious affiliation. About 15 percent place themselves in this category, on a par with 16 percent in the United States. (These figures drawn from 2010 census data may have shifted slightly since that date; see Pew Research Center 2012.)

In none of these nations, according to the most reliable census data available, is there a significant population who identify primarily as adherents of traditional religion. They make up fewer than 5 percent of the population in most cases, fewer than 1 percent in Uganda. These figures should be taken with caution, however, given the prevalence of traditional practices among those who identify primarily as Muslim or Christian. It is statistically irregular but probably accurate, for example, to describe Nigeria today as half Christian, half Muslim, and half traditionalist.

Turning to the specific situation of the nation of Uganda, we find that the population is overwhelmingly Christian, with a significant Muslim minority. In 2010, Christians made up 87 percent of the population, Muslims 12 percent. In population numbers, approximately 29 million Ugandans identified themselves as Christian and 4 million as Muslim. These numbers from 2010 have been updated in Uganda's 2014 census, which also provides a more fine-grained analysis: nearly 40 percent of residents are Catholic, 32 percent Anglican (Church of Uganda), 11 percent "Pentecostal/Born Again/Evangelical," and 2 percent Seventh-Day Adventist. Taken together, the percentage of Christians in the 2014 census results is slightly lower than in the 2010 figures, at 84 percent. During the same period, the number of Ugandans who adhere to Islam has increased slightly to 14 percent (Uganda Bureau of Statistics 2016, 19).

What do these statistics mean in the daily life of the people of Uganda? A Muslim minority as large as 14 percent in an overwhelmingly Christian country might well be a source of deep division and hostility. In the nations of Europe, far smaller Muslim communities—just 4 percent in the United Kingdom, 6 percent in France, 8 percent in Belgium—feel a sense of exclusion and alienation, grounded in both religious and ethnic differences with the majority population. Protests often erupt in response to government action or police intervention that seems to target the Muslim minority. Violent attacks on Muslims have occurred occasionally in Europe, frequently in Russia and China.

Fortunately this has not been the case in Uganda. Christians and Muslims have lived side by side, and even if they have seldom worked closely together for common ends, their differences have not led to open conflict or violence. The Muslim and Christian communities of Uganda have lived alongside each other, separated to some extent by geography, for many centuries. But very seldom have these communities collaborated closely for the common good, as they did in the 1990s when ARLPI was formed. An awareness of the religious history and the contemporary demographics of Uganda helps underscore what a remarkable accomplishment this has been.

On one of my visits to Uganda Martyrs University, a Catholic institution located about two hours by road southwest of Kampala, my wife and I were taken on a walking tour of the campus by a member of the faculty who wore the blue habit of the Little Sisters of St. Francis. As we walked, Sister Cecilia recounted her life story. Born in the West Nile region, she lost both her parents as a young child and was raised by grandparents. Her extended family members, like most of her neighbors, were Muslim, but after attending a Catholic school she wanted to learn more about Christianity, and eventually she decided to convert. She was baptized as an adolescent and joined a Catholic parish. A few years later, she joined the community of sisters, and at the end of her novitiate period she was ready to affirm her vows and join the order permanently.

At the ceremony in which new members of a religious order are welcomed, if they are not yet adults, it is customary for each candidate to be accompanied by his or her parents. The parallel with the marriage ceremony is evident: when a young woman becomes a bride of Christ, her parents formally send her with their blessing into her new life with another.

That was not possible in this case. Even if her parents had been living, moreover, they would not have been expected to accompany her to pronounce her vows, because Muslims do not normally enter Christian places of worship. But in this case, one of Cecilia's Muslim uncles insisted on accompanying his niece to the front of the church. In a very visible way he was announcing, as one of her closest living relatives, that she was taking holy orders with the family's blessing.

The story illustrates both the persistent tensions and the potential for cooperation that mark the coexistence of Christianity and Islam in Uganda, as elsewhere in Africa. In different families, and often in different villages, the two communities remain separate. In cities and towns they live side by side but have relatively little contact. But family connections are more important than religious disconnections. And in the case of ARLPI, the events of the period from 1998 to the present demonstrate, a larger and more inclusive family can emerge in response to dire threats to the welfare of the people in which religious differences no longer impede close cooperation.

Having set out some important aspects of the religious environment of Uganda, it is time now to return to the story of the birth of the ARLPI and the factors in Ugandan life that shaped its early history. One of its first priorities was to advocate an amnesty provision for returning LRA officers, a controversial position that proved essential for the eventual resolution of the conflict. We will trace these developments in the next chapter.

Notes

1. An exception to this narrative is Ethiopia: it has been a Christian nation since the 4th century CE, in comparative isolation from the Western church, but today also has a substantial Muslim population as well as a number of active primal traditions.
2. Every visitor to Ghana has a collection of mental pictures of favorite shop signs: among those I have observed and photographed are "Jesus Will Do It Roof Repair," "God's Time is the Best Time Furniture Shop," "That Rock is Jesus Drinking Water," and "God and Sons Mobile Phones."
3. The distinctive political vision of the first generation of African leaders, seeking to harmonize Western structures with African values, is a topic I have discussed elsewhere (Hoekema 2013).

5

Conflict, Displacement, and Interfaith Activism

What we have done is a lesson to the whole world in peaceful coexistence. We are trying our level best as religious leaders to show the world that we can live together, and this we would like to consolidate and continue. . . . What is taking place in Nigeria [conflict between Muslims and Christians], what is spilling over to other countries like Algeria and Mali—for us as ARLPI we want to be one of the world's advocates joining hands with other interfaith, interreligious bodies in the world so that we can continue educating children in the schools. We want to teach coexistence and tolerance despite our different faiths.

—Sheik Musa Khalil, Khadhi of the
Muslim community of Gulu (Khalil 2014)

In recent years, an alternative vision has emerged to end the conflict in northern Uganda, mainly inspired by the religious and traditional Acholi leaders. The approach involves pursuing peace talks while simultaneously offering amnesty to LRA rebels and reintegrating them into their communities.

—2005 report on northern Uganda
conducted by MacArthur Foundation and the
government of Canada (Baines, Stover, and Wierda 2006, 56)

THE LEVEL OF VIOLENCE endured by the people of the Acholi region during the first two decades of the LRA insurrection ebbed and flowed considerably. In Chapter 3 we heard many voices describe the cruelty and manipulation inflicted on abductees and the destruction wrought by LRA raids on villages. The Ugandan government's military campaigns against the LRA failed utterly to achieve their purposes and only compounded the people's suffering. Repeated attempts were made to bring a resolution, and sometimes these led to temporary lulls in the civil war. But then one side would violate the ceasefire, the other side would retaliate, and brutality would return.

Mercifully, the period from the mid-1990s to the mid-2000s proved to be the last decade in which the LRA waged its war of terror on northern Uganda. Peace negotiations brokered by outsiders took place at last in 2005 and 2006. As they moved slowly forward—and sometimes backward—LRA forces reduced the number and intensity of attacks, began to withdraw from Uganda, and permitted abducted soldiers to return home. The people of the region, having lived under intolerable conditions in IDP camps for the last years of the conflict, were at last able to return to their villages. But this resolution came only after several periods of expanded and intensified violence perpetrated by the soldiers on both sides of the conflict.

Several developments that occurred during this ten-year period helped prepare the way for the end of the LRA movement in Uganda. They will be described in this chapter in approximately chronological order. The first—the focus of more extended discussion in subsequent chapters, and the principal subject of this study as a whole—was the formation of the Acholi Religious Leaders Peace Initiative (ARLPI). This organization was formed in the late 1990s as a joint undertaking of Christian and Muslim leaders in Kitgum and Gulu, working patiently but persistently to reduce suffering and bring the warring parties to the negotiating table.

The second development, one in which ARLPI played a critical role, was the enactment of an amnesty law allowing rebel soldiers to return to their communities and families without fear of being put on trial as war criminals and sent to prison. Amnesty was not offered to senior commanders in the LRA, but others who had served in LRA armed forces were encouraged to return home without fear of prosecution, regardless of whether they had joined the rebel movement voluntarily—as did many who joined in its early years—or as a result of raids and abductions.

A third important event of the late 1990s and early 2000s, mentioned briefly in the previous chapter, was the creation of massive temporary camps for internally displaced persons (IDPs) across the northern region of Uganda. Relocation to these camps, residents were told, would offer protection against LRA violence, a promise that often proved to be empty. What began as a voluntary relocation option soon became a government policy of forced removal. Residents outside the major towns who refused to abandon their homes and farms for an IDP camp were regarded as LRA sympathizers, and the Ugandan army left them unprotected.

This created intolerable risks for those who chose to remain in their rural homes, enduring repeated LRA raids. This situation created the fourth important development of the period highlighted in this chapter: the phenomenon of children walking from their villages into the towns to sleep in safety at churches and schools. As the story of these "night commuters" came to be known outside the Acholi region, on the basis of reports from church leaders and a few journalists, it helped to heighten awareness of the LRA conflict in Uganda and beyond.

All these developments prepared the way for the critical events of the mid-2000s that will be discussed in the following chapter. Neighboring governments, global NGOs, and ARLPI all redoubled their efforts to bring the two sides together. The ceasefire initiatives of the 1990s had all failed, and after each of them collapsed, each side blaming the other, reprisals took a deadly toll. A decade later this pattern was broken at last, when—thanks to the urging and the assistance of several agents who had an interest but no direct involvement in the conflict—20 years of civil war at last came to an end.

Before turning to these developments, we should also note some changes in the conduct of the government campaign against LRA forces in the north, motivated mainly by the concerns of outsiders who began to look more deeply into what had been going on rather than simply accept President Museveni's narrative at face value. Already in the early 1990s, international human rights groups and some foreign governments had begun to put pressure on the Museveni regime to rein in its soldiers, who were frequently and credibly accused of human rights violations including murder, rape, and kidnapping. Foreign governments, some of them regular suppliers of arms and others simply concerned observers, also called on the regime to undertake more effective measures to defeat Kony's movement.

The adoption of a new Ugandan constitution in 1995 led to the formal disbanding of the National Resistance Army, the banner under which Museveni had staged his military coup in 1985. National armed forces were reorganized under a new name, the Uganda People's Defence Force (UPDF). Little changed except the name, however. The military campaign against Kony's forces continued much as before, with comparable levels of destruction and few signs of progress toward victory, let alone a negotiated resolution.

In chapter 3 the account given by a visitor to the Uganda–Sudan border who witnessed just one episode was cited: in a few days' time in January 1997, an LRA attack killed 550 in one district of the Acholi region, and then a retaliatory bombing raid by government forces killed 417 more (Whitmore 2010, 158). But few heard such reports at the time. Most Ugandans, and most international observers, continued to rely on government reports that the LRA was on its last legs. Even a top official at the US State Department, we noted earlier, gave credence to Museveni's assertions that his army respected the human rights of both rebels and civilians and tried to act as humanely as possible.

One reason that the conflict endured for so long had to do with international entanglements with neighboring governments and with other governments far beyond the region. The Sudanese regime in Khartoum supplied arms and funds to the LRA movement and offered rebel soldiers free passage over the border, while the Ugandan government provided support to Sudanese rebel militias opposed to Riek Machar's government in the semi-autonomous region (later to be the nation) of South Sudan. Sudan's Omar al-Bashar was viewed as sympathetic to the enemies of America and Europe, while Uganda's Museveni was a valued ally. In effect, each government was waging a covert guerrilla war against its neighbor while also playing a part in a proxy war between the superpowers for global influence.

In 1999 the regional rivalry that had helped to sustain the LRA insurgency was resolved at last when the governments of Uganda and Sudan came together and agreed to cease supporting rebel groups in each other's territory. Sudanese weapons and materiel were no longer freely available to the LRA for its struggle against the UPDF forces.

Uganda's government stood aside as the Machar regime set out to destroy the rebel militias across the border that had formerly enjoyed Ugandan assistance.

Three years later in 2002, in an unprecedented gesture of cooperation, the authorities in South Sudan gave their permission for a major Ugandan military assault on the LRA on both sides of the Sudanese border, code named Operation Iron Fist. The United States lent political support, as well as the assistance of military advisors, to Uganda in this campaign. But the result fell far short of the Ugandan government's goals and brought no relief to the people of the region. Both LRA and civilian casualties were high. UPDF soldiers laid waste to many Ugandan and Sudanese villages as they pursued LRA units fleeing north to the border regions.

When UPDF forces returned to Ugandan soil, they claimed to have won a significant victory—but LRA operations on both sides of the border continued unabated. In news media loyal to the Museveni government, these were depicted as the death throes of the LRA, but more accurate reporting from independent sources reported lower LRA losses, greater losses on the government side, and numerous incidents of UPDF forces engaging in unjustified attacks on suspected rebel sympathizers. The 2003 report commissioned by ARLPI, "War of Words," documents in detail the ways in which the government sought to conceal its failure in the military campaign by suppressing accurate reporting from the field (ARLPI 2003).

Residents of the region reported that a principal result of the Iron Fist campaign was to increase the frequency and cruelty of retaliatory attacks by the LRA on Ugandan civilians who were suspected of having supported the soldiers of their government. What was billed, domestically and abroad, as a final death blow to the LRA served in reality as a provocation leading to even more suffering for the innocent.

Creation of the Acholi Religious Leaders Peace Initiative

Let us return now to the early 1990s, when the UPDF and the LRA were locked in a stalemate, each launching frequent attacks on the other, neither able to gain the upper hand. LRA tactics became dramatically more harsh in this period. Rather than seize only the food they needed, LRA commandoes kidnapped increasing numbers of boys and girls, and they often killed or mutilated those who were too old or too young to be desirable captives. Historian Margaret Angucia, who lived in Gulu through this period, observes succinctly: "In the early 1990s, the LRA started to mutilate and maim civilians. People's noses, lips and arms were severed" (Angucia 2010, 18).

Government forces responded with equal ferocity. In 1993 and 1994, each side was guilty of massive and egregious violence against ordinary residents. And although each party to the conflict claimed repeatedly to be on the verge of achieving a decisive victory, the residents of the region knew that these were empty boasts. The elephants fought on, and the grass continued to suffer.

Parliamentarian Betty Bigombe, then serving as State Minister for the Pacification of the North, made a courageous attempt to mediate the conflict in late 1993. For a few months the level of violence declined, while government and rebel representatives discussed provisions for a ceasefire. But when President Museveni announced a one-week ultimatum—the LRA must surrender or face the consequences—the result was not a pause in the conflict but rather an escalation of tactics on both sides, each blaming the other for provoking it to respond (Allen 2006, 44–50).

A few years later, as the civil war raged on, a new organization emerged from discussions among the religious leaders in the heart of the conflict zone. Protestant, Catholic, and Muslim residents were suffering in equal measure from the depredations of the LRA's soldiers. Seeking ways to relieve the suffering of their people, their priests, pastors, and imams began to explore ways in which they could come together and speak in one voice on behalf of the suffering population.

This was an unexpected and unprecedented cooperative venture, in a region where the three religious communities had historically wanted little to do with each other. From the early missionary period, we have observed in the previous chapters, there had been intense rivalry between Catholic and Protestant missionaries for land, for converts, and for alliances with traditional authorities. Working in close collaboration with the governors-general, the Anglicans viewed the Catholic presence in the region as a dangerous foothold for European powers who sought to displace Great Britain. Lord Frederick Lugard's 1892 military campaign against *kabaka* Mwanga was also an attack on the White Fathers, whose schools, chapels, and residences were destroyed. What historians describe as a "civil war between Catholics and Protestants" simmered for several decades (Shorter 2006, 9–10). As late as 1913, Father Giuseppi Beduschi, a leading figure in the Catholic mission, complained of Rev. Arthur Brian Fisher, head of the Anglican mission, that "Mr. Pastor and his most fanatic wife work to steal our boys from our schools, and have managed to attract quite a few" (Cisternino 2004, 392).

By the time Uganda achieved its independence, relations between Catholic and Protestant were less confrontational. Each community regarded the other with respect, and yet there was little cooperation, or even communication, between them. Most Ugandan Catholics lived in Catholic villages or neighborhoods, attended Catholic schools, were married and were buried with Catholic rites. Anglicans—by far the largest of the Protestant denominations in Uganda—carried on their own largely separate religious and social lives. These divisions were not drawn along ethnic lines, though they are to some degree regional, with the Protestant presence stronger in the south, Catholic in the north. They have been strongly correlated with political alliances, however. We noted earlier that the Democratic Party (DP) was formed at the time of independence to represent Catholic interests. It was said by some in the 1960s that DP actually stood for *Dini ya Papa,* Luganda for "the Pope's religion." In the same period Anglicans were the most numerous adherents of the Uganda People's Congress (UPC). Some said with tongue in cheek that the initials actually stood for "United Protestants of Canterbury" (Lukwiya Ochola 2006, 135).

Present in smaller numbers in Uganda are Eastern Orthodox and Seventh-Day Adventist Christians. Some rapidly growing religious communities such as Pentecostals—the "born-agains" in Ugandan parlance—have drawn members from those who found both Catholic and Anglican churches lacking in fervor. With the exception of the Orthodox, who joined the organization very early, these groups were not participants in the work of ARLPI in its first decade but became affiliates later.

The Muslim community in Uganda is relatively small, composing only about one-eighth of the population in the 2014 census. Tensions between Muslims and Christians have been repeatedly stirred up by po-litical and ethnic divisions, particularly under Idi Amin, who reaffirmed his Muslim identity during his years in power and set out to reverse the dominance of Christians in Ugandan politics. In the relative stability that followed Museveni's rise to power in the 1980s, relations between Christians and Muslims in most areas including the north have been neither openly hostile nor closely collaborative.

Uganda has not entirely escaped the epidemic of purportedly Islamic terrorism around the globe. The group calling itself el Shabaab, based in Somalia, sent two suicide bombers to World Cup viewing sites in Uganda in July 2010, killing 74. Fortunately this was an isolated in-cident, never repeated. Uganda has no history of attacks on Christian communities by Muslim extremists, or on Muslim communities by Christian extremists, like those that have occurred in northeastern Nigeria, in Mali, and from time to time in Egypt and Sudan. All the same, there has been relatively little cooperation or mutual understanding.

For much of the past century, then, the three large religious communities of northern Uganda—Catholic, Protestant, and Muslim—lived side by side but seldom came together in pursuit of common goals. After the LRA reign of terror had already lasted for a decade, resorting more and more often to kidnapping, rape, and mu-tilation as well as theft of crops, the three groups began to see that the urgent needs of those who suffered from the protracted civil war should take precedence over their social, cultural, and theological divisions. In the words of Monsignor Matthew Odong, Rector of Sacred Heart Seminary, who served as vice-president of the organization for its first twenty years:

> In 1997 we came together as religious leaders in the Acholi sub-region as the Acholi Religious Leaders Peace Initiative, an interfaith organi-zation comprising Catholic, Anglican, Muslim, and Orthodox, and a couple of other denominations have also come on board.
>
> Why did we come together? Because of the suffering of the people. The war forced people out of their homes into refugee camps, what we called internal displacement camps. They had to leave their homes because of abductions, killings, rape, and all forms of violations of human rights. As religious leaders we saw people dying, and the

government was not doing much to end this war. Then we said: we will be the voice of the voiceless. We have to speak and let the world know of the problems in northern Uganda. (Odong 2014)

Nearly as challenging as establishing trust with government and LRA commanders, in the early stages of ARLPI's work, was winning trust and facilitating cooperation between Christian and Muslim communities in the Acholi region. I asked a staff member of ARLPI, Abdala Latif Nasur, how this had been achieved. He commented:

There has always been bias in the way [Christians] talk about Muslims. I don't know why; maybe because of preaching, or the way the religion was embraced in Uganda. But when you open your Bible and I open my Qur'an we can learn from each other. And the war forced us to work together. When the LRA is coming, it doesn't select whether you are a Catholic, a Protestant, a Muslim. We all suffered in the same way. And then also the religious leaders of these areas—I think they played a key role in trying to understand. They moved away from their traditional beliefs and attitudes. We would see the bishops, the pastors and the imams saying we are one people for peace, for our people. Sitting together, eating together, chatting—it was not easy at the beginning for people to accept, but with time, people came to realize, yes, we are one people. The motivating drive was the war, the urge for peace. They met a lot of resistance themselves from their congregations. But time and again, people came to realize that we can work together – we will not ask you to become Muslim, you will not ask us to become Catholic. You will preach from the Bible and we will preach from the Qur'an, and then we will do our planning and implementation together. (Nasur 2014)

The founders of ARLPI came together in a determined effort both to mitigate the effects of the decade-long campaign of terror and civil war and to prepare the way to a resolution of the conflict, which would require major concessions not only from the leaders of the LRA but also from the Ugandan government.

The first event jointly planned by representatives of the three religious communities together—the first step toward the founding of

ARLPI—was a prayer service held in Kitgum on August 15, 1997. The event was a response to heightened attacks by the LRA in the previous months, including the abduction of 139 schoolgirls from St. Mary's School in Lira in October, 1996, and the brazen display of the bodies of LRA victims along the major roads to and from Gulu in subsequent months. An additional incentive for this meeting in Uganda was the news of the first of several meetings of expatriate Ugandans in London, meetings that were referred to as "*Kacoke Madit*," which means simply "big meeting" in the Luo language of the Acholi. At the London meetings, sympathizers and opponents of the LRA came together to consider how they could help bring about a resolution of the civil war (Lukwiya Ochola 2006, 44; Conciliation Resources 2002).

Catholic and Protestant leaders began meeting in Kitgum, in a district to the east of Gulu that was frequently caught up in LRA attacks and government counterattacks, and they invited Muslim representatives to join them both in planning and in the public prayer service. They decided to form a new organization, the Joint Justice and Peace Committee, as an extension of the work of the Peace and Justice Committee of Kitgum that had been created by Comboni missionary Fr. Carlos Rodriguez Soto in order to record and document human rights abuses, property theft, and acts of physical violence. Initially rebuffed by the Catholic hierarchy in Kitgum, Fr. Rodriguez reached out to the Anglican bishop of Kitgum, the Rev. MacLeod Baker Ochola, and together they began planning the August gathering.

Positive response to the August prayer meeting led to further discussions, both in Kitgum and in Gulu, and resulted in the formal establishment of a new entity, the Acholi Religious Leaders Peace Initiative, in February 1998. A five-member task force would oversee its activities: the Rev. Nelson Onono-Onweng, Anglican bishop of the Northern Diocese of Uganda, as chairman; Sheik Musa Khalil as deputy chairman; Bishop Baker Ochola as treasurer; Monsignor Matthew Odong as secretary; and Fr. Rodriguez. At this organizing meeting the following statement of goals and objectives was adopted:

> **Goal and mission:** To actively engage the entire Acholi community to effectively participate in the process of healing, restoration, reconciliation, peace and development in Acholiland. ARLPI is committed

to contribute to bringing about a transformation of the current violent armed conflict by promoting sustainable reconciliation and peace building activities.

Objectives: (a) To unite as believers in God Almighty in order to mobilise the people of Acholi for peace and development; (b) to advocate for social justice and human rights; (c) to train in conflict analysis, conflict transformation and undertake community peacebuilding; (d) to foster the spirit of peaceful co-existence among different communities in Acholiland and with its neighbours; (e) to work collaboratively with the local leaders, members of parliament, local and international NGOs and all community based stakeholders to promote the culture of dialogue as a basis for resolving and transforming conflicts within communities; and (f) to undertake any other activities which may contribute to the creation and promotion of love, harmony, forgiveness, reconciliation, healing and peace. (Lukwiya Ochola 2006, 132–133)

In January 2014, supported by a grant from the Nagel Institute for the Study of World Christianity, I conducted interviews with residents of Gulu who had been involved in this collaborative effort or had benefited from it. The early activities of ARLPI were described to me by John Bosco Komanech, director of Caritas, a Catholic social service agency, in the diocese of Gulu.

I think the activity of the church and its leaders was very instrumental in trying to stop this brutality and the war in the north. First of all, the religious leaders united among themselves. The Catholics, Anglicans, Muslims, and Orthodox—they united and said that this is a common front where all of us, the leaders, have to come together.

Then they started with a kind of peaceful demonstration intended to gain the attention of the government of Uganda and the international community. What they did was to join the night commuters—the people who would run around and then go to sleep under verandas at night. They said, "These are human beings, and we advocate for them. We will be the voice of the voiceless. Let us come together, and join them in town." So they started sleeping in the open spaces, in the bus parks, under the verandas. That is when the international world started saying there is a problem in northern Uganda and we need to intervene.

We will return later to the phenomenon of nightly migration by children. Komanech's summary of the goals and tactics of the newly formed group identified three further commitments that shaped its activities from the beginning:

> Secondly, they did not side with any party. Whether you were a government soldier or in the bus with the LRA, they [religious leaders] had a common position condemning the wrongdoing in northern Uganda. They would go on the radio and say, "Kony, stop this brutal killing. If you want to attack the government, the barracks are there." And then also they would speak to the government of Uganda. . . . Not all of the killing which took place here was the LRA. The government soldiers also killed people. So they were also condemned by the church leaders.
>
> Thirdly, all the churches and mosques were open to receive any person. Whether you were a rebel who wanted to surrender, you were welcome. Whether you were a person running away from the rebels, you were welcome. And if you look on maps for their locations, you will find that most of the IDP camps were created around church institutions. People were given protection by the churches, and then the government created camps in those places.
>
> Fourth, the religious leaders set out to broker peace. At the beginning the archbishop and his colleagues got in touch with some of the commanders of the LRA around Pader and told them: come home, the people are bitter, yes, but they are ready to welcome you. They want you to abandon rebel activity. So they had started the peace process even before the Juba peace talks started. (Komanech 2014)

One of the first actions of the new group was to draft a memorandum addressed to President Museveni, "A Call for Peace and an End to Bloodshed in Acholiland." It called on the Ugandan government to work toward a ceasefire, advocate for a negotiated end to the conflict, and begin preparations for mediation in which all parties would be represented. In an important breakthrough that helped establish the leaders' credibility, they were invited to meet with the president on March 8, 1998. The response they received to their recommendations was guarded but not entirely dismissive. Participants in that meeting reported that Museveni acknowledged the legitimacy of ARLPI concerns over the futility of military confrontation, although he made no promises to change government tactics. Moreover, they add, "a reluctant Museveni was forced to concede the message of reconciliation when they reminded him that even God forgives sinners" (Khadialaga 2001, 4).

The meeting with the president yielded no immediate results—UPDF forces continued their attacks, and the government offered no opening for mediation—but it gained ARLPI a higher profile and legitimized its efforts in the eyes of the community and the representatives of government. Much later, both local and national government officials would agree to participate in the reconciliation efforts that ARLPI set into motion. A short-term benefit came in the form of financial assistance from the United Nations Development Program. Its local administrator, Babatunde Thomas, recognized the importance of the new organization's work, and he provided funding for meetings, community workshops, and travel (Khadialaga 2001, 5).

In June 1998, ARLPI convened a three-day consultative meeting, calling it *Bedo Piny pi Kuc,* "sitting down together for peace." Community members were invited to gather and share their recommendations for "Active Community Participation in Healing, Restoration, and Development." More than 150 residents of the Acholi region attended, including parents of the abducted, teachers and community workers, traditional chiefs, community elders, and local government officials. Few of those attending believed the Ugandan government could provide adequate protection against LRA violence, and yet there was little hope that peace would come through a negotiated settlement either. The efforts of Parliamentarian Betty Bigombe four years earlier had collapsed, after all, making it evident that neither side was willing to compromise. A few years before this unsuccessful effort, three traditional leaders who had sought out LRA representatives to urge an end to the rebellion had been murdered (Latigo and Baker Ochola 2015, 16, 17).

A few months later, an ARLPI delegation brought the recommendations of this gathering to the second *Kacoke Madit* gathering in London. Among their findings: a military solution could not succeed in ending the insurgency; an invitation to the negotiating table must be extended to Joseph Kony; a law granting amnesty to those who give up their arms should be enacted; Uganda and Sudan should reestablish diplomatic relations in order to help resolve the conflict; and the religious leaders of all communities should launch a mass education campaign concerning the possibility, and the benefits, of restoring peace (Lukwiya Ochola 2006, 134–135).

In the accounts of these early efforts to set a peace process in motion, it is evident that there was considerable public resistance to the goal of reconciliation and reintegration with a movement that had caused such indescribable suffering to so many for so long. In a report published in 2015, two observers and participants recalled:

> The ARLPI stressed the importance of non-violence and alleviating the suffering of the people, and argued that most of the rebel fighters did not go to the bush of their own volition and that there was therefore a moral imperative to safeguard the lives of these abducted girls and boys. The ARLPI's work was key to changing the way the community spoke about the LRA: rather than simply being perpetrators of violence, some were seen as the victims of abduction whom the government had failed to protect. (Latigo and Baker Ochola 2015, 16)

In an overview of ARLPI activities written in 2002, Fr. Carlos Rodriguez, the man whose local committee was the seed from which the interfaith movement had grown, recalled some of the challenges that it had faced from its founding.

> In 1997, Bishop Ochola chaired a series of meetings between Catholic and Anglican, and later Muslim, officials to discuss the situation. That August, they organised a peace rally and issued an unequivocal message asking the LRA to stop its violence against civilians and calling on the government to seek a negotiated end to the conflict. This event was followed in September by a workshop that produced a strongly worded publication denouncing the UPDF's attempts

to force villagers into the displacement camps. This letter was read in most churches and met with an angry response from political leaders. . . .

Since its inception, ARLPI has sought to draw the senior LRA leadership into peace talks. While meaningful high-level meetings remain elusive, discreet contacts by some religious leaders with field commanders have taken place. The main focus has been around implementation of the amnesty law, which allows combatants to report to religious leaders. These initiatives have encountered difficulties, particularly in co-ordination with local UPDF units. One of the 'bush peace talks' with junior LRA officers was attacked by a UPDF unit on 26 April 2001— even though Fr Tarcisio Pazzaglia alerted the military authorities prior to the meeting. Despite the risks, ARLPI and other traditional leaders remain committed to continuing these efforts that offer hope for demobilising the LRA. (Rodriguez 2002)

Adoption of an Amnesty Law

ARLPI leaders realized from the beginning that an appeal to combatants to lay down their weapons and rejoin Acholi society would not be heeded if arrest and conviction for actions they carried out in battle were likely to follow. In our interview in 2014, Monsignor Matthew Odong, a founding member, cited advocacy for enactment of an amnesty law as one of the most important initiatives that the organization had undertaken:

Another contribution that the Acholi Religious Leaders made is this: we proposed amnesty—I went to the Parliament with a few others, and we presented our position. Because now we had to find a way of giving confidence to the rebels that when they came back, in spite of the atrocities that had been committed, they would be forgiven.

We had to build trust. We didn't take sides with either the government or the rebels. You know when two elephants are fighting, it is the grass that suffers. The government and of course the LRA were the two elephants, and the people on the ground, the people are the grass. And the grass is crying out, I am innocent! I am innocent! And we are the voice of this grass! And we are ready to die for that! So that is what really made us friends to both sides. We remained completely neutral and that is how we built confidence. But it was also a learning experience, and we felt that we were representing God, and that he would give us the means, and he did it. It was difficult, but God was with us. (Odong 2014)

Seeking to lay the groundwork for an end to hostilities, ARLPI urged enactment of a law to ensure that LRA soldiers who laid down their arms and renounced violence would be granted amnesty from prosecution for acts committed while they were serving in Kony's forces. ARLPI leaders insisted that without such a provision the conflict would continue indefinitely, and even those who had been abducted and compelled to serve as LRA soldiers would remain in hiding rather than risk prosecution if they tried to return to their families and communities. But the idea of a general amnesty was strongly opposed by some members of parliament, and some international human rights groups lobbied against it also. Opponents believed that heinous acts of murder, maiming, and abduction needed to be punished, not excused. Some also objected to the omission of any mention of abuses by government forces, as if only one side had been guilty of atrocities.

After extended debate, the Uganda Amnesty Act of 2000 was approved by Parliament and enacted into law, with these key provisions:

(1) An Amnesty is declared in respect of any Ugandan who has at any time since the 26th day of January, 1986 engaged in or is engaging in war or armed rebellion against the government of the Republic of Uganda by (a) actual participation in combat; (b) collaborating with the perpetrators of the war or armed rebellion; (c) committing any other crime in the furtherance of the war or armed rebellion; or (d) assisting or aiding the conduct or prosecution of the war or armed rebellion.

(2) A person referred to under subsection (1) shall not be prosecuted or subjected to any form of punishment for the participation in the war or rebellion for any crime committed in the cause of the war or armed rebellion. (Parliament of Uganda n.d.)

The passage of this act had the desired effect, and defections from LRA forces became more numerous. Immunity against prosecution brought about what a decade of military pressure had failed to achieve: significant reduction in the LRA forces remaining under Kony's command. Julius Omony, a staff member of the Peace and Justice Commission of the Catholic diocese of Gulu, commented in an interview:

> Amnesty has been so instrumental in bringing the formerly abducted persons out of the bush. So many of them feared to come out because they would be prosecuted. But the religious leaders really advocated for the amnesty provision. It came into place and it has been so helpful in ensuring that many return from captivity, and it has contributed to the peace we have been having. (Omony 2014)

Ugandan human rights lawyer Barney Afako cited evidence of the success of the amnesty initiative, despite the misgivings of many in the national government: "It is a mark of its relevance that since 2000, over 26,000 people have responded to the amnesty, abandoning armed rebellion and returning home under the oversight of an Amnesty Commission" (Afako 2006).

Senior officers of the rebel force, including Joseph Kony, were excluded from applying for amnesty. In the year 2000 indictments by the International Criminal Court for genocide and war crimes were not yet on the horizon, but when they came (as will be described below) they did not invalidate the amnesty provision for rebel soldiers. Amnesty was available to all who had taken part in the LRA rebellion except those who had initiated and directed it.

Many years after LRA withdrawal from Uganda, however, some of the high-level commanders in the rebel movement sought to apply the amnesty provision to their cases too. Even though the law had released only ordinary LRA soldiers and not their senior officers from criminal liability, officers protested that they too had acted under compulsion.

These appeals sparked heated debate among human rights activists in East Africa. Representative of these responses is that of IRIN (formerly Integrated Regional Information Network), a United Nations spinoff that operates today as independent media agency with a focus on human rights issues around the globe. An unnamed commentator writing for IRIN in 2012 urged that "a balance should be drawn to accommodate the calls from northern Uganda for reconciliation and forgiveness against the mandate of the state to ensure that crimes do not go unpunished" and added that the Amnesty Act "has undermined all efforts of accountability for war crimes and is [a] recipe for impunity among others" (IRIN 2012).

The IRIN report was written partly in response to the legal complexities that followed the arrest of Thomas Kwoyelo, a mid-level LRA commander. Kwoyelo was captured by Ugandan forces across the border in the DRC in 2011 and charged with planning and directing attacks against civilians in northern Uganda before 2006. He appealed to the Amnesty Commission for immunity from prosecution, but his appeal was denied. In February 2017, after numerous delays, further rulings, and procedural disputes, he appeared before a special International Crimes Division of the High Court of Uganda. He protested that, because the acts for which he was being indicted had occurred before the creation of this special court, it had no jurisdiction. In November 2017, however, Judge Susan Okalany ruled that he is "properly charged before the court for offenses of murder, rape, sexual enslavement, taking hostages and torture of people in IDP camps," and ordered him to stand trial. The proceedings are expected to be lengthy and complex (Kabahumuza 2017).

Another senior LRA commander, Caesar Acellam Otto, was captured in the Central African Republic in 2012, and he told reporters that he too would apply for amnesty. At the time of his capture a military spokesman stated that he would be held as "a prisoner or war," pending a decision by the Ministry of Justice. In 2015, however, he was granted amnesty (IRIN 2012, 2015).

An account of the Kwoyelo indictment by a writer for *The New Yorker* questioned the inconsistencies in the courts' treatment of LRA commanders, as well as the way in which amnesty provisions were enacted, allowed to lapse, and then reenacted. One of Kwoyelo's defense lawyers charges that his client is the victim of government efforts to make amends for its failure to defeat the rebel forces: "In doing away with amnesty, Uganda may very well be trying to show the donor countries that have poured money into the war-crimes court, and the U.S., which has now sent arms, equipment, and troops, that it is taking action against the L.R.A. despite having been unable to stop the group for the last twenty-five years." Reviewing the actions of Uganda's courts, it is difficult to discern any consistency in the way in which some officers have been put to trial while others are judged to be eligible for amnesty (Okeowo 2012).

In the face of these perplexing legal and moral questions, the religious leaders of northern Uganda stood fast in their advocacy of amnesty as a necessary step toward reconciliation and healing.

> "As religious leaders, we believe in restorative justice, not punitive. We believe in restoring broken relationships rather than punishing the offenders," Bishop John Baptist Odama, a member of the Acholi Religious Peace Initiative, told IRIN.
>
> Odama, who called for the establishment of a Truth and Reconciliation Commission, added: "The LRA has destabilized and committed atrocities in the four countries. We need to rebuild the relationships of the affected countries. Dialogue, truth, reconciliation and forgiveness I believe are the best solutions." (IRIN 2012)

Another testimony to the importance of reconciliation can be found in the example of Sister Mary Tarcisia Lokot, the first woman to serve on the board of ARLPI. She traveled with other ARLPI leaders into the bush to persuade LRA commanders to work out a negotiated end to the conflict, and later she established a training center for the "child mothers" who were abducted and forcibly assigned to rebel commanders, bearing their children in the camps. Peace activist John Paul Lederach reports that he pressed her for an explanation of how she could welcome child soldiers and abducted girls who had witnessed, and in some cases participated in, indescribable horrors during the conflict. Her reply was brief and straightforward: "Because we must . . . because both rebels and victims are part and parcel of my own people." She added:

> I look at those people as my brothers and sisters who have been misled. Especially the LRA soldiers, the Jinjas, the children abducted and forced to do such things. My presence might draw some of them to come back. "I know you have not chosen this. Make a choice

to come back." I must love and forgive and help them. (Lederach 2010, 43)

A general amnesty for crimes committed in a civil war, especially one as protracted and brutal as that conducted by the LRA in northern Uganda, is a risky and controversial measure. Families ripped apart by decades of unrestrained killing, kidnapping, and rape are asked to forego the sense of closure and moral restoration that can only be achieved by holding the perpetrators to account for their crimes. Communities who have seen their young people transformed into brutal killers must take them back into their homes if only they will lay down their weapons and request immunity from punishment. In effect, every measure offering post-conflict amnesty is a policy that sacrifices justice for the sake of reconciliation.

The Morality of Forgiveness: The South African Precedent

The cost of such a trade-off was seen most vividly in the process of reconciliation that followed the end of apartheid in South Africa in the early 1990s. That nation's transition to multiracial democracy offers useful comparisons with the situation of Ugandans in the post-conflict period.

In the early 1990s, following a period of extremely difficult negotiations between the National Party, which was preparing to relinquish a half-century of white rule, and the newly unbanned African National Congress (ANC), it was agreed that it would be unwise— indeed, impossible—to bring charges against all those responsible for decades of government and antigovernment violence. Any attempt to prosecute all the human rights violations committed under apartheid would strain the judicial system past the breaking point and undermine any sense of national unity and common purpose in planning for the future. It also became evident that without a general amnesty provision for members of the South African military there would never be a majority of parliamentary votes for a new constitution.

Eventually a guarantee of amnesty was incorporated into a new bill of rights, with assurances that human rights violations would in the future be considered criminal offenses and subject to legal punishment.

The linking of these two provisions helped secure approval of the new constitution in 1994, opening the way to the nation's first multiracial general elections and the formation of a new government representing all the people of South Africa.

In 1995 the newly formed Government of National Unity, which included representatives of the National Party and the Inkatha Freedom Party as well as the dominant ANC, formulated legislation to create a Truth and Reconciliation Commission (TRC) that would investigate human rights violations committed by both government and anti-government agents between 1960 and 1994. The commission created one committee to review evidence of human rights abuses, another to consider reparations, and a third to accept and assess applications for amnesty.

For a period of five years after its creation, the TRC convened panels in meeting halls in every major city, in many towns, and across rural areas of South Africa, inviting those who had suffered from the repressive violence of apartheid to present their testimony. Victims of ANC counterviolence were also invited to testify, despite the opposition from some who argued that urgency of the struggle against apartheid should excuse any excesses committed.

The TRC regularly released reports on the disposition of requests for amnesty. One of the last such reports, issued on December 13, 2000, gives a clear picture of the ways in which this tribunal sought to close the books on a half-century of racial separation and oppression. In the period under review, seventeen applicants had been granted amnesty and two requests had been denied. Among those granted amnesty, despite having been responsible for a variety of violent acts, were both ANC partisans and government soldiers (TRC 2000).

By the time the TRC completed its work, it had received testimony from 21,000 South African victims of political violence, and of those charged with human rights abuses 7,112 had applied for amnesty. Only 849 of these requests were approved (USIP 2002).

In the hearings, complete disclosure and unswerving honesty were conditions for granting amnesty. The details that emerged concerning government measures to silence and intimidate opponents, and about extrajudicial interrogation and punishment, horrified observers around the globe, but they also provided victims and their families with accurate accounts—at last—of the government's actions.

It was evident to all that the TRC process amounted to giving up any hope of holding the perpetrators of violent human rights abuses responsible for their actions. For the sake of healing and reconciliation, justice was given a lower priority. Opinions vary widely, in South Africa and abroad, over the long-term effects of this difficult compromise. Fears that the TRC process would in effect absolve even the most egregiously guilty from criminal liability proved to be largely fulfilled.[1]

The example of the TRC in South Africa has profoundly affected other countries struggling to recover from prolonged civil conflict. As many as 40 nations have established post-conflict commissions with mandates similar to that adopted in 1994 by the new South African government. Some have had considerable success in healing wounds and rebuilding trust after conflict, while others served only as a cover for new regimes to hide their own complicity in past abuses.

Ugandan president Museveni convened a Commission of Inquiry into Violations of Human Rights shortly after seizing power in 1986, with intentions very different from the later South African model: its avowed aim was to identify and punish those responsible for kidnapping, killing, and torture in Uganda during the Amin regime (1971–1979) and the second Obote regime (1981–1986). The work of this commission was hindered by political opposition, lack of funding, and lack of commitment on the government's part. No individuals were identified as responsible for human rights abuses, and when the commission eventually issued its final report in 1994 it contained only a few cautious policy recommendations: that laws authorizing detention without trial be annulled, for example, and that human rights education be incorporated into school curricula and into military training. A report on this commission by the United States Institute of Peace notes that, in the judgment of many observers, "the Commission only served as a political strategy to provide legitimacy to the new government." It had little credibility and has had little effect on the subsequent history of Uganda (USIP 1986).

A generation later, the example of the TRC in South Africa shaped plans and expectations for Uganda's amnesty policies. The amnesty provision, many feared, might be abused to exculpate senior commanders who did not simply carry out orders but directed others to wage campaigns of wanton killing, kidnapping, and rape. Lack of accountability for past crimes might encourage and empower some to profess their renunciation of violence but to take up similar tactics if their power should be threatened in the future.

Even more worrisome was the inevitable, even if unintended, message conveyed by a general amnesty: that the political dimension of civil conflict must be disregarded in order to overcome a troubled past and move on. Political theorist Bronwen Leebaw has mounted a powerful argument for the inadequacy of post-conflict provisions in an important comparative study of the Nuremberg trials of Nazi war criminals and the South African TRC. In her monograph *Judging State-Sponsored Violence, Imagining Political Change,* Leebaw argues that both the retributive model of Nuremberg and the restorative ideals of the TRC overlooked the political foundations of violence, and for that reason they contributed very little to building a just and workable postwar order. A satisfactory transitional justice process, she argues, must begin with an honest assessment of the political institutions and values that made violence possible and the complicity of those who permitted it to continue (Leebaw 2011).

The Ugandan amnesty law of 2000 was limited in its scope, applying only to acts committed after 1986, and it was written with the sole intent of enticing LRA soldiers to lay down arms and return to their families and communities. UPDF soldiers were guilty of many abuses, but according to the account of the conflict put forward by the Ugandan government—and accepted too readily by observers and donors—these were regrettable but justified countermeasures against an entrenched enemy. Government soldiers did not need to request immunity from criminal prosecution, because there was no possibility that they would be held to account for what they had done. The amnesty law was put forward as a generous measure of reconciliation toward those guilty of atrocities in warfare, but only one side's guilt was acknowledged. The autocratic rule of the NRM prevented any honest reckoning with the politics behind the protracted civil war, and the pretense that abuses had occurred only on one side was not challenged.

All the same, the passage of this measure brought major improvements to the lives of the people of northern Uganda. Many thousands of LRA fighters escaped to government-controlled territory and surrendered their weapons. Family members who were able to communicate with those still serving under Kony encouraged their relatives to do the same.

From the earliest years of the conflict, LRA commanders had been issuing dire warnings to their young captives. Attempting to escape was pointless, they said, because government soldiers would capture and kill anyone who was known to have taken up arms under Kony's command, no matter what their age, regardless of whether they had joined the LRA voluntarily or as a result of a kidnapping raid. As word filtered into the bush concerning the amnesty law and its implementation, this story became less credible.

The intent of the amnesty policy was to encourage LRA soldiers to return to their families and their former communities. But the massive displacement caused by the war often made this impossible. Unless they lived in one of the larger towns, such as Gulu or Kitgum, their family members had been forcibly removed from their farms to overcrowded internal refugee camps. Houses had been burned, crops uprooted, livestock stolen and slaughtered. This is the third development of the early 2000s that fundamentally changed the experience of war for the Acholi people: a massive concentration of the region's people into camps utterly inadequate to the enormous numbers who were crowded together there.

Migration at Gunpoint: IDP Camps

The creation of "protected camps," effectively acknowledging that government forces could not ensure the safety of rural communities, has already been mentioned. The rural residents of northern Uganda were forced to abandon the farms and villages where they had lived for many generations and move to overcrowded camps for internally displaced persons—IDP camps.

Before the huge camps were created, many villagers had relocated to towns for safety. A 1997 report by Michael Gersony to the US Department of State and the UN Agency for International Development documents the tactics that were employed and the results. In five months' travel in northern Uganda, during which he interviewed several hundred residents, officials, and military officers, Gersony noted

that some residents had fled to government-controlled towns for protection, while others had sought protection from government soldiers
by relocating to LRA-controlled areas.

The first population movements were voluntary, albeit motivated by
fear of attack. By the time Gersony visited the region, however, the government had launched a policy of forcible relocation from villages to
areas that the UPDF could defend. Gersony describes one incident in
the implementation of this policy in which tens of thousands of rural
residents—75,000, by Gersony's estimate—were ordered to abandon
their homes and farms. On arrival in the towns they had to build their
own huts in designated areas.

> In October 1996, the UPDF ordered the remaining rural population
> of Gulu [District] to move into trading centers, in which it desig-
> nated the locations for the construction of their temporary grass-
> hut accommodations. In most cases, civilians were given a three-day
> deadline for moving. Although reluctant to leave their homes, they
> were advised that if found in rural areas they would be "treated as
> rebels." The Government had made no advance arrangements for
> health, sanitation, food or other assistance, aggravating the increased
> infant mortality which predictably arose in these locations. (Gersony
> 1997, 49)

The areas provided for resettlement were usually close to military bases
in the towns. The intent was to assure that UPDF forces were close at
hand should an LRA raid occur. But the siting of the camps violated
a fundamental international principle: resettled civilian settlements
should be well separated from military bases in order to reduce the possibility of civilians being caught in the crossfire of government–rebel
clashes. The residents of the IDP camps were indeed frequent victims of
such skirmishes. In one 1996 incident, for example, LRA looters seized
food and supplies from shops that supplied camp residents and fired
at the government soldiers assigned to protect the camp. The soldiers
returned fire with mortar rounds that killed eight camp residents
(Gersony 1997, 50).

Rural residents who remained in their homes were often subjected
to abuse by government soldiers, who regarded anyone unwilling to

relocate as a probable LRA sympathizer or supporter. "Brutal beating of civilians during questioning in rural areas was described as routine," writes Gersony. Sometimes the residents attempted to help the government by reporting LRA troop movements, but the UPDF response often came too late to find the rebels—and then the army accused the residents of misleading them and facilitating the insurgents' escape.

In these circumstances any men of military age who ran from UPDF forces were likely to be fired on or subjected to brutal interrogation tactics. Some incidents were reported in which young men who did not give satisfactory answers to the soldiers questioning them were executed immediately. These practices were not systematic, nor did they reflect a general policy of the UPDF forces, Gersony adds, but were ordered by individual commanders in the field. Across the region, he notes with uncharacteristic understatement, "Rape appears to be a continuing problem" (Gersony 1997, 46).

In the few years following Gersony's visit, the pace of relocation accelerated rapidly, and to accommodate the huge numbers forced from their farms, large IDP camps were established near each of the larger towns. A 1998 report published in a Canadian journal of refugee affairs summarized the mass displacement of rural residents in Uganda, to that point in the conflict. A Ugandan author living in Toronto, Ogenga Otonnu, chose a chilling title for his account of the campaign of forced relocation: "The Path to Genocide in Northern Uganda." Otonnu observes that the stated purpose of the population transfer to IDP camps, to assure the safety of the population, was only a partial truth: it was also intended to "make it difficult for the rebels to mobilize new recruits; deprive the rebels of food supplies and other support from the population; punish the Acholi for not voting for Museveni in the 1995 election; and deter the insurgents from attacking army detachments in Acholiland" (Otonnu 1998).

When this article was published in 1998, 27 IDP camps had been established in Gulu District and ten more in the neighboring district of Kitgum. The total number of residents of the camps was estimated at 470,900. In the years following, this number would grow to as many as two million, representing a large majority of the population of the entire region.

Food aid from the United Nations Food Program and other re-lief agencies was distributed to camp residents, since they could not could venture safely into agricultural lands nearby to cultivate their traditional crops. Food shortages were chronic, malnutrition epidemic. Medical care was woefully inadequate, with the result that death rates from infectious disease, complications in childbirth, and early child-hood disease were far higher than in other areas of the country. Robert Lukwiya Ochola, the Comboni priest whose account of ARLPI's founding has been cited above, mentions in passing that he lived for several months in a camp whose 18,000 residents had to line up for hours to obtain water from just three unreliable wells (Lukwiya Ochola 2006, 78).

An American Catholic priest who traveled to Uganda each summer during the last decade of the LRA conflict provides a chilling first-person account of the camp at Pabbo.

> The living conditions I observed in the camps are shockingly in-human. People wait in line for many hours to fill a single container of water. Many tell me they have stopped bathing altogether; the water is just too precious for anything other than cooking and drinking. Inadequate privacy and a total lack of sanitation add to the frustra-tion of everyday life. The gravest and most long-term danger is severe malnourishment. The best estimates suggest that upward of 40 per-cent of children less than five years of age have seriously stunted growth due to malnutrition, which will have an effect on their health for the rest of their lives. Many die in infancy; these camps have the worst infant mortality rates in the world.
>
> There is a moral degradation here, a spirit of defeatism unlike anything I have witnessed. . . . . Suicides mount. It is highest among young mothers, who despair at their inability to provide for their young. (Dunson 2008, 97–98)

Media agency IRIN reported on a flare-up in the same camp in February 2004—the largest in the region, housing 62,000. On this occasion, and others, the alleged protection offered by UPDF forces proved to be nothing of the sort.

Kampala, 3 February 2004: A row has broken out between the army and residents of Uganda's biggest Internally Displaced Persons (IDPs) settlement, Pabbo camp, in the northern Gulu District, with the army claiming that the camp harbours rebel collaborators and the IDPs accusing the army of starting a fire which destroyed much of the camp during an operation to arrest suspects. . . .

The army announced that it had recovered 800 rounds of ammunition and some uniforms after a raid on the camp mounted in the early hours of Monday morning. . . .

But residents told the Acholi Religious Leaders' Peace Initiative (ARLPI)—a prominent local advocacy group based in Gulu town—that the claims that the army had found ammunition were a lie intended to divert attention from a fire that soldiers had started in the camp during a roundup of 6,000 people whom the army "suspects" of being collaborators. (IRIN 2004)

In a 2012 overview of review of postwar recovery efforts, an international agency reviewed the catastrophic effects of the government's policy of relocation:

By the height of displacement in 2005, nearly 2 million people—approximately 90–95 percent of the population of Acholi, 33 percent of the population of Lango, 200,000 people in Teso and 41,000 in West Nile—had become internally displaced as a result of the conflict. There were over 240 IDP camps during the height of the conflict in the Greater North. IDP households were largely unable to access land for cultivation owing to the threat of attack outside the camps and dense populations within the camps. The residents of IDP camps suffered from 'malnutrition, high mortality rates, low life expectancies, high primary school dropout rates, and early pregnancies and marriages.' (Secure Livelihoods Research Consortium 2012, citing Lehrer 2010)

Another observer writes, "in effect, by the late 1990s, most of the Acholi parts of Uganda were being kept in rural prisons, often in appalling conditions" (Allen 2006, 14). According to an estimate by the World

Health Organization, in 2005 there were one thousand "excess" deaths each week in the IDP camps—deaths as a result of malnutrition, disease, and violence that exceeded the mortality rate of other rural communities in East Africa (Whitmore 2010, 176–177).

Less obvious, but no less disruptive of the fabric of northern Uganda culture, was the effect of poor housing, lack of land, and overcrowding on the traditions that sustained Acholi culture. In the IDP camps families had no privacy, and there was no room for the evening cooking fire at which elders would retell Acholi folktales and teach traditional dances, a ritual that Monsignor Odong described as "like a classroom—and it is like the Parliament. All the members of the family gather to have their meal and to share about their experiences of the day. . . . But when children are taken from their families, and even when families are crowded together in IDP camps, there is no more 'factory of society' around the evening fire circle" (Odong 2014).

In an interview I conducted on a brief return visit to Uganda in 2016, an administrator at Gulu University, George Openjuru Ladah, described the disruption experienced by his family and many others:

> An entire generation of children has been born and raised in camps, in a very limited and very restrictive environment. They never saw their parents go to work the fields in the morning. Now the insecurity is ended, and they can return home, the world is wider, but what can they do? They can ride boda-bodas [motorcycles], and what else? How will they learn to farm? Who will teach them to plant millet, keep chickens, and milk cows? (Ladah 2016)

His colleague Stephen Langole added this observation:

> We must recognize the problems in the way education is packaged today. Technical knowledge without knowledge of spiritual and community values is useless! It is essential for us in Uganda to integrate beliefs, rituals, and values as part of education. This may not make sense from a Western point of view, but if it is ignored it will only lead to further collapse of our communities. (Langole 2016)

Voluntary Migration by Children: The Night Commuters

Residents of the larger towns were not forcibly relocated, and they continued to carry on their occupations as best they could. Food was scarce, owing to the destruction of crops and their seizure by the LRA, and trade with the outside world nearly ceased because travel on the roads connecting the Acholi region with southern Uganda was unsafe. But the towns, where UPDF forces were quartered, were relatively secure from LRA attack. Raiding parties who tried to seize boys and girls from larger towns rather than small villages were less likely to succeed and more likely to suffer casualties. The primary targets of the LRA throughout this period remained small farming villages, often located far from roads and other means of communication. Life for those attempting to carry on their traditional way of life outside the major towns became more and more precarious—far more so for children than for adults.

In the early 2000s, children of northern Uganda who were still living with their families in rural villages discovered a new means of protecting themselves against attack: an informal and spontaneous program of voluntary migration. They began to walk each evening from their home villages to the towns of the region such as Gulu, Lira, and Kitgum. There they would simply lie down to sleep for the night in open spaces—railway and bus stations, parks, and church and school yards—under blankets, if they had brought them from the village, or simply in their clothes. Early in the morning they would walk back to their villages. Some walked just a mile or two, while others had to traverse distances of ten miles or more.

Of all the sources that attempt to convey the displacement caused by the LRA conflict, and the ways in which the people of the region responded, Jagielski's *Night Wanderers* is the most thorough and the most vivid. He describes the fear and antipathy that greeted the first wave of "night commuters" when they began to show up in city streets in the evening. Local residents gave them a wide berth, wondering whether there were child soldiers among them. The children seldom spoke to the city residents, and they had little money to buy goods in the shops. In the morning they set out before sunrise to arrive at school before the opening bell.

As the children returned, night after night, week after week, local leaders began to take notice. Jagielski conveys the experience of a visitor to Gulu during this period, sitting outside his hotel on the outskirts of Gulu as evening fell.

> Then the children began to come into town.
>
> They appeared suddenly, almost imperceptibly. They loomed out of the darkness, from under the ground like apparitions. They were heading on foot, by the dozen, from every direction, toward the almost deserted town, now plunged into silence before the storm. They walked confidently, not in a hurry, like someone repeating for the thousandth time an act that's entirely familiar and no longer holds any mystery.
>
> Some were dressed in school uniforms and had satchels full of textbooks and notepads on their backs. Others, in rags and barefoot, were carrying blankets, bundles and parcels of some kind, as well as sheets of newspaper and pieces of cardboard picked up from roadside ditches or gutters. The older children were leading smaller ones by the hand, and the girls had babies strapped to their backs, like village women on their way to work in the fields.
>
> In the market square the gray river of children, quietly murmuring in the darkness, divided up into several smaller ones. The biggest offshoot headed toward the bus station, while a smaller one ended its journey in the courtyard of the large red-brick church of the Blessed Virgin Mary. Others continued to the yards of local schools and hospitals. The rest of the children ended their march on the main street, where they spread their makeshift beds on the ground. (Jagielski 2012, 3)

Initial suspicions gradually subsided as the children returned, night after night, and as local residents began to realize that they were simply seeking to escape the risk of abduction from their homes.

By this point in the conflict, LRA forces were consistently targeting older boys and girls—preteens and early teens—as kidnap victims. Raids early in the conflict had swept up young adults as well, but Kony's senior commanders had come to the conclusion that older abductees were less reliable and less malleable. Younger children could be turned into relentlessly effective child soldiers, or compliant sex partners for officers, by a few months of indoctrination backed by dire threats of the consequences of any attempt to escape. Older children, the commanders feared, might be more resistant to being recast in the LRA mold, and they might be too quick to attempt escape and too often successful when they did.

Adults were seldom targets for LRA abduction. In some cases, after the rebel soldiers had searched a village for food and supplies and perhaps destroyed houses and barns, the adults were left unharmed. In other cases, particularly if rebel commanders had any grounds for suspecting them of harboring or aiding UPDF forces, they were subjected to rape, mutilation, and torture. In any case it was impossible, whatever the treatment of adults in rural villages, for parents to protect their children from abduction. So the children had devised their own defensive tactic: they became night commuters.

As children settled in for the night on the grounds of police stations, bus stations, schools, and churches, and as it became evident that they were simply victims of the continuing conflict and not rebel child soldiers, the administrators of these institutions—police officers, schoolteachers, and pastors—began to visit them. Priests and pastors urged their congregations to respond with compassion, not hostility, to the uninvited visitors who filled the churches' grounds and other open areas every night. Some organizations created shelters for the children, and many made latrines and water sources available to them.

Leaders of the religious communities of Gulu and Kitgum began to carry their own bedclothes outside to sleep in the open air with the night commuters. A Catholic priest commented on the nightly ritual of his archbishop in 2002:

> Archbishop John Baptist Odama may have never performed a more unusual ritual in his life. For four consecutive days, in the evening, he quietly left his residence carrying a sack containing only a blanket, walked the five kilometers distance to Gulu town and on the way met with a good number of children, carrying their own sacks and blankets on their way to the verandas for the night. Odama greeted all of them warmly: "These are my colleagues, my fellow night commuters," he remarked with a smile, and continued on foot

followed by the children some as young as five to the bus park."
(quoted in Otim 2009)

The nightly migration of children was an effective, if burdensome, pre-
ventative against capture in LRA raids. The columns of children each
morning and evening on the roads and footpaths of the region grew
steadily. While government forces repeatedly assured the international
community that their military campaign had crippled the LRA to the
point that its collapse was imminent, in fact the situation in the villages
remained as dangerous as ever. Rebel forces were increasingly desperate
to obtain grain and meat, after the movement of much of the population into camps caused the collapse of northern Uganda's agricultural
production, and the small villages from which residents had refused to
move became ever more tempting targets. The number of number of
attacks and their brutality increased to levels not seen in a decade.

Reports of the children's long journey to safety, and of the welcome
extended by local religious leaders and officials, captured the attention
of news media in Uganda and beyond. Until now most domestic and
international media had repeated the official account of the conflict
given out by Museveni and his government: the LRA movement was a
dangerous and rapacious rebel force, but it was backed into a corner and
would soon surrender, if the government stayed the course. Reassured
that the end was near, international partners kept up the flow of arms
for government soldiers and food for the displaced. The phenomenon
of tens of thousands of children who chose to walk several hours to the
nearest town each night, rather than risk kidnapping and rape in their
home villages, opened the eyes of many observers to the falsehood of
this narrative and the suffering of the people.

In 2004, when the director of UNICEF, Carol Bellamy, visited
Uganda to observe the situation first-hand, it was estimated that more
than 44,000 children had joined the ranks of nightly commuters. In
Gulu alone their numbers had reached 14,000 (UNICEF 2004). In the
International Herald Tribune, Bellamy wrote:

The 18-year conflict in northern Uganda has obliterated the idea of
childhood as a protected time of healthy growth. It has left parents
so desperate to shield their children from abduction and murder that

sending them trekking miles into town by themselves at night is their only hope, a contrarian act of love.

Every afternoon, as the sun starts dipping in the sky, children emerge from the tall grass of fields and converge on the dusty roads. The little ones are carried by older children, or ride on the center bar of bicycles. Babies are carried by their mothers, but most of the night commuters are children on their own.

The lucky ones find shelter in a handful of temporary assistance centers, where they can get water and blankets and use latrines. Others sleep in empty churches, bus stations or dusty doorways. In the morning, they walk back home or to school.

"Uganda is rightly considered a development model in Africa," she added, but "northern Uganda stands in dreadful contrast" to advances in other regions: "The night commuters offer a vivid image of what happens when parts of a society are left completely unprotected" (Bellamy 2004).

In August 2005 the story of the night commuters was recounted in a special report aired on NBC in the United States, a "Dateline" report on "Children of War in Uganda." The program featured images of children on their morning and evening walk, and of church yards and bus stations where they slept at night, accompanied by interviews with both night commuters and LRA captives who had been released or had escaped (NBC 2005).

The first half of the program was primarily devoted to first-hand accounts of the atrocities committed by the LRA, including episodes in which abducted children were forced to kill their parents. The second half featured two interviews. The first was with an American preacher, unaffiliated with any denomination, who had created an orphanage near the Sudan border and hired and armed 45 Somali guards—to protect his wards and, he boasted, to track down and kill Joseph Kony and his commanders if possible.

The second interview was with the mother of a young woman who had been abducted and assigned to an LRA commander as one of his wives. Several years later the mother was told that her daughter would be released, but only if her mother ceased stirring up opposition to the LRA. She refused, explaining to the network interviewer: "If I had asked for Charlotte and she came back—what about the rest? What about the other parents?" The mother interviewed by the American television crew was Angelina Atyam, mother of one of the girls abducted in 1996 from St. Mary's School near Lira. Her leadership in organizing the parents of other abductees to overcome their anger and reach out to returning rebel soldiers in a spirit of forgiveness has been cited above in the first chapter (Katongole 2011, 155–157).

The NBC report implicitly challenged the Ugandan government's claim to be on the verge of a military victory over the LRA, but it gave no indication of the complex history of the conflict or of the Museveni forces' brutality. Nor did it mention the efforts of religious leaders and others to assist the night commuters and to press for a negotiated end to the conflict.

NBC's report was also seriously out of date by the time it aired. LRA raids were infrequent by 2005, and a UNICEF report estimated the number of night commuters as just 4,000, most of them now housed in shelters built by churches and NGOs. Protection against kidnapping was no longer necessary; but thousands of children were suffering because of broken families and dire poverty (IRIN 2006).

By the last months of 2005, thankfully—and contrary to the impression still given in the international press on the rare occasions when the conflict was mentioned—the LRA rebellion was at last beginning to relinquish its two-decade grip on the lives of the residents of northern Uganda. In 2006, after numerous false starts and ceasefire violations, representatives of the Ugandan government and the LRA at last sat down and began working toward a negotiated end of the conflict. Within two more years, Kony's rebel army withdrew from Uganda and almost completely disbanded.

The Lord's Resistance Army remains in existence to this day, in 2018, as a band of perhaps a hundred loyal officers and fighters concealed in remote and inaccessible areas of countries bordering Uganda. But the people of northern Uganda have been set free at last from the reign of terror under which they lived, and they have left the squalid conditions of the IDP camps and have returned to their long-abandoned farms and homes.

The causes of these developments will be explored in the next chapter. Many parties collaborated to bring them about, representing not just the government and the rebels but also the government of Sudan, the United Nations, and several international and local NGOs. A particularly important actor in these developments, we will see, was ARLPI, which was at last able to lead the region on the path toward peace. But the absence of war, as we will see, is only the first step toward the restoration of peace and the rebuilding of broken communities.

Note

1. The literature of apartheid and the TRC is vast. Among the most insightful commentaries are Tutu 2000, Krog 1999, and Boraine 2000.

6

Peace Comes to Northern Uganda

I myself believed what Kony used to teach. I took that teaching as though it was true. I thought that what he was saying was correct. He used to say that our fathers, our mothers, our people are not able to help us—Museveni is raping them, killing them, taking them to work on his plantations. There is nothing for the Acholi there any longer. So why would we want to go back? Why don't we fight hard so that we can take control of the government, so that we can be the government? I took this as a right thing, and true. Even if we went back home, it would be useless. Who would we stay with?

But then I realized that what the LRA is doing is not good. Even though Kony is telling people he is the Lord's Resistance Army, and he calls on the name of the Lord, it is not right what he is doing. So that is why he [one of my LRA commanders] told us one day: we are going to leave, we are going to escape with all of you [31 soldiers in all]. We are going home. We are leaving the LRA. Do you understand? We said yes—but we were afraid that maybe these people were playing with our minds. Maybe they were going to kill us. Some of the soldiers ran away. But we continued, and a driver came, and we entered the car. That's how we reached Juba. That is how we escaped from the LRA.

—Issa Mubarak, abducted at age 7,
former LRA sergeant (Mubarak 2014)

The church leaders like our bishops and the Muslim leaders had international contacts, and they appealed to the international community. They took up the issues and the rest of the world began to know. And they had discussions with the government about what was taking place. Many times our religious leaders were telling the government that this conflict will not be solved by the use of the gun and they were encouraging peace talks and negotiations. If we continue fighting, they said, we will keep killing our people and we will not find an end to the conflict. And it was mainly the force of the religious leaders that led to the Juba peace talks that brought the peace that we know at the moment. It is relative peace, but it is significant—we don't have any active fighting, even though there are still LRA in other countries.

—Julius Omony, member of
diocesan Peace Commission (Omony 2014)

AGAIN AND AGAIN DURING the 1990s, the Museveni government boasted that the Lord's Resistance Army was on the ropes, lacking the means if not the will to continue the fight, and predicted that it would soon surrender and lay down its arms. Foreign governments, donor organizations, and even residents of southern Uganda often took these reports as truthful. But the residents of the north knew better.

The promised collapse of the rebellion did not happen, and the conflict raged on into the 21st century. Village residents of the region continued to suffer from brutal attacks by LRA forces and from UPDF counterattacks, some of them equally destructive of civilian lives and property. The elephants fought on and the grass continued to suffer. In a few more years, however, the end was at last in sight. By the middle of the first decade of the new century, opposing sides were sitting at the negotiating table, attacks were fewer, and plans for LRA withdrawal were taking shape.

The prospects for peace had changed very rapidly. We have already described the collaborative cross-border military campaign launched in 2002, "Operation Iron Fist," that was supposed to lead to total defeat of the rebel force that had held northern Uganda in its grip for nearly 20 years. Having secured the cooperation of the Sudanese government—a dramatic break from its past support for the LRA—the Museveni government and the UPDF also received generous assistance from US and other Western advisors, while keeping these allies' soldiers well away from the battlefield. But the military campaign failed disastrously. The LRA suffered significant casualties, to be sure; but so did the government forces. LRA units initiated severe reprisals against communities in Uganda that they suspected of aiding the UPDF campaign. UPDF soldiers, for their part, demonstrated a shocking lack of training and disregard for discipline, looting and killing village residents on any suspicion of collaboration with the rebels. By 2003 the national army was weakened and demoralized, but they were ordered to launch attack after attack, with little result. An ARLPI report on the slow disintegration of the military effort used an ironic wordplay in its title: "January 2003: New Year, Tired Fist?" (ARLPI 2003, 11).

These years brought the region to its lowest point since the LRA had achieved effective control over the region in the 1980s. Raids on villages, looting of crops, abduction of young people, and murder and mutilation of village residents became more frequent. What was billed as a short military incursion that would achieve a final and decisive defeat of the LRA instead heightened tensions, increased the level of violence, and made the anticipated end of the war recede far into the future. What had been advertised—and sold to international allies—as a decisive final blow that would bring an end to the people's suffering served in the end only to compound and prolong it.

In late 2003, the United Nations Undersecretary-General for Humanitarian Affairs, Jan Egeland, visited northern Uganda for two days, to assess the prospects for an end of the conflict. A public statement that he issued while still in transit in Nairobi, on his way back to UN headquarters, offered a dismal assessment of the situation. To those in Uganda and abroad who had been inclined to believe the government's claim that the LRA was on its last legs, Egeland's statement—quoted earlier as an epigram to the introduction of this study—was a rude awakening:

> The conflict in northern Uganda is the biggest forgotten, neglected humanitarian emergency in the world today. . . . We should ask ourselves: how can we as an international community accept that a war is continuing that is directed and targeted against children . . . who are abducted, brainwashed and made into child soldiers or sex slaves and forced to attack and kill their own families in their own villages? . . . I know of no place in the world where such a bad situation has so little international presence and so little international relief. (Al-Jazeera 2003)

Observations such as Egeland's heightened international awareness of the LRA rebellion, yet very little changed on the ground. Life for the residents of northern Uganda was uncertain and dangerous for those remaining in rural villages, comparatively peaceful but economically difficult for residents of the larger towns, and intolerable for two million living in the poverty, squalor, and epidemic disease of the IDP camps. Children continued to stream into towns for safety at night, but few goods came in or out of the region while LRA ambushes lurked in the bush along transit routes. Fear of attack along the roads not only prevented agricultural goods from reaching markets in the major cities, and needed supplies from being brought to the north, but also deterred journalists from attempting to report from the field. Government assurances that everything was under control, or would soon be, went unchallenged.

John Bosco Komanech recalls that, just at the time when international attention was beginning to focus on the previously neglected region, the situation on the ground became worse than ever for the people of the region.

> Around 2003 was the peak of the war here, with massive killing and intensified fighting. Just now it is around 3 pm, right? At that time you would not dare to go out or to come to our offices here in Gulu town. . . . All of this area was being patrolled by the rebels.

As a result, many of the international agencies previously active in the Acholi region closed their local offices and evacuated their staff. Caritas, the Catholic relief agency, was one of a very few whose offices remained open and whose programs continued.

> Even the U.N. put Gulu in the red zone, the "no go" zone. And in that same year, I was driving to the IDP camps to carry out verification exercises so that the people there could receive food and non-food items, and we drove into a rebel ambush. I was shot in my thigh and lower abdomen. We were two in the car and both of us were hit, but we both survived. At the end of that year, one of our staff on his way to monitor a project was shot in an ambush and died. In 2004 we lost a staff member in Kitgum, and another was shot in the

leg and it was amputated. These were some incidents that happened with Caritas staff, but we did not withdraw. (Komanech 2014)

Activities and Priorities of ARLPI

Throughout this difficult period, alongside agencies such as Caritas that were supported by one or another of the participating religious communities, ARLPI continued its patient efforts to bring the two sides to the negotiating table in order to arrive at a ceasefire and an end to the violence. In 2004 the vice president and a founding member of the organization, retired bishop Rt. Rev. Macleod Baker Ochola II, presented a paper to a conference organized by Swedish churches who had provided support for peace efforts in Uganda in which he included a summary of the origins and priorities of the organization.

The organization had been launched in 1997, he said, as "an interfaith forum that brings together Muslim and Christian (Catholic, Orthodox, and Anglican) leaders in Acholiland to promote reconciliation and peaceful settlement of conflicts." Its objective is "proactive peaceful resolution of conflicts in Uganda through community-based mediation services: advocacy, capacity-building, peaceful resolution including negotiation, community mobilization and awareness creation." Representation from diverse religious groups helps ARLPI "to unite and mobilize the people of Acholi, [and] other people and groups in Uganda, for peace and development" (Baker Ochola 2004, 4).

Bishop Ochola went on to enumerate specific programs to achieve these ends. The first was promotion of peace education in local religious communities, with particular emphasis on extending a welcome to former LRA fighters who escaped, or were released, and sought to rejoin their families and communities. Ugandan and international NGOs had created camps and rehabilitation centers to assist those who had spent a decade or more in the bush, but the transition back to life in towns and villages posed enormous challenges all the same for the returning individuals and for their families. ARLPI worked with local churches and mosques to overcome fear and hostility and to rebuild relationships with those who had been separated from their families for long periods, even though some of them had been responsible for attacks on their own villages.

A second major area of the work of ARLPI was lobbying and advocacy in the political realm. It was noted in the previous chapter that Uganda's amnesty law was enacted by Parliament over the objections of some who urged criminal prosecutions instead. The amnesty law required periodic renewal, and ARLPI support was a critical factor both in its initial approval and in its periodic extension. Already in 2004, Bishop Ochola noted, 6,000 returnees had been reintegrated into society.

Another strand of advocacy, one that would soon bring dramatic results, was ARLPI's persistent lobbying of President Museveni, urging him to appoint a "peace team" to negotiate terms for an LRA ceasefire and withdrawal. At the time of Bishop Ochola's presentation, unfortunately, these efforts were "in limbo," in his words, owing to an inappropriate show of force by government troops that had effectively scuttled a new round of peace talks. His account of this debacle, and of the response of the religious leaders, conveys the strength of the commitment to seeking peace that motivated their work.

> When the religious and cultural leaders and government team were planning to meet the LRA's [representatives], government forces who were duly informed of this process and [had] made the arrangements attacked the venue before the meeting. This created a very high ground of suspicion on the part of the LRA, who concluded that Government was using our initiative to locate and kill them. [For this reason] the LRA leader (Mr. Joseph Kony) issued an ultimatum to kill any religious leader trying to initiate peace talks. However, we are determined to continue with peaceful dialogue in ending the war. (Baker Ochola 2004, 6)

Bishop Ochola also brought to the attention of his Swedish audience the work of ARLPI in bringing representatives of different ethnic communities into dialogue with each other and with religious leaders, in order to overcome divisions that had contributed to the suffering of the people. LRA incursions into neighboring regions of northern Uganda had targeted Lango and Isetot communities, he related, exacerbating already high levels of mistrust between these groups and the Acholi. This gave credence to widespread rumors that all Acholi were either openly or secretly supporters of the LRA.

ARLPI worked to overcome this misunderstanding with concrete actions as well as words. An example can be found in its response to the Bunyoro massacre in February 2004 in a Lango community near Lira. In one of the most savage attacks of the 20-year conflict, rebel forces shot, hacked, and clubbed to death nearly 300 residents of an IDP camp there. Most victims were from the Lango and Teso groups, and many survivors blamed the Acholi, since that was the ethnicity of LRA soldiers. UPDF forces had been completely unable to protect the camp, but they too fueled the flames of division. Some Ugandan generals, after all, had spoken publicly of the inherently violent character of the Acholi people as the soil in which the LRA movement had grown. There was good reason to fear retaliatory violence from the Lango communities against Acholi residing nearby (Justice and Reconciliation Project 2009).

ARLPI representatives called on the elders and the religious leaders of Lango and Teso communities to assist the survivors of the attack, prevent any acts of reprisal, and pray together. They also sent an appeal to the Ugandan government and to international agencies active in the region, urging more effective protection of the vulnerable from such attacks. Their intervention prevented a brutal massacre from serving as the trigger for more rounds of ethnic violence. Without this rapid intervention by ARLPI representatives, the situation might well have spiraled into a genocidal conflict like that between Hutu and Tutsi that had engulfed Rwanda ten years earlier—or the one between Hema and Lendu groups in the DRC that was raging not far to the west in 2004, leading to as many as one million deaths (Lukwiya Ochola 2006, 151).

Bishop Ochola's colleague Monsignor Matthew Odong underscored the overall aims of the group when I interviewed him, recalling that Pope John Paul II had delivered a similar message during his visit to the Acholi region in 1993 when the LRA movement was less than a decade old.

> Back at the beginning of the war in 1993—if only the government and the international community had listened to the voices of religious

leaders and of the Holy Father: Let us seek what unites us, not what divides us. Let us seek a better way of ending this conflict than the military option. That has been our slogan: no to war, no to military responses, yes to dialogue. This has been the pillar of our mission. (Odong 2014)

Other areas of ARLPI activity that were highlighted in Bishop Ochola's 2004 report to supporters in Sweden—improved primary education opportunities, networking with North American and European relief agencies—all helped to advance its highest priority in this period: "to influence government, development partners, and other stakeholders to pursue a peaceful rather than a military option in resolving the Northern Uganda conflict." Closely aligned with this overall objective were investigation and punishment of gross human rights abuses, including rapes committed by both LRA and UPDF soldiers and detention of suspected rebels without trial. A recent study has documented the high incidence of sexual violence against women that occurred not just in situations of abduction and forced "marriage" but also in families and communities disrupted by the war (Tiessen and Thomas 2014). The Ugandan government took little notice of the situation, and outside observers were left in the dark. ARLPI representatives brought it into the light and called on communities to take steps to protect the vulnerable.

In pursuit of these goals of preventing and countering all forms of human rights violation, Bishop Ochola related,

ARLPI has sent advocacy missions both to the Government of Uganda (including the President and the Members of Parliament) and internationally to the UN and [to] governments and other civil society and faith-based groups in the US, UK, EU, Germany, and Sweden in the hope of bringing to light the forgotten conflict in Northern Uganda. (Baker Ochola 2004, 8–9)

The retired bishop made no mention in his conference presentation of ways in which the LRA conflict had affected him personally. The brief biography on an ARLPI website fills this in: he had endured losses that would have sent many into despair and withdrawal but instead motivated Ochola to devote himself to sparing others similar suffering. In 1987, one of his daughters committed suicide after she was the victim of a savage LRA attack. Ten years later his wife, Winifred Ochola, was killed in a landmine explosion. The bishop had experienced the worst of the war's brutality, yet he continued to seek opportunities for dialogue and reconciliation (ARLPI 2016).

De-escalation and Progress toward Resolution

The conference where Bishop Ochola presented his paper reviewing ARLPI activities occurred in 2004. By this time the Iron Fist military campaign, begun two years earlier as an all-out assault on the LRA in northern Uganda and southern Sudan, had been drastically scaled back to a lower-intensity military effort on the Ugandan side of the border. Government attacks on suspected collaborators were less frequent than they had been in the 1990s.

LRA attacks had also diminished in frequency and severity, except for a few major incidents such as the one just described at Bunyoro. Government sources attributed this reduction entirely to military actions and the losses inflicted on the rebels. This was no doubt true in part, but local residents reported that the worst of LRA atrocities had been committed in direct reprisal for UPDF attacks in 2002. Fewer government assaults in the next two years generated fewer LRA responses.

It is likely, too, that the reduction in overall violence resulted as much from the Uganda military's weakness as from its strength. A diminished UDHP presence in the region left LRA forces greater freedom to seize crops and livestock whenever and wherever they wished, without needing to drive away government troops guarding rural villages. Villagers were still being robbed of their food supplies, but shootouts between the two sides were less frequent.

Life in northern Uganda was now much as it had been in the late 1990s, an improvement over the devastating violence of 2002–2003 but still beset by fear and vulnerability. Two million residents remained crowded into poorly supplied IDP camps, where they had no means of livelihood, inadequate medical facilities, and limited supplies of food from international aid agencies. The government continued to insist that complete defeat of the LRA was imminent, and few foreign governments or aid agencies had sufficient evidence from the field to challenge this claim. But local residents knew that these claims had little relation to reality on the ground.

The events of following four years, from 2004 to 2008, brought fundamental changes to the region, including—at last—withdrawal of the LRA from Uganda, cessation of hostilities, and release of abducted men and women. Some of the most important developments occurred in northern Uganda; others in the Ugandan capital, Kampala; and still others in distant cities such as the Hague.

The efforts of ARLPI and other advocates began to bear fruit as the long struggle for peace in the Acholi region became more widely known. For most of the two decades of de facto LRA rule in the region, the people's suffering was little known even to residents of other regions of Uganda and East Africa. As travel became somewhat safer, the numbers of international aid workers and journalists visiting the north increased, and their reporting conveyed a bleak picture of the situation to the outside world. The LRA crisis came to be seen not as a geographically isolated ethnic clash—another of the perpetual but unimportant tribal conflicts that many regarded as endemic to the region—but as a major humanitarian crisis, necessitating more effective efforts for its resolution from the Museveni government and more coordinated international assistance. Jan Egeland's impassioned 2003 appeal to the world to open its eyes was beginning to bear fruit in the form of both heightened international awareness and increased humanitarian assistance.

The first event that brought major changes to northern Uganda occurred many thousands of miles away in 2005, when indictments against Joseph Kony and his senior commanders were handed down by the International Criminal Court (ICC) in the Netherlands. The filing of charges had been recommended by the Museveni government, and it was supported by some human rights groups. But the effect was to make the process of seeking a ceasefire and withdrawal even more protracted and more complicated.

Indictments in the Hague

The ICC was a newly created tribunal whose purpose was to enforce United Nations statutes prohibiting war crimes and crimes against humanity in situations where national systems of justice lacked the resources to do so, or where they had failed to take action against egregious violators of human rights. The need for such a body had been discussed since the founding of the United Nations in 1945, and indeed for decades beforehand. Two years of consultation by a preparatory committee in 1996–1998 led to the endorsement of the Rome Statute of the International Criminal Court, adopted by an overwhelming majority of UN member states. Following ratification by 60 states in 2002, the court convened for the first time in the Hague early in 2003 (Coalition for the International Criminal Court n.d.).

Later in the same year, the government of Uganda formally submitted a request for ICC indictment of the leaders of the LRA. This was the first such request to come to the new body from any member of the United Nations. The indictments were controversial, in Uganda and abroad, for several reasons.

In the first place, the ICC was created primarily to provide justice in situations where national governments were either complicit in, or unable to prevent or punish, gross violations of human rights. The first conviction handed down by the court did not come until 2012, and the case fit this pattern. The defendant, Thomas Lubango, was found to have recruited and deployed children as young as nine years of age as soldiers in his Union of Congolese Patriots, one of several factions in the long and devastating civil war in the eastern regions of the Democratic Republic of the Congo (DRC). That region of Africa, then and now, is effectively without a functioning central government, even though the DRC government was successful in arresting Lubango and turning him over to ICC authorities for trial.

Uganda, in contrast, has a functioning system of criminal, civil, and appeals courts. But it requested ICC indictments without even attempting to bring charges in its own courts. This appeared to violate the terms under which the new court would operate (BBC 2012).

There were several other reasons for questioning the government's request for ICC action. Many feared that the indictments would make it impossible to bring Kony or his commanders to the table to discuss terms for a ceasefire and withdrawal, because they would fear being arrested and extradited. This fear, as we will see, proved to be well-founded. The long-suffering residents of northern Uganda, and many international observers, also deplored the court's readiness to consider charges of human rights violations by commanders of the rebel forces without also exposing the savagery of NRA and UPDF tactics.

The ICC accepted the Ugandan government's request and launched an investigation of LRA activities, leading to its first criminal indictments in 2005. Arrest warrants followed, but since the ICC has no police powers it was up to the government of Uganda or one of its neighbors to apprehend the accused and extradite them to the Netherlands to stand trial. No charges were lodged—nor had they been requested—against officers of the UPDF national army who authorized and committed acts of rape, kidnapping, and use of child soldiers.

Of the five named individuals in the ICC's 2005 indictment, two have since died. One was killed in an armed conflict with Ugandan forces, and the other was reportedly executed by Kony in summary punishment for disloyalty. A third, Dominic Ongwen, was captured by a rebel army in the Central African Republic in 2015, then turned over to US forces stationed nearby. The Americans in turn placed him under arrest and sent him to the Hague to stand trial (BBC 2015). The indictment against him identified 33 counts falling under seven categories classified as war crimes or crimes against humanity in the Rome Statute: murder, enslavement, inhumane acts, cruel treatment, attack against a civilian population, and pillaging (International Criminal Court 2005).

Hearings related to Ongwen's trial began in January 2015, ten years after the court's initial indictment. One year later the court reviewed and confirmed the appropriateness of the charges, and another year elapsed before the defendant made his first court appearance and entered a plea of innocence (International Criminal Court 2017). Since February 2017 the court has heard testimony from its prosecutors and collected witness statements. A news report summed up the opening of the trial in its headline: "Trial of ex-child soldier Dominic Ongwen to hear prosecution case: Former LRA commander on trial at the ICC accused of war crimes says he was victim not perpetrator of atrocities in Uganda" (Burke 2017).[1]

Ongwen has been singled out by survivors of LRA raids as one of the most relentless officers in its ranks in ordering the abduction, maiming, and killing of village residents. An important element of Ongwen's personal history, setting him apart from the others named in ICC indictments, is the way in which he joined LRA ranks, which some regard as a mitigating factor: he was abducted as a boy of ten.

As soon as the Museveni government announced that it would seek action by the ICC, ARLPI expressed its concerns over the likelihood that the intervention of the international tribunal might impede progress toward a resolution of the conflict. Its concerns were expressed in several public statements, distributed both before and after the issuing of arrest warrants in 2005. A position paper distributed in 2009 summarizes the ARLPI position:

ARLPI recognizes the ICC as a legal world body along with the Rome Statute to which Uganda is a signatory and its attempt to address issues of impunity around the world. ARLPI by no means is against the formation of the ICC as a structure and supports the important role it can play to stand up against injustice, however ARLPI has the following reservations regarding the role which the ICC is playing in northern Uganda:

— ICC has not maintained an appearance of neutrality. By failing to address crimes committed by the Ugandan United Peoples Defense Force (UPDF), it appears as though it is playing a partisan role in investigating the conflict. . . .
— The ICC lacks sensitivity for current initiatives taking place to bring about peace and justice and does not consider how its actions will affect the outcome of such.
— The ICC fails to act in a complementary way with other transitional justice mechanisms. While it seeks justice, it forgets about other core principles such as forgiveness and reconciliation which are needed to realize sustainable peace. (ARLPI 2009)

For better or worse, the search for a resolution of hostilities between the Ugandan government and the LRA movement had to be conducted after 2005 in the shadow of the ICC's charges. Arrest warrants issued in the Hague created a potent incentive for the leaders of the LRA to remain in hiding and to refuse any invitations to engage in dialogue with government representatives or third parties hoping to serve as intermediaries. Nevertheless, ARLPI continued to press for separate meetings with each side and for future discussions bringing all factions together.

Another Election, Another International Court

Several other developments in 2005 had an important but more indirect effect on the progress of the conflict. In November, opposition leader Kizza Besigye returned from abroad in order to campaign for election to the presidency the following February, seeking to prevent Museveni from extending his rule for another five-year term. He was immediately arrested and brought before a military court for trial. The charges against him, including treason and illegal weapons possession, were eventually dropped. But he was held in detention through the election, in which he was defeated.

Museveni claimed a clear mandate from the people of Uganda when he won a 59% majority, even though this was a smaller margin than in previous elections. Museveni has been elected twice more, in 2010 and 2015, and he has given no assurance that his current term will be his last. When he was first elected to the presidency the Ugandan Constitution limited any president to two five-year terms, but he has persuaded Parliament to remove any such limits. In 2017, his party removed the only remaining obstacle to lifetime rule, an upper age limit of 75 years on presidential candidates. Opposition parliamentarians, we noted in an earlier chapter, were forcibly expelled from the legislative chambers when they protested this consolidation of power.

In December 2005, another important event occurred, one that offers another window into Uganda's relations with its neighbors. A stern rebuke was handed down in that month by the International Court of Justice (ICJ), a United Nations judicial body in the Hague that deals with disputes among member nations. It is separate from, and was established long before, the ICC.

The Democratic Republic of Congo had lodged a complaint about human rights abuses and misappropriation of resources by Ugandan forces who intervened in internal conflicts in its territory from 1997 until 2003. The court's decision, which drew little attention from the international press, affirmed the validity of the charges. Its verdict was framed in stark terms:

> In its Judgment, which is final, binding and without appeal, the Court . . .
> — By sixteen votes to one, finds that the Republic of Uganda, by the conduct of its armed forces, which committed acts of killing, torture and other forms of inhumane treatment of the Congolese civilian population, destroyed villages and civilian buildings, failed to distinguish between civilian and military targets and to protect the civilian population in fighting with other combatants, trained child soldiers, incited ethnic conflict and failed to take measures to put an end to such conflict; as well as by its failure, as an occupying Power, to take measures to respect and ensure respect for human rights and international humanitarian law in Ituri district, violated its obligations under international human rights law and international humanitarian law;
> — By sixteen votes to one, finds that the Republic of Uganda, by acts of looting, plundering and exploitation of Congolese natural resources committed by members of the Ugandan armed forces in the territory of the Democratic Republic of the Congo and by its failure to comply with its obligations as an occupying Power in Ituri district to prevent acts of looting, plundering and exploitation of Congolese natural resources, violated obligations owed to the Democratic Republic of the Congo under international law.

The court then ordered Uganda to pay reparations to the DRC for these egregious violations of international law.

The DRC was not entirely absolved of responsibility in its dealings with its neighbor, however. The court affirmed the veracity of one of Uganda's counterclaims, ruling that Congolese forces had mistreated Ugandan diplomats at the embassy in Kinshasa and at Ndjili airport and had illegally seized Ugandan property and papers. The DRC was ordered to compensate Uganda for these offenses. These findings related to a limited number of incidents in the capital, far from the conflict zone in eastern Congo. Ugandan misconduct, on the other hand, had been long-lasting and pervasive (International Court of Justice 2005).

The ICJ decision provided corroborating evidence for the claims of many residents of northern Uganda that UPDF soldiers were un-disciplined, opportunistic, and guilty of gross abuses of the rights of the people whom they were supposed to be protecting against the very crimes that they were themselves committing. Donor nations and NGOs paid little attention to this finding, however. Development aid and military advice continued to be provided to the Museveni government in exceptionally generous measure.

Negotiations Begin At Last

An initial round of negotiations between the Museveni government and the LRA command began, at last, in 2006. They were conducted in Juba, the capital of the semi-autonomous region of South Sudan, at the instigation of Riek Machar, Vice President of the regional government. (When South Sudan attained independence in 2011 he became the new nation's vice president.) The path to the negotiating table had been pre-pared by several other groups, among which the most important were ARLPI and another organization that has not yet been mentioned: the Community of Sant'Egidio, a Catholic lay order.

Founded in 1968 in Rome, and named after the church in which its first meetings were held, the Community of Sant'Egidio claims 70,000 members in 73 countries. From the beginning, taking its cue from the reforms implemented by the Second Vatican Council, the members of the community have sought opportunities to assist those trapped in cycles of poverty and to mediate seemingly irreconcilable conflicts.

A notable event in Africa's recent history was the contribution of the Sant'Egidio community to the resolution of 15 years of civil war in Mozambique. Both the ruling Frelimo Party and the armed resist-ance agreed to recognize members of the Community as mediators be-tween them, leading to a comprehensive ceasefire and peace agreement in 1992. As a result, a war that had caused one million deaths ended at last in a ceasefire and demobilization that was honored by all sides (Community of Sant'Egidio n.d.). The Community had not been pre-viously involved in the LRA conflict, however, so far as I have been able to determine.

ARLPI, for its part, had been working quietly and persistently since its founding in the 1990s to bring both sides of the conflict to the negotiating table. Those whom I interviewed in Gulu recalled the deep suspicion that greeted these efforts from both sides. Representatives of the LRA were very difficult to contact even through intermediaries, and meetings had to be held in the bush, far from any towns or camps where UPDF forces were stationed. In some cases the religious leaders who initiated these conversations were transported blindfolded or in closed vehicles on long journeys to the LRA's hideouts, with no assurance that they would find anyone waiting for them with the authority to discuss the possibility of a ceasefire. Indeed, they could not be certain whether they would be allowed to return to their homes, rather than be held as hostages or killed.

In 2015 a former LRA commander responded to questions from an interviewer, James Latigo, about how it had been possible to arrange meetings with the leaders of a group so completely closed to outsiders and so protective of its secret bases. Former Captain Ray Apire recalled:

> The LRA does not trust anybody. That is why it has survived for so long. When I say LRA, I mean Joseph Kony. He gave the orders and decided for us, although he would often say it is the "spirit" in him talking. For example, when he decided to convene a general parade he would tell us that the spirit had directed him to do so.
>
> We did not know the ARLPI as an organisation. But we knew certain members who were prominent religious leaders. . . . I overheard a conversation about dropping a letter to the Archbishop's residence [Anglican Archbishop Odama]. That was how they gave directions and instructions on where to meet. Because of a lack of trust, Kony did not want the religious leaders to be accompanied by the army. They kept changing the location to confuse the army.

Even community leaders who accompanied ARLPI representatives to some of the secret meetings were mistrusted, he added.

> Kony used to say the Acholi community is like *dogiryo*—a two-headed snake that changes direction at its convenience. They will speak to you nicely and then say something different to the government. Out

of respect for the religious leaders, those who accompanied them were tolerated.

Apire added that when ARLPI pressed LRA leaders to stop the atrocities being committed by its commandoes, Kony responded—dispatching subordinates to deliver this message, because he was not willing to participate personally in these meetings—that he was acting on the orders of the spirits who communicate through him. But the LRA's leader took the highly unusual step of offering a public response to the charges of misconduct by means of a telephone call to a Gulu radio station, Mega FM.

> He said that people were aware of the ongoing war between the LRA and Government of Uganda, and if they put themselves in harm's way the LRA was not responsible. He said that government soldiers were doing most of the killing and then blaming the LRA. On the question of abduction, he said that the Acholi people were infected with evil and it was his responsibility to start a new, clean tribe. (Conciliation Resources 2015)

The response typifies the complex blend of elements that characterized both the LRA and Alice Lakwena's short-lived Holy Spirit Movement. The Acholi people had indeed suffered from governmental neglect and military misconduct. None of this was acknowledged by the Museveni regime, and little of it was known outside northern Uganda. To claim that all of those victimized by LRA raids had "put themselves in harm's way" was hardly credible, and yet everyone hearing the radio broadcast would have known of instances where UPDF soldiers committed murder and rape but tried to pin the blame on the LRA.

But juxtaposed with this claim was the familiar—and chilling— ambition to cleanse and purify the people by whatever means might be necessary. This had been the supposedly spiritual justification for Lakwena's shift from spiritual disciplines to training an army, and it was part of the propaganda drilled into LRA soldiers to persuade them that they must follow the orders of their commanders, no matter how brutal, in order to bring deliverance to their people.

Apire adds one more important detail, not reported in other sources: despite the secrecy maintained in LRA camps concerning meetings with ARLPI representatives, word began to spread that negotiations were underway, and this provided some encouragement to the residents of LRA military encampments.

> The possibility of talking peace raised morale in the camps. I think many of them [LRA combatants] were becoming tired of fighting, and increasingly unconvinced by the promise that the government would be overthrown. But they were afraid to express their true wishes; they feared that Kony had the power to know when he was being discussed. It was serious psychological torture on the combatants. (Conciliation Resources 2015)

From the government side, too, the persistence of ARLPI in seeking opportunities to talk to LRA leaders created suspicion and mistrust. Because the leaders of the Christian and Muslim communities were Acholi, and because they evidently maintained indirect contacts with the LRA, government commanders suspected that they were covertly rebel sympathizers. Abdula Latif Nasur, a project officer today for ARLPI, was not yet working for the organization at this time, but he recalled in our interview what he had learned from the leaders of the Muslim community about their accomplishments and their frustrations.

> When things became tense the government would call the religious leaders collaborators. That was not easy, but they stood their ground. At last the government realized that it is only the religious leaders who can influence [the negotiations], because the rebels would talk freely only to the religious leaders. Through the influence of the religious leaders, the Juba peace talks yielded results. The Christian and Moslem leaders never wanted to play a role that was visible, only to make contact and talk to all sides.

Their intervention sometimes brought unexpected results, small in scale but significant indicators of what might be possible. Nasur described a project with which he had assisted.

We realized that there were a lot of firearms and ammunition in the small towns bordering Sudan. The government knew about it but could not do anything. So we launched a project there, a small arms collection project, and in three months we collected more than 200 guns. We told the army, let the people turn in their weapons to the religious leaders, and then we will give them to you to destroy.

People know us, and they know that we don't shout or fight [with those who do not share our religion]. They know us by our reputation, and by the ways that we give back to the community. (Nasur 2014)

In a follow-up interview in 2016, Nasur described the key to winning trust from those initially suspicious of adherents of religions different from their own.

We make sure to get wide representation, and we recruit leaders from each community. We find spiritual leaders who preach peace and offer counseling—their goal is not to convert but to help! And our staff gives an example of cooperation. I will go to a community along with a pastor, and people will see how we work together. That helps them to understand that it is necessary to cooperate with each other—not only on our projects, but also to come together in prayer. (Nasur 2016)

ARLPI leaders insisted that their purpose was to open a dialogue, not in any way to condone the LRA reign of terror or the brutal countermeasures of government troops. They pressed repeatedly for meetings with the regional commanders of the UPDF, and eventually their representatives were invited to meet once again with President Museveni, this time in the conflict zone.

Inevitably, contact with the government fueled suspicion in the LRA and created obstacles to further contact. Kony's forces feared that the apparent neutrality of the religious leaders was only a smokescreen for future betrayal. But the leaders of ARLPI showed their integrity, and their courage, by their continued willingness to meet with LRA representatives in remote and undisclosed locations, after making certain that government forces would not follow them.

In 2004 ARLPI's efforts to bring peace in the region were recognized by the Niwano Peace Foundation, a little-known Japanese NGO devoted to religious tolerance and interreligious dialogue. Its annual Niwano Peace Prize is awarded each year to an individual or organization whose work advances peace and reconciliation through dialogue and public advocacy. The 2004 prize was awarded to ARLPI with this commendation:

> The ARLPI is an organization in northern Uganda in which the members of different religions, including Islam and Christianity (Catholic, Orthodox, and Anglican), work together. Since its establishment in 1998, it has acted non-violently to end armed conflict, to nurture human resources for the task of creating peace, and to provide assistance to war victims through the work of over 400 volunteers, including its core membership of religious leaders, as well as individual staff members, peace committees in various districts, and peace supporters. (Niwano Peace Foundation 2004)

Five years later, in 2009, the Niwano Peace Prize was awarded to ARLPI's close partner in facilitating the Juba peace talks, the Community of Sant'Egidio.

ARLPI received another honor in the same year, 2004: the Paul Carus Award for Outstanding Contributions to the Interreligious Movement, which was formally given to Bishop Ochola as a representative of ARLPI at the Barcelona meeting of the Parliament of the World's Religions. This was the first such award; subsequent awards in 2009 and 2015 were given to another interfaith activist group in Africa, Interfaith Action for Peace in Africa, based in Johannesburg, and to British interfaith theologian Karen Armstrong (Lukwiya Ochola 2006, 153; Parliament of the World's Religions 2015).

Formal dialogue between the Ugandan government and the leaders of the LRA began at last in Juba in July 2006. Initially the LRA was represented by expatriate Acholi who were supportive of Kony's movement and claimed to speak for the movement in their desire to arrange a ceasefire. No one from Kony's circle of close associates was present, but messengers kept them informed of what was being discussed. Representatives of the Museveni government asserted that they too sought an end to hostilities, when both sides would lay down their arms and the long civil war would come to an end at last.

Caritas staff member Julius Omony recalled in an interview how critical ARLPI efforts had been to bringing the opposing sides into dialogue.

> The churches did much to make the conflict known. As the conflict went on many people outside Uganda were unaware of it. But through different international contacts [ARLPI leaders] appealed to the international community and informed them of what was happening in northern Uganda. And that also led to interventions by several international bodies that came to help the people.
>
> The church leaders and Muslim leaders also had discussions with the government about what was taking place. Many times the religious leaders emphasized that this conflict will not be solved by the use of the gun. So they were encouraging peace talks and negotiations.
>
> It was mainly the force of the church leaders, I believe, that led to the Juba peace talks and that brought the peace we have achieved at the moment. The church leaders were also involved in some international conferences where Acholi and other Ugandans in the diaspora came together to help find solutions to the problems of northern Uganda. (Omony 2014)

A Peace Agreement Is (Almost) Signed

At the beginning of August 2006, Kony's top military commander Vincent Otti announced a unilateral ceasefire and called on the Ugandan military to reciprocate. A mutual ceasefire was declared shortly afterward, while negotiations for a permanent resolution continued. But during the following year the guns were not quite silent. Repeated charges of attacks by one side or the other brought the dialogue to a halt, and only after protracted discussions and assurances that the alleged attacks would not be repeated did the two sides return to the table. UN Undersecretary Jan Egeland, the UN official who had decried "the world's least-known humanitarian disaster" after his 2003 visit, made a courageous return visit to the region, allowing himself to be taken to a secret location where Kony and his commanders were stationed, in order to move the process forward.

After many stops and starts, it was agreed at last that a final, comprehensive agreement would be drawn up and signed in two years' time, in February 2008. Its provisions would include a permanent ceasefire, withdrawal of all LRA forces from Uganda, and release of any men and women who wished to return to their families. The agreement was drafted, a date for its signing was fixed, and a war of more than 20 years' duration appeared at last to be coming to an end through a negotiated settlement.

But Joseph Kony did not appear as promised to sign the agreement. It was reported that he was unwilling to risk arrest and deportation to the ICC. The Juba peace talks collapsed, and the Juba accord resulting from two years of difficult negotiations remained nothing more than a proposal, lacking any force.

The government of Uganda had initiated the indictments against Kony and his commanders, and it now recognized that they posed a serious obstacle to any peace agreement. The government petitioned the ICC to withdraw the charges, proposing instead that LRA leaders appear before a new Ugandan court created to adjudicate war crimes in civil conflict. UN official Jan Egeland recalled that, during this period, Museveni's administration seemed to believe that since it had asked the ICC to prosecute Kony and his commanders, it retained the prerogative of rescinding this request and dropping the 2005 indictments. But this was impossible: the charges, and the warrants for the arrest of five LRA commanders, had been drawn up by prosecutors at the court, and only they had the authority to withdraw them. They refused to do so.

Several attempts were made to assure Kony and his deputies that they would not be arrested if they turned up to approve a settlement of the conflict. Signing dates were postponed repeatedly, from February 2008 to March, then to April. At last Kony sent word that on a designated date in May he would come to a remote location in South Sudan, where his forces could ensure his safety, to sign the accord. But once more he failed to show up.

The fear of UPDF attacks on LRA leaders traveling to the sites designated for the signing of a peace agreement was by no means unfounded. Earlier meetings between religious leaders and LRA representatives had been broken off because of UPDF harassment and surveillance. Jan Egeland recalled, in a book published in 2008, that in the course of the planning for the meetings scheduled to take place in Juba, President Museveni had stationed UPDF troops in locations inside Sudan where they would be able to intercept any LRA officers who were on their way to the signing site. In effect, the Ugandan government intended to sabotage the entire process of negotiation, and it was only after Egeland voiced his outrage that the president agreed to move army forces out of the way.

Egeland also reported that Museveni regarded the effort to negotiate an end to the conflict as a useless exercise. In a meeting in the Parliament buildings in Kampala, Egeland recalled having said, with satisfaction, that "we have, for the first time, an absence of fighting and terror thanks to the peace process." Museveni retorted: "No, that is only due to the efforts of our army." He rebuked Egeland for his efforts to initiate direct talks with Kony, and he added, "No, those talks were not to our benefit. Let me be categorical—there will only be a military solution to this problem" (BSN 2008, citing Egeland 2008, 211–213).

This shocking dismissal of the entire effort to negotiate an end to the war took place four months after the peace talks in Juba had begun. In public statements, on the other hand, the Museveni administration continued to affirm its desire to come to a ceasefire agreement and its readiness to suspend its own military operations if LRA violence would stop. Indeed, just a few months after this reported conversation, the Ugandan government changed course and agreed to the ceasefire that had been initiated unilaterally by the LRA. Negotiations continued for two more years. Although attacks and counterattacks continued to occur, inside Uganda and across its borders, the level of violence on both sides was now dramatically lower than it had been in the preceding decade.

An LRA Remnant Relocates Outside Uganda

After the Juba talks collapsed in 2008, with no peace agreement signed, conflict between government and rebel forces flared up again, but now it occurred outside the borders of Uganda. Just one month after the meeting at which a comprehensive agreement was to have been signed, the LRA staged an attack in South Sudan that killed 24 people, including 11 Ugandan soldiers. The Ugandan military responded force-fully, and pressure on LRA units in Sudan pushed them west into the Garamba National Forest area, across the Congolese border.

Late in 2008 the United States government stepped up its support for the Ugandan government in its campaign against the LRA. For several years it had offered technical assistance and military advice, without any public acknowledgment. Now President George W. Bush publicly signed a directive to provide intelligence, military planning assistance, and $1 million in fuel to the Ugandan army in its northern campaign.

Shortly afterward, the Ugandan government was joined by the governments of South Sudan, newly independent, and the DRC in announcing a major collaborative military initiative, the first of its kind in the region. Back in 2002–2003 "Operation Iron Fist" had been undertaken by Ugandan troops, with the approval and assistance of the governments in Sudan and in Washington. "Operation Lightning Thunder" in 2008 would deploy a multinational military force representing three nations. It was launched with great fanfare as a campaign—this was by now a long-familiar boast—that would confront LRA units and commanders in their forest hideouts and destroy the movement once and for all (Gettleman and Schmitt 2009).

Negotiations had been tried and had failed, this initiative implicitly declared. After all, as President Museveni had stated privately two years earlier, the solution to the LRA problem must in the end be a military solution. Negotiations had failed, he claimed, because of LRA duplicity and noncooperation. The coordinated joint campaign would at last eliminate the LRA as a force in East Africa—so said its advocates in Kampala and Kinshasa and Juba.

"Operation Lightning Thunder" succeeded in driving the LRA farther into hiding in the DRC, despite many problems of coordination and communication. But it failed to achieve any of its major objectives, and it inflicted massive civilian casualties. Worse yet, it provoked round after round of cruel reprisals. An observer from an international monitoring agency summed up the outcome of the campaign in these words:

> Operation Lightning Thunder was a joint offensive on an LRA camp
> in northeastern DRC, led by Uganda, the DRC, and South Sudan.

Seventeen U.S. military advisers provided logistics, communications, and intelligence support. The mission was a failure. Leaky intelligence allowed the LRA leadership to get advance warning of the bombing raid that was supposed to begin the operation. Bad weather meant the air strikes were conducted with slower moving helicopters rather than Ugandan fighter jets, further reducing the element of surprise. Poor coordination meant the ground forces that were supposed to swarm into the camp immediately after the bombing raid didn't turn up for a week. Finally, mutual antipathy among the three main militaries involved—those of Uganda, South Sudan, and the DRC—meant that Kony's forces were allowed to slip across the border into South Sudan unchallenged. The costs of the failed operation were devastating for civilians. In the weeks that followed, almost 1,000 people were killed in a series of bloody reprisals in northeastern Congo. (Downie 2011)

Military operations continued for several months, until Uganda announced that its forces would withdraw in March 2009. The stated reason for withdrawal was an agreement recently reached with the government of the Congo, which promised to continue the fight against the LRA using only its own forces. But the government and the people of the DRC also remembered the brutal tactics employed by UPDF soldiers a decade earlier, which had led to international condemnation and sanctions. Their return, fully armed, was not welcomed.

Neither the multilateral campaign nor the Congolese army actions of the next few years succeeded in capturing or killing Kony or any of his closest associates. LRA loyalists retreated into inaccessible areas of the DRC and the neighboring Central African Republic. In retaliation for the recent military campaign against them, they increased the frequency and violence of their attacks on civilian populations near their camps. A report from the monitoring agency The Resolve summarizes the horrors of this period:

From March 2008–March 2010 Kony ordered his fighters to conduct brutal massacres and child abduction campaigns in DR Congo and eastern CAR, abducting more than 3,000 people and killing another 2,480. Many of these attacks were reprisals, an intentional show of strength following poorly executed military operations by regional governments that failed to capture Kony in December 2008.

Before long, however, unfavorable publicity, increasing numbers of defections, and fears of being tracked down caused Kony to scale back. The number of soldiers who remained loyal to him dwindled, according to observers' estimates, to no more than a few hundred. The Resolve report notes:

> Since 2011, high-profile massacres and child abductions by the LRA have dropped dramatically and most attacks have been focused on acquiring needed supplies without drawing attention to the rebel group. . . .
>
> As LRA violence tailed off beginning in 2011 and the explosion of civil conflicts in CAR and South Sudan drew more focus, attention on the LRA has waned and deployments of African Union troops have shrunk, slowing military operations. Defection campaigns driven by the US military continue to get results, but few Ugandan LRA members have defected in recent months. As 2015 drew to a close, the LRA's attrition rate had slowed considerably and LRA groups seemed relatively secure within their safe havens. (Invisible Children 2017)

The LRA Crisis Tracker is a reporting site created by Invisible Children and another US-based nonprofit group focused on the conflict, Resolve LRA Crisis Initiative, in order to collect and verify all reports of LRA activity in the Great Lakes region. Its website makes it easy to compare one period with another (Invisible Children 2017). Consider this year-by-year comparison of reports from August in successive years, for example: in August 2011 there were 14 reported incidents and five reported deaths from rebel activity; in August 2012 and August 2013 there were 13 and eight incidents and no deaths. August 2014 reports cite 19 incidents, two deaths; in August 2015 and 2016 there were 17 and 12 incidents, with no deaths. In August 2017 there were ten incidents, with one reported death. Clearly the violence has not stopped, but its level is far, far below what Uganda experienced until the LRA withdrew.

Looking more closely at these reports, the picture becomes even more hazy—and much less supportive of the claims of some outsiders that the LRA remains a major source of internal conflict in the Great Lakes region. For each reported incident, the LRA Crisis Tracker assesses the likelihood that it was carried out by the LRA, not by one of the many other militias and rebel armies that are active today in the DRC and the CAR. Most are labeled as undetermined. Only a very few are verified actions of Kony and his small remaining band of loyalists (Invisible Children 2017).

In August 2017, for example, only one of the ten incidents has a "high" confidence rating—and it is a very unusual one, a far cry from the atrocities of the long Ugandan civil war:

> August 14, 2017, Kpatanabu, Haut Uele, DRC: 6 armed LRA combatants ambushed 30 travelers, one after the other, near Kpatanabu, DRC. They looted the victims and forced them to shell peanuts for a few hours. (Invisible Children 2017)

Confirmation that the Lord's Resistance Army is now an army in name only, and poses little threat to regional stability, has also come from one of the two groups that created the LRA Crisis Tracker. Project Director Paul Ronan explained in January 2017, in a farewell blog posting.

> This week The Resolve LRA Crisis Initiative is closing its doors. . . .
> In the summer of 2005, I joined a small group of students in Washington, DC, in founding an organization now known as The Resolve LRA Crisis Initiative. All of us had spent time studying in Uganda and had been deeply impacted by what we saw and heard from communities surviving the conflict between the LRA and the Ugandan government. . . .
> Nearly 12 years later, much progress has been made towards our founding goals. In 2008, LRA leader Joseph Kony had approximately 800 combatants under his command. Today, he has less than 140. In 2009 alone, the LRA killed more than 1,000 civilians. Since 2014, the LRA has killed less than 50 civilians in total and has largely lost its ability to commit the large-scale massacres for which it became famous. Thousands of children and adults abducted by

the LRA have escaped captivity and returned to their families. In northern Uganda, nearly two million displaced people have returned home, while increased international scrutiny has helped reduce some abuses by the Ugandan government. USAID [United States Agency for International Development] and other international donors have pledged tens of millions of dollars to help protect and rebuild communities affected by the conflict.

Of course, much remains to be done. Joseph Kony still roams free, and the frequency of LRA attacks and abductions in the Central African Republic and the Democratic Republic of Congo remain stubbornly persistent. . . .

Still, the LRA is undeniably far weaker than it was in 2005 and we are closer than ever to permanently ending its ability to commit atrocities. Members of the Resolve team, past and present, are grateful to have played a small role in the progress that has been made. (Ronan 2017)

Despite the reduced level of violence and the complete withdrawal of LRA forces from Uganda, U.S. Special Forces soldiers continue to be stationed in Uganda. Based near the Entebbe international airport, they travel across the entire region to offer advice and to assist with the debriefing and reintegration of defectors. The organization Invisible Children continues to lobby members of Congress to press for increased troop strength and additional military assistance. On its website it cites, as one of its important achievements, the passage of a 2013 bill offering a $5 million reward for information leading to arrest or conviction of individuals under indictment for war crimes. Kony and his associates were mentioned as prime targets of this legislation (Invisible Children 2016).

In 2014, despite controversy over an anti-homosexuality bill introduced in the Ugandan Parliament that led the White House to issue a strong warning to Uganda to respect the rights of all citizens, the US administration nevertheless approved a further expansion of US military involvement. The *Washington Post* reported in March that President Obama had expanded the number of Special Operations forces deployed to Uganda and had sent US military aircraft there for the first time. The Americans "provide information, advice and assistance" to an African Union military task force in pursuit of Kony. Although armed, the US soldiers are barred from engaging LRA forces except in self-defense (DeYoung 2014).

As I was preparing to depart from Gulu at the end of January 2014, a few months before this expansion of the US presence, I had an unexpected opportunity to talk with a member of the US Special Forces about his work during the two years that he had been stationed in Uganda. His primary responsibility was to interview LRA soldiers who defect, and it was that task that had brought him to Gulu. Most of the defectors, he told me, come from Sudan, DRC, and CAR. Very few of those who escape from LRA camps are Ugandans who accompanied the group across the borders ten years ago, although some of Kony's Ugandan senior officers remain loyal to him in their camps in the bush.

In the previous year 37 LRA soldiers had succeeded in escaping from LRA camps, he said, and African Union soldiers had conveyed each of them to US interviewers in Uganda. Normally a debriefing interview lasts just a few days, Sam told me.[2] But he had just completed an entire week of interviews with a recent defector. He could not tell me what new information this man might have been able to provide about Kony's location or his plans. What Sam was willing to disclose is that, on the basis of many recent interviews, he is convinced that Kony's small remaining band of loyalists has no intention of returning to Uganda, let alone any ambition to overthrow the Museveni government. There has been very little talk of overall strategy in the Kony inner circle, reported Sam, for several years. Their goals at present are simply to evade the African Union forces searching for them and to obtain food and supplies. Raids continue to occur, but there are very few direct conflicts between Kony's soldiers and those of the African Union.

I told Sam of the interviews I had just conducted with religious and community leaders in Gulu, and we talked about the dashed hopes for a comprehensive resolution of the conflict a few years earlier. Sam evidently shared the judgment that only military force could put an end to LRA violence, and he insisted that Kony had only given the appearance of wanting to negotiate even when it appeared that a comprehensive ceasefire was within reach in 2008. This is his standard way of operating, said Sam: Kony plays along with donor countries and NGOs and pretends to be ready to come to the negotiating table, he collects the shipments of food and other supplies that are given as a good-faith inducement to stop raiding villages—and then he slips back into hiding, much the richer, waiting for the next round in this game.

Sam was interested to learn about the work of ARLPI during and after the LRA occupation of northern Uganda. Although he had spent much of the previous two years in Gulu, he had never heard of it, he said. He was very familiar with the agenda and the activities of Invisible Children, however. Radio transmitters that the organization is installing in remote areas of the DRC and CAR are a featured element of their campaign to "make Kony visible" to the outside world and track his activities, he added, confirming what I had learned from the organization's website.

These transmitters, said Sam, are funded by the US military as part of its support for African Union units in pursuit of Kony. I have not been able to verify this assertion from government sources. It is clear from the Invisible Children website, all the same, that it regards military action as the best, if not the only, way to put an end to the LRA movement ("Sam" [U. S. Special Forces] 2014).

Peace Returns to Northern Uganda

For several years following the Juba talks and the LRA withdrawal, conditions remained very difficult in northern Uganda. But gradually life returned to normal. By 2012, LRA attacks on Ugandan soil were only a memory—a recent memory, to be sure, and a painful one, but not a current reality. IDP camps had been dismantled and their residents had returned home. Families were being reunited with members whom they had last seen decades earlier. The LRA war in Uganda was at an end, and there was no sign that the rebels intended to return to the territory they had controlled for two decades.

In June 2016 a spokesman for the Ugandan army announced that all Ugandan troops—numbering about 2500—would be pulled out of the African Union forces serving in the Central African Republic before year's end. Lt. Colonel Paddy Ankunda told a reporter from the Associated Press that the LRA no longer poses a threat to Uganda, because "the rebels have been sufficiently degraded." He added that the LRA "is reportedly in decline, with many of its fighters surrendering or killed in firefights with African [Union] troops" (Muhuzuma 2016).

Northern Uganda is at last at peace. Major roads are once again safe for travel. Goods can be brought in from Kampala, and agricultural and other products can be shipped out, without fear that they will be seized by bands of LRA soldiers along the way.

But this is a difficult peace, given the enormous dislocation of the life of the region and the removal of most residents from their farms, and therefore from their livelihood, when they were forced into IDP camps. Between family members who suffered from LRA attacks and others who had become part of the movement that initiated those attacks, high barriers of suspicion and mistrust remain. Even after several months in rehabilitation centers, returning abductees frequently feel unwelcome in their families and in their home communities.

ARLPI is one of the few organizations that has worked steadfastly and courageously to help the people of Acholiland carry on their lives through the worst years of the LRA conflict. For that reason it is particularly well prepared to assist with the process of post-conflict restoration. In the next chapter, we will review these efforts to explore what the organization has done, how it sees its work as an expression of the religious life of the various communities, and what ideals it serves in doing so. ARLPI holds up a vision of a restored community, and its work is indispensable in translating that dream into reality in northern Uganda.

Notes

1. The slow progress of this proceeding in the ICC parallels that of the trial of Thomas Kwoyelo in the Ugandan courts, described in the previous chapter, but the two tribunals are entirely separate.
2. "Sam" is a pseudonym. Although the Special Forces officer gave me his name, he may have disclosed some facts without authorization. It seems prudent to conceal his identity here.

7

Perpetrators and Victims Return Home

*When I came back [from captivity in an LRA camp], my father had so many
people to take care of, and it was hard going to school and paying my fees. But
I was lucky enough to have a sponsor who started paying my fees, and even now
she pays my tuition and my hostel. I look at myself, and I look at what I went
through, and I say, God, what am I going to do for other children who are still
behind? How can I help support them? How can I have the strength to help a
child who is in need? Even if I am going to be earning a salary that is not very
much, let me take care of that child. Let me educate that child the way I am
educated, up to now! . . . And if God blesses me and I have a lot, then maybe
I can create a home for children who are helpless and can't help themselves.*

—Lucy Okwarmoi,
abducted at age 13 (Okwarmoi 2014)

*When I had just come they had some fear. They handled me with care because
they thought I could harm them since I had undergone a bad experience. I told
them they were my people and I could not harm them. I told them I had seen
greater havoc than what they were thinking. I added that if I started hurting
them it would not be good. Then they relaxed and started living with me freely.
Now we live very well.*

—Formerly abducted young man
in IDP camp (Angucia 2010, 168)

FROM ITS FOUNDING IN the late 1990s through the last years of the LRA
presence in Uganda in the late 2000s, ARLPI had played a vital role
in relieving the suffering of the people of the region and in preparing

the way for LRA withdrawal and the return of the population from IDP camps to their former homes. Its activities had been initiated by leaders of the Catholic, Protestant, and Muslim communities, with assistance provided by Orthodox, Pentecostal, and Adventist pastors and priests as well. Despite initial misgivings from members of their respective communities, who found it hard to believe that anyone trusted by the government could ever talk to the LRA or vice versa, their efforts eventually earned broad support. The efforts of ARLPI leaders to bring the suffering of Ugandans to the attention of the wider world bore fruit also, leading to invitations to address government leaders, legislatures, and church groups in Europe and North America.

Yet the most important contributions of ARLPI to the life of the people of northern Uganda were still to come. The IDP camps had closed, the guns had gone silent, and as a result nearly all of the international donors had packed up and moved on to other crisis areas. The international attention that had been directed to the LRA rebellion dwindled. Few realized just how great were the challenges of rebuilding communities torn apart by kidnapping, forced relocation, and decades of war. Disputes over land, mistrust toward former soldiers on all sides, and hostility toward children born in the LRA camps divided families and communities. Through this trying time, ARLPI continued to work for reconciliation, acceptance, and renewal at every level. Its principal focus in the post-conflict years was building a wide network of local committees in which these initiatives could be advanced in ways suited to local needs and local priorities. We will review these efforts in the present chapter.

The dislocation caused by LRA violence, beginning in the late 1980s and continuing until 2008, had been compounded by the Ugandan government's forcible relocation of the population into IDP camps, which housed as many as two million people in the early 2000s. Very little agricultural land was available in proximity to the camps, far too little to feed all the residents. As a result—so I was told repeatedly by those who had lived through this experience—a generation of Ugandans grew up believing that food comes from trucks with the letters "UN" or "USAID" on them, not from soil they had cultivated.

Even when land was available, venturing beyond camp boundaries meant risking capture or rape by LRA soldiers. Security was supposed to be assured inside the camps by UPDF soldiers stationed there, but this assurance often rang hollow. Rebel soldiers frequently came into the camps to steal supplies and abduct children, while government soldiers looked the other way—sometimes because they had been paid to do so. Most camp residents simply waited for the relief trucks to arrive.

In 2006, with an end to the conflict within sight at last, the Ugandan government declared that internally displaced persons living in the northern region's camps were free to return to their home communities. Within a few years more than 250 camps were officially closed. The return migration was as slow as the corralling of the population into camps had been quick. And it was not free from problems.

As residents returned to their former communities, there was little to welcome them home. The livestock they had left behind when the army demanded immediate evacuation many years earlier had long ago been stolen or eaten. Farming tools and household goods too had gone missing. In many villages the dwellings and farm buildings were no more than piles of overgrown ashes after they were burned to the ground by government or LRA troops in pursuit of each other. Buildings that remained standing, such as churches and schools built from brick or block, were empty shells after LRA soldiers stripped them of their roofs in order to use the materials in their camps.

In villages that were not destroyed, houses and fields had been taken over by newcomers who found them unoccupied and unused. Many of these squatters, having repaired the dwellings and cultivated the fields for a decade, now refused to leave. Those whose farms had not been stolen faced other problems as they set out to clear the overgrowth. Fields left uncultivated for even half a year, given Uganda's abundant rainfall and warm climate, soon revert to bush. After several years it can be difficult to tell what was once a farm and what has always been forest.

Some of those who had been forced to join the LRA movement chose to remain in its reduced ranks even when given the opportunity to return home. It is difficult to estimate their number, which was in any case only a small minority of the 65,000 who had been abducted during the conflict. Perhaps as few as a hundred, or a thousand or more, decided not to return home. Most of the noncombatants among them chose to accompany LRA soldiers who were relocating outside Uganda.

Church leaders were called upon to help ensure a peaceful exit from Uganda for both civilians and LRA soldiers who decided to withdraw elsewhere rather than return to their home villages, fearful of the hostility of their neighbors and parishioners who had suffered from LRA violence for so long. Caritas staff member John Bosco Komanech described the delicacy of this task in our interview.

> In July 2006, we were requested to deliver food and non-food items to the women and children of the LRA, and to some LRA combatants with them, who were moving from Uganda to South Sudan. You can see the tricky situation we were in. We did not do this as Caritas, under the auspices of the organization, but as individuals concerned to help—but we were conducting our distributions at a church. The government of Uganda was aware of what we were doing, and we delivered these items in the presence of district leaders. The government had offered safe passage for all the LRA camps' residents to leave Uganda.
>
> The intent was to prevent them from carrying out ambushes or looting as they moved to South Sudan. So we would try to move with them as they were going. And we were again requested to deliver food, non-food items, and medicine to the LRA former soldiers and other camp residents after they had resettled in Sudan. (Komanech 2014)

Far more numerous than those who elected to accompany the LRA across Uganda's borders into a neighboring country were residents of rebel camps who returned to their former communities in the towns and villages of northern Uganda. More numerous still, by far, were two million residents of IDP camps who were now permitted to return to the villages and homes from which they had been forcibly displaced a decade earlier. What they found on arrival was the same displacement and dislocation that greeted LRA returnees: squatters in the houses that were still standing, charred remains of others, roofless churches and schools, and fields taken over by others. Systems of community care and governance, too, had broken down, and the central government had done very little to rebuild them. Nearly two million no-longer-displaced persons began the arduous task of rebuilding their lives, back on the soil that had sustained their families for many generations until civil war drove them away.

In 2006 the United Nations High Commissioner for Refugees (UNHCR) opened a new field office in Gulu. Observing the inadequacy of Ugandan government provisions for the IDP camps, the UN took responsibility for supplying them and preparing for the return of their residents to their former communities. A UN dispatch from 2012 notes that the Gulu office was established "to manage 251 camps and provide protection to an estimated 1.84 million internally displaced people in 11 districts." As camp populations began to move back home after 2006, coordination of food aid and other assistance became the primary task of UN representatives.

An international organization, the Association of Volunteers in International Service (AVSI), published a joint report with UNHCR documenting the reintegration process at approximately its midpoint, when more than half of the camp population had dispersed back into local communities. The report summarizes the recent history of the camps thus:

> As of today, this large displaced population is taking advantage of the new freedom, moving steadily outside the camps toward the areas of their origin. This return pattern is challenged however by the lack of services in the return areas, the difficulties in accessing several sites, the lack of governance at parish level, and by the incapacity of a coordinated approach at parish level by the humanitarian actors. (AVSI 2009)

In the previous four months, the report estimated, 100,000 people had moved from IDP camps to their former communities. One by one, all of the camps were officially closed, which meant that there would be no more food assistance, medical help, schools, or other services. In camps that had not yet been closed, and even in those that supposedly no longer existed and therefore received no services, many residents remained behind, not knowing what would be waiting for them at home. In 2009, it was reported, more than 600,000 residents still remained in IDP camps (Lambright 2011, 173).

Most of the camps were eventually razed. A few remained unofficially open, housing a small number of residents who eked out a living as traders. A visitor to the Gulu region in 2014 could still find a few small clusters of huts, in out-of-the-way locations, that were the remnants of IDP camps but were now being used as permanent settlements.

"With such great numbers of people moving, and with great improvements to return-area services necessary for a safe return, it is urgent now to understand where people are moving, and the service gaps still present," the AVSI report urged (AVSI 2009). These "service gaps" were many, and daunting in their extent. UNHCR and other international NGOs provided assistance to many returnees, including building materials, livestock, seeds, and tools. NGO and government representatives provided legal assistance to some so that they could regain land once theirs on which others were now farming. In settlements where returnees put up new houses, NGOs assisted in digging latrines.

AVSI also worked with other organizations to provide wheelchairs for the physically disabled. The Gulu Youth Development Organization took up the task of building crutches and canes, thus providing employment for young people and assistance to war victims and others in need. Even more challenging than the injuries and physical disabilities many had suffered were the lasting psychological wounds of decades of war, which had divided communities and families and built up an atmosphere of mistrust and mutual suspicion that would not be quickly dispelled. Margaret Angucia has documented the many ways in which both government agencies and community leaders have sought to facilitate reintegration of the formerly abducted and to bridge the enormous gap between services that are needed and resources that are available (Angucia 2010).

On January 6, 2012, a UNHCR spokesman announced in a Geneva press briefing:

The UN refugee agency has ended its assistance to nearly 2 million internally displaced persons (IDPs) in Uganda as the vast majority have returned home.

Last week, we closed the UNHCR office in Gulu, northern Uganda, after five years of assisting and protecting people displaced by fighting between the Ugandan army and the rebel Lord's Resistance Army. . . .

247 IDP camps [of 251 that were open in 2005] have been closed after making sure that the land was cleaned up and rehabilitated before being handed back to the original owners.

Further actions and interventions on behalf of the returned IDPs have now been integrated into the government's long-term development and recovery programmes so as to ensure that the transition from humanitarian/relief to recovery/development efforts is as seamless as possible, and in order to maintain the sustainability of returns. (UNHCR 2012)

It had been more than a quarter-century since the LRA began its campaign against the Ugandan government, five years since it withdrew from Uganda and allowed its soldiers and the residents of its remote camps to return to their communities. At long last, the roads of the region were safe for travel, and the markets were open once again in every town and village. Crops were planted, houses rebuilt, and schools reopened. Life returned gradually to its established patterns of buying and selling, sowing and harvesting. But the scars of the protracted civil war remained deep and fresh.

New Priorities for ARLPI (1): Local Organization

In this period the work of ARLPI shifted dramatically to respond to the changing situation of the people of the region. Founded in 1997 to facilitate interfaith cooperation, promote nonviolent conflict resolution, and pressure both government and LRA to come together and negotiate an end to the civil war, the organization could now look back on remarkable successes achieved in all of these areas. But communities were struggling now with issues of poverty, mistrust, and dislocation.

John Bosco Komanech recalled what happened as people began moving back to their former communities.

The government of Uganda had promised that people who were living in the IDPs who returned to their villages and to their former homes would be provided with what they needed to start a new life there. But these promises were never kept. The organizations that we can give credit to [for helping in resettlement] are very few. The UN provided vulnerable ones in the community with houses and latrines, and for people with special needs they would provide lands. They would organize youth in the area to open the land [to clear weeds and plant crops] and give them a token or a small payment. UNHCR did a lot of that in our region.

UNHCR by its mandate works through partners, so Caritas and the Church of Uganda took the lead on shelter construction, digging latrines, and distributing walking sticks and other items for the blind.

The challenges of readjusting to life in the village were numerous. Access roads to villages were very poor. Government assurances that all land mines had been removed proved to be unreliable, and concealed explosives posed a constant danger on formerly contested ground. Drinking water in the villages was often contaminated, but the people lacked the money either to buy bottled water or to buy fuel to boil their water. Diseases transmitted by contaminated water became common.

There were also problems of cultural readjustment, especially between young and old. Komanech explained:

> There were some elderly persons who were abandoned even by their own children. The youth who lived in towns, or in the trading centers that developed around the former IDPs, did not want to return to their villages. So that was another challenge, one that is attached to our cultural identity as Acholi. You know, we used to respect our parents; we used to respect elders. But there is a lost generation of youth who do not even respect their parents. When they are told "this land belongs to us all" they hurry to divide it and sell it to gain quick money.
>
> When people started going back home there were many cases of suicide in our communities. Land conflicts arose, and families fought with other families or clans. (Komanech 2014)

International agencies had offered generous help to the residents of IDP camps, and also to transit camps where former LRA soldiers and camp residents were housed for several months of rehabilitation. In these camps the NGOs ensured that housing, sanitation, and food supplies were at least minimally adequate to meet immediate needs. But just at the time when former residents were moving back to their villages in large numbers, organizations cut back on their budgets and staff levels, closed their local offices, and withdrew. Far less assistance was offered to residents after they returned to their homes and farms than during their stay in temporary camps, and this exacerbated the problems of resettlement and readjustment.

ALRPI leadership recognized that in order to promote healing in northern Uganda it would be essential to form a broad network of local leadership and to foster initiatives that would reflect the residents' own assessment of their needs. For too long the lives and choices of the Acholi people had been dictated by others. LRA forces had effectively cut off access to the outside world, Ugandan government troops had forced them into IDP camps, and international aid agencies had created a system of food distribution to replace the crops that the people were unable to grow for themselves.

In a comprehensive report on its activities and its plans issued in 2011, ARLPI identified the new challenges of life in postwar Uganda. Its work would benefit, it was noted, from the support of two religious organizations that had just become affiliates: the Seventh-Day Adventist mission in Acholiland and a group of evangelical churches called the Born-Again Faith Federation. A central focus of current work related to issues of land ownership. One recent project in this area was publication of an Acholi translation of the Uganda Land Act, to help those returning to their former homes understand their legal rights. Other areas of emphasis included "women's empowerment" in the community, HIV/AIDS prevention and care, election monitoring, and a "SALW" initiative—a campaign to reduce the number of small arms and light weapons in the possession of residents of the region, like the exchange program described in the previous chapter.

Some unexpected efforts to influence national and international leaders are also highlighted in the report. ARLPI had asked the Kampala government to release Thomas Kwoyelo, for example, to honor the spirit if not the letter of the amnesty law that had been enacted, then allowed to lapse, then reinstated. Under its terms Kwoyelo and other LRA commanders were liable to criminal prosecution, but the Museveni government had refused his request for release, as has been recounted above in Chapter 5. This appeal was ignored, and in 2017 and 2018 Kwoyelo's trial moved forward—very slowly, with numerous postponements and adjournments (Ogora 2018).

ARLPI also sent a letter to the President of the United States, protesting against its bombing campaigns in Libya and urging avoidance of unnecessary force. Killing Libyan strongman Muammar Gaddafi, they urged, should not be a goal, since it would not advance peace in the region. Gaddafi was killed a few months later, by Libyan rebels and not by US forces. Peace in Libya, regrettably, remains a distant ideal (ARLPI 2011).

The observations and recommendations of this report were confirmed in my interviews with members of the staff of ARLPI, when I asked how the organization's priorities had changed in the period since the withdrawal of LRA troops and the closing of IDP camps. Two emphases stood out in their responses: strengthening local ownership and control of interfaith activities, and addressing issues of land ownership.

The shift toward stronger local involvement resulted both from a realization of past shortcomings and from changing circumstances. Reviewing the earlier stages of their own work, ARLPI leaders realized that they had made most of the key decisions at the level of top leadership, in the organization itself and in the supporting religious communities, and then had announced their decisions to the community. When the highest priority had been to set negotiations for a settlement in motion, despite high levels of suspicion and risks of interference, the planning and implementation of ARLPI activities had of necessity been highly centralized—and highly confidential. There had been extensive consultation with the leaders of each religious community, but little information had been shared with their congregations or with others in the community for fear of stirring up controversy or raising hopes prematurely. The challenges now facing the northern region of rebuilding communities long disrupted by war would require a fundamentally different approach.

Pastors, priests, and imams, however deep their desire to rebuild, could not know just what challenges the members of their communities were grappling with or what means were available to cope with them. What was needed for postwar rebuilding, they realized, was a wide network of local involvement, with members of the community setting priorities and implementing programs. The religious leaders would need to provide support and encouragement, but the leadership must now come from below rather than from above. They were learning an important lesson of political philosophy in practice: that social and political change arising from the initiative of local communities seeking to address their most urgent problems is more effective, and more likely to endure, than change mandated by experts who believe they understand local needs.

Komanech described some of the mechanisms for nurturing local leadership that were undertaken by religious leaders.

> The money from international agencies was no longer adequate to support our activities, and there were areas where we feared land mines, although the government of Uganda assured us that these places were safe. We wanted to continue with agricultural services like providing seeds and seedlings. But as a civil society organization we did not want to duplicate government services but to work with the government to strengthen it [the local community].
>
> So in some areas we trained local leaders at the lower levels—the LCs, who are local councilors, some of them in charge of one parish, others of a sub-county. We built their capacity and helped them learn to make local government structures effective. (Komanech 2014)

As the difficult task of rebuilding communities moved slowly forward, these efforts were greatly facilitated by the networks of interfaith collaboration that ARLPI had created in the most difficult years of the conflict. As an organization that sought the welfare of the entire community, not just of one of its constituent groups, ARLPI had earned the respect of the residents of northern Uganda, and its efforts at community organizing soon yielded results. Komanech recalled what he learned in this time of transition:

> This is a personal lesson that I can share with you. I learned that networking with different faith organizations is the best way forward.

Whether you are Catholic, Protestant, born-again, or Muslim, this conflict affected you in the same way. So working together is necessary.

When we provide services to the affected people, we should not segregate them. I am a Catholic and I work for Caritas, but I should not seek to benefit only Catholics. And what I've learned is that during a conflict some people are sacrificed for the sake of others' ends. Many church leaders were discredited and regarded as collaborators [with the government or with the LRA].

Another lesson learned is that it's not only during the emergency that help is needed but also after the conflict is over, when people need to rebuild their lives and rebuild their homes—and to come back to the sense of being a human being. The need is not just for physical things but for psychological healing. (Komanech 2014)

For that reason a Counseling and Training Institute was created in Gulu, under the sponsorship of Caritas. It continues to offer services to all residents, from all religious and ethnic communities.

Another participant in church-sponsored programs to assist in community building, Jessica Aeko, emphasized the importance of teaching schoolchildren what it means to respect human rights and seek reconciliation in situations of conflict.

Our program [offered by the diocesan Peace and Justice Commission] teaches the young people who are our future generation that, although we have suffered from the violence of the LRA in this war, if we promote dialogue we can achieve healing. Hearing the testimony of those who have been hurt by a neighbor helps us understand what others have suffered, and then we can seek a peaceful reconciliation.

We know that the young people who were in the camps learned behaviors which disrupt their families. There was low attendance in the churches, and there was conflict in the schools, after the war ended. So we teach the children other ways to behave, so that we can all live together in a peaceful way.

By encouraging young people to respect others' rights and seek non-violent resolution of conflict, she added, we can help prevent future outbreaks of violence. A community whose members know their own rights and respect the rights of others is unlikely to sustain a war such as the LRA conflict.

> An empowered community can provide for its needs. When a war erupts in a country people may be led away to join the rebel team. But if the people are empowered, then nothing can come to divide them. (Aeko 2014)

New Priorities for ARLPI (2): Land and Community

Rebuilding communities in northern Uganda proved to be a long and difficult task. Those who had lived for a decade or more in IDP camps needed to reclaim their homes and their plots of agricultural land, which sometimes meant evicting illegal occupants of ten years or more. The settlement of land disputes, I was told by those I interviewed, is one of the most serious challenges today, and one of the most difficult to resolve.

Even if access to farmland could be assured, those who had relied on aid shipments from NGOs needed to become self-sufficient. A generation of young people had grown up without seeing their parents go off to work the fields, without being sent to weed, without helping with the harvest. The children who had been forcibly relocated to IDP camps were now young adults, more familiar with mobile phones than with hoes and shovels.

Reintegration of former LRA camp residents, especially those who had served in the rebel army, posed even greater challenges. The Ugandan government and the NGOs active in the region set up rehabilitation camps, where all returnees—those who escaped, and those who were given their freedom as the LRA forces left Uganda—were expected to spend several months undergoing training and counseling to prepare them for life back at home.

Not everyone responded positively to the regimentation and restricted freedom that were imposed on residents of these camps. Some wanted to return directly to their communities, bypassing the centers. But that posed difficult challenges too. Paul Rubangageyo Okello of Caritas commented:

> For those who go to the [rehabilitation] center, everything is scheduled. They have breakfast at the same time every day, then lunch, and so forth, and the people in the reception center are very nice. But then they return to the community, and everything is opposite. In the community they will be abused—there is so much stigmatization. (Okello 2014)

Okello estimated that the number of LRA camp residents who avoided the rehabilitation camps, slipping back into their former communities quietly and without reporting to local authorities, was even greater than the number who reported to the camps for formal reintegration. It is difficult to confirm or challenge this assertion. Certainly the number who completed formal rehabilitation procedures was far less than the estimated 65,000 abductees, and Okello's conjecture is plausible.

Those who returned directly home had to make the adjustment from the bush to the village on their own. Some received assistance and support from family members and neighbors, but others encountered bitter resentment and hostility. A girl who had been abducted at age 9, then escaped with a companion after just a few months in an LRA camp, returned home to find that her parents had been killed, but she was welcomed by her grandmother. She told Margaret Angucia:

> When I saw my grandmother, she received me and took me home. She bought for me clothes. I stayed and stayed, then I started going to fetch water. The children at the well would look at the girl who has returned from the bush, look at her red bulging eyes; the spirits of those she has killed will make her kill us; let us get away. The children disturbed us and I would cry at the stream. That is what happened. (Angucia 2010, 110)

Even those who received help from local and international staff in refugee transit centers found the transition to the next stage—returning home—to be very difficult. The rehabilitation process typically ended after a few months with simple discharge, and the international agencies could not spare staff for follow-up counseling or visits back in the villages. Some found their communities even less welcoming to them than to those who had returned quietly and unofficially. Many of those who bypassed the reintegration camps simply kept silent about where they had been in the intervening years, to protect their families from embarrassment and themselves from ostracism. Anyone who spent time in a rehabilitation center, however, was identified as a former rebel. They and their families were sometimes shunned by neighbors for this reason (Okello 2014).

A 2017 documentary film, "No Place for a Rebel," documents the challenges of readjustment for a former LRA commander now united with his family. Made in Uganda by a Greek director, Ariana Asamakapoulos, and a Dutch producer, Maartje Wegman, it has been selected for several international festivals and as part of the Africa World Documentary Film Festival. Dutch reviewers describe the film as "an intimate story exposing a large-scale issue," the issue of "how difficult reconciliation can be" (Asamakopoulos 2017).

Issues of land ownership have been a constant source of conflict for returnees. Abdula Latif Nasur explained why, and described some ways in which ARLPI has sought to resolve these issues.

> When people were going back home [from the IDP camps] boundaries had been lost. And people started looking at land only as a means of getting money. This war destroyed the cultural cohesion that existed before the war. . . .
>
> The issue of land can only be resolved by the people themselves. They need to be empowered. That is why we use the alternative dispute resolutions mechanism, and it has worked tremendously well. . . . The poor people have lost their land to the people who have money. But now there is a way forward, through dialogue and dispute resolution. In the subcounty with the largest number of land title issues we have been able to resolve 40 different land disputes. Boundaries are demarcated, trees are planted [as boundary markers], and people have applied for a certificate of customary ownership so that their land cannot be taken away again. (Nasur 2014)

The problems of regaining farmland are not caused only by ownership disputes, I was told by one interviewee, Stephen Langole, a program head at Gulu University. Even when ownership has been established, land is being misused as a source of cash.

> Young people who do not want to farm are selling their family land in order to buy motorcycles! Communal responsibility for land—ownership of land as part of the community—is collapsing. Today the land families once farmed has commercial value, so it is being sold to outsiders, from other regions of Uganda and from other countries. But land in our culture is not something to be sold! It is to be used. Land can be yours as long as you use it. (Langole 2016)

He took note of one encouraging sign: rural communities still respect the inviolability of family granaries. Those who have returned to their former homes, he said, are building or rebuilding granaries, so that when they harvest grain crops such as maize and millet they can provide for their families in the future.

Several of those involved with ARLPI initiatives in the area of land ownership mentioned that the usual remedy for disputed ownership claims in Europe and North America—consultation of government land records, and appeal to the courts to honor ownership claims if necessary—is not available in most areas of rural Uganda. Land ownership has long been assigned, and adjudicated, by community leaders and traditional elders. Families could maintain their claim to farmlands by keeping them under cultivation. As sons and daughters married and began new families, they would receive portions of the family land for their own use. The title to a plot of land consisted of its having been used by a family for generations, with no survey records or legal documents to serve as recourse when disputes arise.

As has been mentioned, ARLPI undertook to expand residents' awareness of their legal rights by publishing a translation of the national code regarding ownership rights. Yet it was clear that disputes would need to be resolved through negotiation and mediation, not litigation. Families who returned home to find others working their farms could appeal to the Local Council, and many disputes were resolved at that level on the basis of customary law rather than formally recorded property rights.

Obtaining needed tools, seed, and draft animals was no less difficult. Monsignor Odong told me in our 2016 conversation that the recovery will probably take longer than the LRA rebellion itself.

> It will take fifty years to rebuild! The guns are silent, yes. But it is not just a matter of whether the guns are active or silent: think of what the gun has done to the people. The entire region now lives in abject poverty. Nearly all of our income in the northern regions comes from traditional agriculture—but those who are returning from the IDP camps cannot afford to buy two bulls and a plow. And often they are told that someone has bought their land, and fenced it off.

Sometimes the returning families can dispute a fraudulent sale and win back the land stolen from them, he added. But they may not succeed. Worse yet, in some cases the returning family members have no memory of what land was once theirs, as is the case for the thousands of orphans whose parents were both killed in the conflict or died in the camps.

> Our goal as mediators in land disputes is simply to be fair and just—especially to orphans and others. Land titles that are not legitimate can be challenged. Lands can be restored to the families from which they were taken illegally. But there are deep wounds, wounds to the mind and to the heart, that law and politics cannot heal. (Odong 2016)

The 2011 Annual Report of ARLPI identifies its Land Conflict Mediation Project, supported by funding from Catholic Relief Services, as one of its major areas of work. Several instances of specific land disputes are listed as having been resolved. This was usually accomplished through mediation efforts by residents in the relevant community who had undergone training in nonviolent dispute resolution offered by ARLPI staff. Other activities listed, from the preceding year, included five "debriefing meetings" for local government officials and land owners; five "refresher training" courses to enhance the skills of mediators enlisted from each community; two radio talk shows on land rights and dispute resolution; five community meetings; and more. In all, it is reported, more than 2,000 residents had participated in one or more of these activities.

The report includes a detailed account of the settling of a long-simmering dispute over a plot of land in the Amuru district. To convey a sense of the complexity of the task, and of the way in which locally based mediation can succeed, I quote a few excerpts from the account:

> The land in question was given to Vicentina by the grandfather of Oceng way back in the 80s, and after return from the [IDP] camp Oceng wanted the land back. Oceng confessed that after listening to the sensitization carefully and receiving clarity from the legal officer, especially on the rights of women and widows, he (Oceng) realized that there was no basis for rivaling with Vicentina over the land [because] he did not know how and why it was given to Vicentina. He promised in front of the participants and asked them to be his witness that he will relinquish the contested piece of land to Vicentina. He also apologized to Vicentina for all the inconveniences caused to her and her family . . . Vicentina thanked him for realizing his mistakes and the truth and forgave him and promised to resume harmony that had for long been lost among them.
>
> Another participant noted, "We shall waste no more money in court now that ARLPI is opening our eyes by teaching us very simple and cheap means of resolving land conflicts." (ARLPI 2011, 22)

This colorful narrative conveys vividly what is meant by ARLPI's commitment to "the community dialogue approach to foster reintegration." Necessary resources are provided by the staff based in Gulu: a thousand copies of an Acholi translation of the Uganda Land Act, training sessions for community leaders and mediators, and informational meetings for officials and landowners. Then the real work of rebuilding can be done by members of each rural community, who seek to persuade their neighbors that seemingly intractable conflicts can be resolved through dialogue and mutual accommodation.

On several occasions above, we have identified the pitfalls of positing some sort of distinctively African human nature: early explorers saw Africans as savages by nature, romantics countered that African societies are attuned to nature and harmonious in spirit, southern Ugandans described the Acholi as violence-prone, and so forth. All these preconceptions rest on discredited notions of racial and ethnic essentialism. All the same, ARLPI has not hesitated to call on certain aspects of local cultures as important foundations for the work of rebuilding. Here is the description offered by participants in the Peace and Justice Commission, for example, of the heart of the community dialogue approach:

> We developed a dialogue and discussion approach where people would sit and talk about [the problems they faced], and this is a part of Acholi culture. If there is an issue the people will talk about it until they find an agreeable and amicable solution.

With the right framework to foster dialogue, they added, "you can face your own killer" but in the end you come to a point of reconciliation and forgiveness, if the necessary context and supporting structures for community rebuilding are present.

The contributions of Acholi tradition extend beyond a willingness to address problems communally. Not just talking, but also singing and dancing, are part of the process of healing, since they reconnect people with their traditional values and culture.

> The success of our reintegration activities is this: the community interactive activities where people would sing their songs and dance traditional dances. This provided the opportunity for people to reconnect with each other. Some in a family were in a camp, others were in the bush, and for five years they may not have been together. The churches promoted intergenerational activities for the people of a village to come together and accept and appreciate one another. (Okello 2014)

Caritas staff member Joseph Ogaba added:

> The different traditional dances have different meanings: some are asking for something, some are about children in the family, some

are about the clan and its leader. In this kind of event so many messages are conveyed and it is left for the people to analyze and respond to them. It is not just "I" coming and explaining to the leader, it is the community coming to explain, and also learning toleration and forgiveness.

When someone who is known for robbing and killing comes back to the community it is very hard to accept. But now you can express your passion in your song, and the returnee can sing his own song to apologize and ask for forgiveness. And the abductees can also complain to the community, asking, "Why did you allow me to be abducted?" The community is blaming the returnee and the returnee is blaming the community, but traditional songs and dances provide a very good means for people to understand one another and learn to live together. (Ogaba 2014)

Topics that are too difficult to discuss in words, in this context, can be resolved through songs and dances, because "there is a power in song and dance." In an earlier period the Catholic and Protestant missionaries alike had condemned traditional rituals as Satanic and demanded that they be abandoned. In many Muslim and evangelical communities even today, such practices are discouraged and viewed with suspicion. But leaders in the religious communities seeking to advance postwar recovery have come to understand how important they are in healing the deep scars of a protracted and cruel war and promoting mutual respect and acceptance. Let us consider a few examples.

Rituals of Healing

Traditional Acholi rituals of reconciliation have been mentioned by many observers of postwar recovery in northern Uganda as an important part of the process of community healing. A detailed and perceptive account of these rituals was provided by Amy Finnegan, writing in 2010 while pursuing a PhD degree at Boston College. She had the benefit of many years' experience working with NGOs in northern Uganda. The background provided by Finnegan helped me to understand the frequent references made by my interview subjects to welcoming ceremonies. Paul Rubangageyo Okello spoke of the churches' support for "many positive things in Acholi culture," and cited as an example that "now people are stepping on the eggs when someone comes back." This phrase baffled me until I learned that it is an English translation of the Acholi name of a traditional practice, *nyono tonggweno,* a rite of purification for those who have been away from the community for an extended period.

Finnegan describes a large gathering of the people of a village to which a group of young people had returned after they had recently escaped from the LRA. Traditional songs were performed by the musicians of the village. While they played and sang, each of the young men stepped forward. Finnegan describes what followed, quoting from the journal she kept during her visit to the village.

The first individual in line, a dark-skinned adolescent boy fourteen years of age, walked briskly with intent and determination, directing the sole of his left foot to the top of a white raw egg that awaited its breaking. Suddenly, the shell crumbled and the thick, yellow yolk burst forth, seeping over the boy's toes and over the symbolically placed branches. Smiles spread across the faces of spectators as the line of returning youth moved forward and each individual stepped on the raw egg. Naturally laid from a hen and with no mouth, to symbolize innocence, the egg had been placed at the intersection of the *Obopo* branch, slippery and soaplike, representing cleansing, and the *Layibi* stick, used to open the granary and thus symbolizing nourishment. With the assistance of a few men from the community, young mothers, some of whom had been forcibly impregnated by the LRA commanders, grasped their children's feet to ensure that they too each touched the yolk of the broken egg and received the cleansing. (Finnegan 2010, 432)

Afterward the young people approached the village chiefs and elders, looking respectfully down rather than meeting their eyes. The elders greeted each of them with a handshake, representing their acceptance into the community from which they had been separated by far more than distance.

Similar ceremonies of healing and reconciliation are described by many of those interviewed by Margaret Angucia. A group of elders whom she interviewed related that, after a large number of children returned to a community but their families were unable to arrange the appropriate traditional rituals, others stepped in to help.

> When they came they were not welcomed in a traditional way and so they could not stay well. But when the paramount chief came he organized the ritual and they stepped on the egg. There were 400 of them. After that they started living well. (Angucia 2010, 178)

"Stepping on the egg" is a community event in which the cultural values of reconciliation and healing are visibly and dramatically enacted. It is an initial step toward full reconciliation, which culminates in the cere-monial consumption of a bitter traditional beverage brewed from roots, along with the sacrifice of a sheep and other ceremonies. Both the bev-erage and the ritual are called *mato oput,* and the shared drinking from a calabash gourd can occur only after several other steps including mock combat and the bending of spears have been completed. In traditional Acholi society this ritual made it possible for someone guilty of a hei-nous crime to return to the community after offering restitution to those whom he harmed and asking their forgiveness. It was also em-ployed symbolically, outside a specific structure of traditional authority, as part of the peace negotiations in Juba that led to LRA withdrawal from Uganda (Afako 2006).

In our interview Paul Rubangageyo Okello related Acholi rituals of reconciliation to those described in Biblical parables:

> In the Bible when the prodigal son returned home, the father ran and jumped on him and ordered a bull to be prepared. Why did he order it to be slaughtered? Culture plays a very big part in people's lives, and religion is a part of culture. In this [situation] there are a lot of positive things about Acholi culture that were very important. And our churches realized very quickly that now people are stepping on the eggs when somebody is coming back from captivity.

It is difficult for a family to accept someone who has been abducted or has run away and now wants to come back, he added. In the time of the slave trade, slaves who escaped and returned home were often rejected, and it was believed that they often brought evil spirits home with them. But a family can accept the one who returns if it follows Acholi tradition, he added:

> . . . and part of it is the eggs. The eggs symbolize innocence. The Acholi live a collective, not an individual, life. You were away because of something terrible that happened, and now we want to welcome you back. And so you step on the egg: it means we still consider you to be innocent. Those things that come out of the egg will stop the bad spirits that may have tried to come with you. (Okello 2014)

It is not just child soldiers who can benefit from these ceremonies of healing. A recent study of the high incidence of sexual violence in northern Uganda, both during and after the LRA insurgency, for example, emphasizes the importance of traditional rituals in enabling victimized women to overcome barriers of mistrust and exclusion in their families.

> An egg, simple and fragile as it is, has the power to bring the young women into their families. By a symbolic act of stepping on and breaking the egg, the woman is allowed access into the homestead. Behind the act of stepping on the egg is the belief that the evil or dirt associated with warfare is left behind and the person entering the homestead is clean and devoid of any contamination. (Tiessen and Thomas 2014, 130)

Some observers warn that these rituals have been given an exaggerated importance by outsiders, who see in them an essentially—and uniquely—African desire for reconciliation rather than punishment in response to acts that disrupt the community. In the article cited above, Finnegan does not entirely avoid this pitfall. She distinguishes between three alternative modes of response to violent acts and other crimes: that of retributive justice, which is secular, behavior-focused, and unilateral; that of forgiveness, which is usually religious in its foundation, person-centered, and can be either unilateral or bilateral; and that of reconciliation, which can be either religious or secular in motivation, focuses on individuals more than behavior, and is essentially bilateral. The ritual practices of the Acholi, she argues, show that Acholi culture emphasizes the third far more than the first two (Finnegan 2010). Finnegan echoes the statement of ARLPI staff quoted above: resolving differences through dialogue is deeply grounded in Acholi culture. These rituals exemplify an underlying ethical stance.

Unfortunately, Finnegan may here be seeing in an African culture the projection of her own ideals and a confirmation of a preconceived notion of Acholi identity. Another longtime observer of northern Ugandan culture, both during and after the LRA conflict, has raised this challenge. In traditional communities, insists Timothy Allen, the response to crime is sometimes primarily a matter of punishment and restitution, sometimes focused on reconciliation The nature of the wrongful act, the relationship of offender to victim, and the community's priorities all influence which approach will be followed in each case. The *mato oput* ceremony is occasionally employed as a means of bringing the community together, now as in the past. But its frequency has increased dramatically, Allen reports, as NGO observers have seized on it as a favored expression of traditional culture. Without discounting its historic roots or its importance in some contexts, Allen warns against the danger that outsiders may be imposing their preferences and their sentiments on the communities of northern Uganda, in a way that invites the people of the region to affirm—and exaggerate—aspects of their culture that hold special appeal to Western aid workers and donors (Allen 2010).

Who is right here: are traditional rituals an important and effective means of overcoming division in the Acholi community, or is their prominence in Western observers' accounts yet another manifestation of the colonialist perception that Africans are "not like us"? We need to take care in considering this question—we are, in the Western and not the Acholi sense, stepping on eggs. Outside observers are not in a favorable position to assess these opposing perspectives, and we need to listen to the voices of those who have been most directly involved in post-conflict recovery.

In the accounts of reunification and reconciliation that were given to me in interviews by those affected by the civil war, it became clear that traditional rituals served as one element among many others in the difficult process of community healing. Many modes of reconciliation, I was told, must be pursued in parallel: talking honestly about the events of the past decades, expressing in song and dance what is too painful to say in words, and engaging in cultural rituals through which mistrust and recrimination can be symbolically put aside. Paul Rubangageyo Okello framed his comments in a vivid metaphor:

> I lived with formerly abducted persons and I know what can happen to them. There are flashbacks and nightmares. They keep re-experiencing what has happened to them. And when you lead them back to their communities you must assure them of their safety. And that is what the egg does in reassuring them—religious leaders and cultural leaders working together. When I look at our community I see a plane, a very speedy plane. And how can you bring it down for a landing? This is what our people are managing to do. It is windy, it is difficult, it is even snowing, but we can land! First let us land! And then we can talk about the situation that we are in now. (Okello 2014)

His Acholi ancestors would have had no idea what a speedy plane was—and even many Ugandans today have never seen snow. (I once met a first-time visitor from East Africa to the United States who said he was shocked to see snow falling from the sky: he had assumed, from what he had seen in photographs, that it seeped up from the ground when it is cold.)

Others share Rubangageyo's conviction that reaffirming tradition is an essential element of postwar rebuilding efforts, difficult as it is today when communities have been so violently torn apart for so long. Archbishop John Baptist Odama, a central figure in the founding of ARLPI, has emphasized the collective and communal elements of traditional rituals as a means of community healing. In his acceptance speech to the Niwano Peace Foundation, he observed that the public ceremonies of the Acholi are part of a complex process that incorporates elements of punishment, restitution, and reconciliation. When a crime has been committed in traditional Acholi culture, he said, the responsibility is not placed solely on one individual, but "the person's whole clan or tribe takes on the guilt as a community." Then the community undertakes to rebalance the moral scales through several successive steps: expressing repentance for the crime, accepting the offer of forgiveness from the clan of the person who was harmed or killed, and then making restitution.

> Compensation was not a punitive imposition but it was deemed a process for healing, affirmation of personhood, and enhancement of life within the community. Compensation, therefore, opened up the gateway of reconciliation so that both sides can walk through and approach each other.

After all these steps have been completed, said Odama, it is time for both parties to join in a ceremony of reconciliation such as *mato oput.*

> Drinking the *oput* juice from the same calabash is highly symbolic. Two people, one each from the offending and the offending [clan], drink the juice, with hands behind their backs. They would then sip the bitter juice simultaneously. . . . This goes on until every member of each community drank of the *oput* juice. (Odama 2004)

Some Western observers may be too eager to highlight the "typical African ceremonies" that facilitate reconciliation, as if they possessed some magical power, or to view them as manifestations of a uniquely African human nature. However charitably intended, such accounts are uncomfortably similar to discredited ideologies that separated human beings into distinct racial types. Many such accounts by outsiders also discuss the ritual practices in isolation from the rich fabric of community life in which they occur.

Okello's comments, and Odama's acceptance speech, correct these errors. The rituals do not stand alone; they have no special healing power; and they do not arise from any inherent or universal African human nature. Yet they remain vital elements in a complex process of recovery from conflict. Drawing on longstanding traditions, they create a means by which communities can come together to heal the wounds caused by war and violence. Their importance was well stated by informants who spoke to Margaret Angucia, responding to her questions about why such practices persist in a context where traditional religion has been largely displaced by Christianity and Islam, and these have been challenged in turn by modernity and secularism. They suggested that

> . . . in theory most Acholi would prefer not to believe in traditional beliefs and practices. However, they cannot isolate themselves from the still highly communal society and the consequences of living in it. . . . It was further agreed that if the reintegration of the formerly abducted children were to rely solely on modern secular solutions, the children would not feel at home, due to the isolating tendencies of secularism. Acholi culture, it was posited, has a way of accommo-dating most issues, including this "new" societal problem of formerly abducted children. (Angucia 2010, 180)

Overcoming the Mentality of Dependence

Most of the 65,000 abducted young men and women returned to their former homes in the period following the LRA's withdrawal, begin-ning in 2006. Not all, very likely fewer than half, had the benefit of a formal program of rehabilitation. The rest simply slipped back into their communities and set out to rebuild their lives. The dialogue pro-cess initiated by ARLPI leaders in local communities, and the observ-ance of traditional rituals, helped overcome the fear and mistrust that greeted them initially and facilitated acceptance by families.

For as many as two million more Ugandans, it was not the LRA but the government's policy of forcible relocation that had driven them from their homes. As the IDP camps emptied out during the period from 2006 until the end of the decade, no cloud of suspicion related to wartime atrocities hovered over these returning men, women, and children. But their reintegration was extremely difficult all the same.

The collaboration that had characterized ARLPI activities during the last six years of the LRA conflict was no less important for communities seeking to restore normal rural life in the years following the closing of the IDP camps. Patterns of dependency, divisions among Protestant and Catholic and Muslim, and epidemics of infectious disease had all been prevalent in the overcrowded camps, whose residents had no land on which to grow food crops and few other opportunities to work. Rev. Patrick Lumumba, head of the diocesan Peace and Development program of the Church of Uganda (the Anglican church), told me, "Our biggest problem in the churches of northern Uganda now is to teach people to come out of this relief mentality." If the churches emphasize their differences, he added, and if they offer only a message of spiritual renewal and healing, they will contribute very little to the rebuilding of functioning communities (Lumumba 2014).

If Protestant churches serve Protestants while Catholics assist Catholics, Lumumba told me, very little will be accomplished. He has observed, and others have corroborated, a tendency in the post-conflict period to separate once again into distinct religious communities and focus on assistance within those communities, in contrast to the ways in which religious leaders came together to provide refuge and emergency assistance at the height of the conflict. At that time, in the words of a Muslim staff member at ARLPI, the religious leaders who became involved in its work had sought not to convert but to help. When life was returning to normal, religious divisions became more visible again (Nasur 2016).

Those were special circumstances, many Ugandans said now, that required special measures. Suffering from daily fear of LRA raids, we all had to come together. But now that we are back in our homes, why should we worry about Protestants if we are Catholic, or vice versa? Why should the Muslim community not look after its own while others attend to the needs of their own people? This mentality frequently impeded ARLPI activities in the years following 2006. Yet its leaders continued to work closely together, sharing information and strategies for development. Catholics shared information and resources with Protestant counterparts, and Muslim residents were included in development initiatives alongside others.

Some expected the churches to concentrate on spiritual needs and leave matters of livelihood and health to government and NGOs, Lumumba told me. But the leaders of ARLPI rejected this as a false separation and a distortion of the holistic nature of Christian teaching.

If we are not involved in physical and economic development to help people who lack food, who lack water, who lack other things, then we will not be a relevant church in northern Uganda. And I think this is why God has called us to be a church. I don't like a church that preaches the Gospel while people are dying from jiggers on their feet.[1] No, the people who have been preached to should also be able to seek health care, to send their children to school, to have a means of livelihood. If the local people are empowered, then they will not look to the church only to support them—they will support the church. (Lumumba 2014)

Among the initiatives that ARLPI has helped launch, with the goal of helping the returned residents provide for themselves and work together, are some familiar ones and some that are less conventional. Several focus on assistance to women and girls. A vocational center for girls has been created, for example, as part of a women's development center. Women in farming communities traditionally work alongside men in the fields, planting and weeding and harvesting, but in the towns many returned camp residents were single women who had no land to farm and needed an independent source of income. At the training center they were given training in occupations traditionally open to women, such as hairdressing and sewing, said Lumumba. Others receive training in finance and business development. "Some of them have opened hotels," he observed, "or have formed groups in the community," referring to financial self-help groups. There are programs to assist children in their school assignments, and others to train adolescent young men and women in employable skills. Funding for these projects has come from government programs and from internationally based NGOs, with ARLPI providing oversight and ensuring that all groups in the community are served.

One of these NGOs will be mentioned again below, since it has been a faithful partner in many development initiatives across East Africa: this is World Renew, the development arm of the Christian Reformed Church in North America (previously called the Christian Reformed World Relief Committee). World Renew activities in Uganda include assisting in the formation of microcredit groups, agricultural training, and training in conflict resolution, in partnership with the Church of Uganda in some areas and with evangelical churches in others. World Renew staff, including country director Joseph Mutebi and northern Ghana coordinator Edward Okiror, are not directly involved in the programs or the planning process of ARLPI but often work collaboratively, for example in a recent World Renew initiative to assist in post-conflict recovery (World Renew n.d.).

ARLPI and the churches that created it also continue to offer development assistance programs. The effectiveness of its work is often enhanced by assistance from other organizations; but their work can also make it more difficult to achieve ARLPI goals. James Ocayo, assistant planning officer for the Anglican diocese, told me that the provision of generous aid from outside NGOs, year after year, with no work requirements or other strings attached, has created special difficulties for implementing locally based programs. "People say that the church does a lot of talking and preaching, but they look to other development partners and the government" for food aid and other consumer goods, he said. But these programs have a limited duration. Before long, the funding is exhausted, donor attention turns elsewhere, and the assistance is phased out. So long as the civil war raged, there were usually new donors ready to take the place of whose who withdrew. But the end of the LRA emergency also meant the end of many international assistance programs.

For that reason, Ocayo told me, the Anglican church offers assistance in the form of a certificate that can be earned by contributing time to projects—a "voucher for work." A similar example related to community road-building will be described below. Persuading community members to participate has been a challenge, said Ocayo. But the challenge has been gradually overcome by the realization that the churches' involvement is long-term and locally based. The UN may close down its offices, and European governments may scale back on funding and withdraw their staff. But the clergy and staff members of the Catholic, Protestant, and Muslim communities of the Acholi region will remain right where they are, and their assistance programs are likely to continue (Ocayo 2014).

In all ARLPI initiatives, Ocayo emphasized, clergy are involved in setting policies, but the managers of each project are community members who have appropriate experience and education. Responsibilities for planning, programs, and land tenure issues are assigned to different people to ensure that if one person moves to another job, others can provide continuity until he or she is replaced. Each program manager works with several organizations, including local churches and foreign

NGOs, so that when one agency's three-year project comes to an end there is a plan in place to provide similar services from other sources.

Programs in agriculture, microfinance, and farmland access are all part of the development efforts that ARLPI helps to coordinate across the region. More unusual is a program that I witnessed with my students in 2012: ARLPI and its partners have undertaken to build roads to remote communities previously accessible only by footpath. Residents who returned to these villages faced great difficulties in obtaining agricultural supplies and in carrying crops to market in the towns. But government funds have been inadequate even to maintain the major connecting roads in the northern region. A request to build new roads to small communities would have been dismissed out of hand. So one of the most urgent infrastructure needs was to improve access by road to the villages where those returning from captivity or from the IDP camps were now resettling.

A personal example will suggest the extent of the problem. On one morning during my 2012 study tour, our extremely capable bus driver set out from a hostel near Fort Portal, west of Kampala, and we decided to use the direct route to our next stop in Hoima, a journey of about 130 miles, hoping that the roads were no worse than had been reported by recent travelers, with some rough patches but generally well-graded dirt surfaces. Unfortunately, recent rains had washed out large sections of the road, necessitating detours and perilous traversals of deep channels across the thoroughfare, and a trip that we expected to take about five hours took nearly twice that long. We would have been wiser to use the routing I had used on my first visit to Uganda: from Fort Portal back to Kampala, then north to Hoima, along well-maintained arterial roads. It would have added 200 unnecessary miles but would have cut the travel time by nearly half. Every sizable city and town in Uganda is linked to its neighbors by road, and trucks and buses ply these roads every day. But Ugandans have no expectation that the roads will be kept in good repair, and in seasons when rain is frequent they know that the journey may take twice as long as it did last week.

In this context, new roads to small settlements, however urgently they are needed, will be completed only if local communities take the initiative. Hence the program to build "freedom roads" in the Gulu district. Ocayo told me that 16 such roads have been completed and many more are underway. My students from Calvin College were invited to observe the progress made by a community near Gulu during the study tour that I led in 2012—and to pick up a hoe or a pick to lend their labor to the project as well. (Only a few local residents were there working alongside them, owing to an unexpected development: an elder of the village had died, and nearly all the residents were attending his funeral.)

World Renew staff members introduced us to community leaders who were coordinating the project, and they in turn explained that it was serving a dual purpose. Not only would the road ease transport to and from the village, it would also help overcome the "relief mentality" instilled by life in an IDP camp, because each family was required to contribute several days' work on the road in order to qualify for crop seeds and fertilizer. The road closely followed a long-established footpath, which was being widened by cutting brush and small trees, then smoothed by removing rocks and spreading loads of gravel. In Europe or North America—or on one of the major arterial roads in Uganda—these tasks would have been accomplished in a day by heavy earthmoving equipment. In rural Uganda, local residents instead spent hundreds of hours wielding machetes, carrying stones, and carrying or spreading gravel. The result would more than repay the effort. Making use of the new "freedom road," village residents would be able to carry crops to market, obtain goods from town, and summon an ambulance when it was needed for a medical emergency.

Dispute resolution is another focus of ARLPI work, and it has been applied to a wide range of problems. In theory one might expect religious leaders to help with personal and spiritual problems but to stay away from economic and political challenges. But this is not possible in the post-conflict situation, because these are often so deeply connected. Patrick Lumumba put it this way:

> People come to the church in case of land conflict, and they come to the church in cases of domestic violence. The church must provide a holistic gospel—something that the government cannot provide. If you look at the PDR document [a proposal submitted by ARLPI to its development partners, including the Ugandan government] you will see that the peace-building component includes building roads and schools. (Lumumba 2014)

Projects such as these exemplify ARLPI's comprehensive approach to economic, political, and spiritual healing in the aftermath of the LRA conflict. What began as a project to build metaphorical bridges between divided religious communities now encompasses teams of village residents swinging pickaxes and pushing wheelbarrows full of gravel to build "freedom roads" to isolated villages.

The Importance of Local Accountability

ARLPI leaders stressed repeatedly that their experience since the closing of the camps has taught them the importance of building local systems of accountability. When development projects have been shaped by consultation with local residents, and when they go forward under the supervision of a qualified team who have the respect of the community, the likelihood that goals will be met is far higher. Projects initiated by outside groups may meet short-term needs, but they reinforce the mentality of dependency and undercut local leadership.

Even when organizations firmly grounded in northern Uganda set the goals and guidelines for development initiatives, if they are administered through centralized and top-down structures they are unlikely to be sustainable or to yield long-term benefits. But when organizations such as ARLPI help to form leadership teams that enjoy the trust of the communities affected, and then assist them with appropriate training workshops and reference materials, the results assist communities to become economically self-sufficient. Equally important, they help local governance become more efficient and more accountable.

Ocayo described the process used for selecting local staff, as he recalled his own hiring by the Anglican diocese, a process very similar to that used by ARLPI in recruiting its staff. "There are quite a number of things that are considered," he said, including education, experience, and "level of maturity," which can be evident, for example, in good relations with one's family and with the community. "One of the key things they look at is whether you are a strong person back home," already known for personal integrity and community leadership.

When I came for the interview I remember they asked me first, "Are you married?" I said I am 80 percent married. "What kind of married?" they asked. I have had a traditional marriage, I said, and I am planning to go to the church [for a Christian wedding ceremony]. When I asked them why they had asked this question first they said, "We need to have people who are settled in mind, who are mature, and who will understand the dynamics of the church very fast."

An applicant's character is very important in hiring, he said. But religion was not a criterion. "We have Muslims who work for the church" (Ocayo 2014). As his Muslim colleague had told me, those who work for ARLPI seek to help, not to convert.

As the displaced population of the Acholi region returned to their homes, free at last from fear of LRA ambushes, the challenges of resettlement were daunting. The aid offered by the Ugandan government and by international NGOs was limited and, in many cases, short-lived. ARLPI, and the Christian and Muslim leaders who supported it, offered essential assistance at every stage of the process. Ocayo recalled:

> When it came to resettlement in the communities that they had been forced to leave, the churches and ARLPI played a very big role. Right from the IDP camps, to the temporary satellite camps, then on to their former homes, we have been working hand in hand with other development partners.

As examples of joint efforts he cited food security programs, distribution of agricultural tools, and a program funded by the American relief organization CARE to address problems of domestic and gender violence.[2] If one organization should decide to discontinue its support for a program, the planning committees in the communities and the leaders of regional organizations come together to seek new sources of support. The diocese and its partners in ARLPI arrange to train board members and administrators in governance and financial management, with assistance from Ugandan staff of World Renew.

> We have signed up with World Renew to offer a training program for the whole year for the board [of the diocese's development programs] so they get to know their role and their responsibilities.

This training—the first extensive training offered since the board was created in 1961—has motivated them, and we see them coming and saying, "I have this idea which I can develop." So now we have made many plans, and we only have to find the resources. (Ocayo 2014)

A project supported by CARE that continues down to the present is the Northern Uganda Initiative for Affected Youth, whose goal is education and economic empowerment of youth affected by the LRA conflict. When I interviewed its field coordinator, Moses Rubangageyo Okello, he provided a specific example of the kinds of community initiative that ARLPI and its Ugandan partner organizations are providing to assist in post-war rebuilding. Working in two districts that are situated between Gulu and the Sudanese border, Moyo and Amuru, the youth organization is providing training, support, and counseling to 2,070 young men and women affected by the LRA conflict.

We support them with entrepreneurship training, human rights education, good governance education, psycho-social support, and peacebuilding. The majority of our beneficiaries were formerly abducted, returned mothers [with children fathered by LRA officers], orphans, and landless youth. So there is a need for psycho-social support and life skills education.

At the moment we are in a situation of "negative peace," but there is continuing conflict arising from land ownership. And the youth in our programs have been both perpetrators and victims in this conflict. Many have been chased away from the land that was theirs under traditional ownership—and in any case youth and women were not permitted to own land. So it is our task to train them in conflict management and mediation, and also to teach them about democracy and human rights. (Okello 2014)

Most of the participants in youth training programs bear the scars of war, and some have been socialized to "go and carry out violence even for something very small." This is no less true of former IDP camp residents than of former soldiers: "in the gun culture of the IDP camp they didn't fear killing."

The training and counseling that Okello and his colleagues offer, he told me, is explicitly based on "God's way"—farming in God's way, treating family members in God's way, caring for others in God's way— rather than following the destructive patterns of behavior that were instilled during the war.

> Wherever we go we try to link the Biblical aspect of livelihood to apply to work and to the life of the community. We do not segregate [by religion] in our training programs—some of the youth are born-again, some are Muslim, some are Protestant, some are even traditionalist. But we counsel them in the Biblical way—and when you go to the Qur'an you get the same message, [to respect] everyone's humanity. (Okello 2014)

The work of the Northern Uganda initiative begins by contacting local government at the district and sub-county level, then continues by building a network of contacts in each parish and in each of its villages. Elders and community leaders are informed that the initiative seeks to offer help to young people aged 16–35 who have suffered as a result of the LRA conflict, and "the local leaders are then the ones to identify the youth who are most vulnerable." But these nominations are supplemented by further inquiries and by what Okello calls a "transect walk," using the term that ecologists use when they conduct a field survey of native species, in order to find those most in need of assistance.

> It is very common here that the most vulnerable are being left out. When you don't have high self-esteem, you don't tend to go and socialize with others. You tend to isolate yourself. In this category are the disabled, the mentally ill, maybe the former child soldiers. So it is our job to carry out a transect walk to identify them. (Okello 2014)

Moses Rubangageyo Okello's Story

Okello himself is an extraordinary example of the transformation of the lives of northern Ugandans in the past decades. During the early years of the conflict he had been a student at a boys' boarding school in Gulu, Sir Samuel Baker Secondary School, which is named for the British governor who established British dominance in the Ugandan interior—the man we met in Chapter 2, who claimed to have stolen his wife from a Bucharest slave market.

Abducted at age 16, Okello served as a soldier in the LRA rebel force for 18 years, a story that has been recounted in Matthew Green's *The Wizard of the Nile* (Green 2009; Green identifies him only as "Moses," without his family names, in ch. 12). In our interview in 2012, he recounted some of the horrors that he experienced.

> From my secondary school 39 were abducted. Out of the 39, 14 escaped before we reached Uganda. Then of the 25 who were still in captivity in Uganda, some died in battle, some died of sickness, and I was the only one who survived. Three of us were abducted from the same family, and I was with my two brothers until they both died in captivity. (Okello 2014)

Like other abductees Okello was subjected to beatings, brainwashing, and indoctrination about the justice of the LRA struggle and the brutality of UPDF military tactics. He provided what amounted to slave labor for his captors. Rules were strictly enforced, infractions punished harshly.

Some of the rules, he said, were "good rules," such as the bans on smoking, drinking alcohol, and sexual relations with anyone who was not assigned to you as one of your wives. Bible texts were used to justify severe penalties: didn't Jesus tell us to cut off a hand or pluck out an eye if it does wrong?

Other rules were more arbitrary: do not shout when crossing a river, for example, and do not sit on rocks. Eating shea butter was forbidden, and new recruits were prohibited from eating chicken. "There were countless rules." But gradually the indoctrination had its intended effect, the beatings stopped, and his living conditions became better as he showed that he could be trusted to complete tasks assigned to him.

Okello rose in the LRA ranks and became a two-star lieutenant. At one point some of the LRA officers who had abducted him were part of the unit that he commanded.

I was leading those who had abducted me. Some of them were under my direct control. But I was not seeking revenge. I took the Bible point of view because I realized that they were forced to do what they did, against their will. So I cannot blame them for what they have done because they were ordered to do so. . . . At one point the same commander who led the soldiers who abducted me was under my direct control, and his wife was the one cooking my food, because he was a junior officer and I was the highest-ranking officer. I don't know how he was feeling! It is very funny that someone whom you abducted can become like your father who keeps you. (Okello 2014)

Okello and other LRA officers were sent to Khartoum for a year of training in intelligence. He was instructed not to say that he was affiliated with the LRA, or even that he was Ugandan—"you are just a civilian who is doing the training." Training programs of this sort were part of the Sudanese government's covert support for the LRA, its ally against the Museveni regime. Okello lived in housing that was arranged for him by LRA contacts, and it was clear that any attempt at escape would fail. "There is always someone spying on you. So even if you are alone, you are not really alone."

Despite these measures, one of his friends succeeded in making contact with a UN staff member, who made arrangements for his escape. "He was taken to the U.S. and went for a medical course, and up to now he is in the U.S. So you can say we were two who survived [and moved on], but he is no longer in Uganda." Moses did not follow his friend's example but instead returned to LRA camps in Uganda after completing his training.

Okello was selected as an LRA representative to the peace negotiations of the early 2000s, and on several occasions he was permitted to leave LRA camps and travel to towns for meetings. He did not attempt to escape at that time, either, even though a Catholic who represented ARLPI in these talks, Father Carlos Rodriguez Soto, pleaded with him to do so. The amnesty period under the law passed in 2000 had run out, and it was widely feared that officers who escaped from the LRA would be prosecuted for war crimes rather than welcomed home.

In March 2004—after Parliament had restored the offer of amnesty—Okello took an LRA child soldier with him and left the rebel camp where he was stationed, explaining to his fellow officers that he needed to go to the nearest hospital to obtain medical treatment for a bullet wound he had sustained in a recent skirmish. They walked all night until he reached the outskirts of the town of Pader. There he gave the boy who had accompanied him a school uniform to wear in place of his military uniform and sent him ahead to a village, instructing him to return with someone from the town who was ready to help ensure safe passage for both of them. Okello encountered an LRA "mobile force" along the road, he related, "but because I was dressed in my full uniform and was walking slowly with my gun they just saluted me."

Evidently the boy could not find anyone to assist, or perhaps he simply slipped away when he had the chance. Moses continued alone, all the way into the town. Government troops stationed there to watch out for rebels did not stop him, he said, because the uniforms worn by LRA and UPDF officers were so similar that they were often confused. He made his way to a clinic, where he identified himself as an escaped LRA officer and requested transfer to a hospital in Gulu for treatment of his injuries.

By chance the UN worker who received this request in Gulu had been among those kidnapped and later released by the LRA several years earlier. He recognized Okello's name as that of the officer who had been his captor and who, he recalled, had treated the hostages kindly and helped to arrange their release. This UN worker, Okello related, came directly to Pader, got him a place on a UN helicopter for the short flight to Gulu, and contacted his family.

Like other returnees, Okello was assigned to a rehabilitation camp. But the counseling provided there, he said, was not well suited to the very different situations of LRA returnees.

How can you mix a commander and a one-week recruit and counsel them together? "Oh, we are so sorry for your suffering in the bush, we know they were always beating you, you had to walk such long distances every day." That was not the experience of someone who had stayed more than six months. After that time you would be relieved from all of that stress, because by that point you have given up thinking of your past life and everything has become positive.

And the counselor told me, "Moses, you have stayed for so long in the bush that you cannot go back to school. The only option for you is to learn bricklaying and building." For someone who was already in secondary school when he was abducted! (Okello 2014)

Father Carlos gave him more encouragement and introduced him to another counselor at the Caritas counseling center. Soon Okello made his own plans to assist those whose lives had been disrupted by the war: he invited a group of the formerly abducted to come together and create the Information for Youth Empowerment Program, with support from the Justice and Peace Commission of the Catholic archdiocese. They focused especially on the difficulties that some returnees faced in their families.

> Some returning from captivity were being rejected. "You came back with a rebel child, and we cannot accept you in our family." These were the kinds of things that we were fighting for in that organization.

Still active today, the organization provides a variety of services to the formerly abducted and their families, including vocational training and "peace camps" in which music, drama, and poetry are used to help overcome the war's effects and motivate members to build new lives (Information for Youth Empowerment Program n.d.). This project is now integrated with the CARE-funded northern Uganda youth initiative that has been described earlier.

Many of Okello's relatives and acquaintances in Gulu, aware of his having been promoted to the rank of lieutenant in the LRA, urged him to take a commission in the government army and continue to serve. That was the path that was followed by many returning LRA soldiers and officers. Their training had taught them many needed skills, and the pay was comparatively good. Moreover, their families sometimes preferred that they stay away from home.

> Just continue with the UPDF, they told me. We can see you are a lieutenant, and by the end of this month you will be collecting a

salary. And I said "No!"—a very big No. I have fought for eight years, and I am not going to go back and fight again. You think I am trying to run away from responsibility and I will disturb you for fees if I go back to school. But I am back home, I am going to stay with my mother, and I will not disturb anyone. (Okello 2014)

Okello defied the advice of those who believed his educational prospects had been destroyed by his years with the LRA. He enrolled in a computer course, began selling fish from his family fish pond and vegetables from his farming plot, and used the money to start a small business. A year later, he enrolled once more in secondary school, and a few years later he was accepted into a BA program in development studies at the newly established Gulu University. Since then he has continued to serve as an officer of the youth empowerment organization in Gulu that he had established, while also assuming the role of field coordinator for the CARE-funded program in two other districts nearby.

The remarkable career of Moses Rubangageyo Okello abducted as a young man, raised to a high rank in the LRA rebel army, denied access to education because of his experiences, then defying expectations to become a highly educated community leader—offers a dramatic example of the capacity of former rebels to rebuild their lives and contribute to their communities. When others told him that his mind had been warped, and his future prospects dimmed, by his time as a rebel commander, he set out to prove them wrong. And many hundreds of young people in northern Uganda have benefited from his vision and his determination.

Remaining Challenges

It is easy to fall into the trap, said Rev. Patrick Lumumba, of expecting that goals embraced by leaders at the top levels of each religious community will be quickly embraced by their local communities. Sustainable development does not work that way, he said: "The religious leaders at the grassroots—the reverends, the priests, the imams—they seem not to understand what the top leaders are saying and doing" (Lumumba 2014). So a great deal of ARLPI's effort is devoted to nurturing local leadership and ensuring that each community is fully committed to the programs offered on the local level.

In each village a group is created that will participate together in training programs and development initiatives. Frequently the most urgent need identified by village residents is for better financial services, since the nearest bank may be a day's journey away. Village Savings and Loan Associations (VSLAs) are established in which community residents can pool their money and request short-term loans, to be used either for agricultural supplies or to purchase goods for resale in the market. When a group is being formed, ARLPI staff or local community members whom they have trained offer education in budgeting and accounting.

> We want a group that can be easily managed, so the maximum number is 30 and the minimum is 15. Currently there are 110 groups that have been formed in Moyo and Amuru districts. (Okello 2014)

Many more examples of grassroots community development in postwar Uganda could be cited, but the examples provided above are sufficient to give a sense of the situation today. After more than 20 years of intractable and unimaginably destructive conflict between a ruthless rebel military force and an equally undisciplined national army, northern Uganda is at last at peace. IDP camps are empty, farms are yielding harvests, and village markets are busy centers of economic and social life once more. Many problems of poverty, disease, and land conflict remain, but the residents of the region no longer live in fear, and their children are no longer in danger of being abducted and forced to become child soldiers.

Northern Uganda remains one of the poorest regions of the country, however, and agricultural productivity is far below pre-war levels. Families disrupted by the war struggle to overcome suspicion and restore trust. Schools are poorly supplied and understaffed. Many roads are nearly impassable, and water and sanitation systems in the towns and cities are woefully inadequate.

In this context ARLPI continues its efforts to bring healing on every level. When one of his colleagues complained that the government in Kampala continues to favor the south over the north in its development assistance, Paul Rubangageyo Okello responded with a forceful reminder that economic assistance is not enough.

> Everybody is talking about infrastructural rehabilitation, and no one is paying attention to social rehabilitation. They think that because the gun is silent everything is OK. But when the people are psychologically not well, we will destroy what has been achieved in minutes.
>
> Our communities are struggling with three situations right now. One is shame. The second is guilt. And the third is livelihood. (Okello 2014)

To restore means of livelihood without addressing the problems of shame and guilt, or to try to achieve economic recovery without social rehabilitation, he insisted, is a recipe for the collapse of society.

Monsignor Odong addressed the same theme in different words when he spoke about the importance of restoring cultural as well as material well-being, words that have been quoted in part in an earlier chapter:

> Another impact [of the war] was the social disintegration of Acholi culture. When you move a family away from its home, village education becomes difficult. In our culture every family has a gathering in the evening around a fire. It is like a classroom—and it is like the Parliament. All the members of the family gather to have their meal and to share about their experiences of the day. And the parents are like the moderators, like the professors who listen carefully to the experience of the children.

If the children admit to doing mischief—stealing a chicken, perhaps—then the parents tell them why it is wrong. Their conversations build relationships between young and old and lend support to shared values. But when children are taken from their families, whether they are forced into a rebel army or merely crowded together in an IDP camp, there is no more "factory of society" around the evening fire circle.

> This social disintegration did not do us any good. It is a blow to the culture of the Acholi. We lost some of our values. (Odong 2014)

If the tradition of a family recounting its daily experience each evening was sacrificed during the war, perhaps we can think of the work of ARLPI as creating a much bigger circle around a more inclusive fire. Not just the members of a family or clan but the members of all the major religious communities of the region have been able to work together to reaffirm their values and address the loss of social integration caused by a quarter-century of war. By means of this study I hope to extend the invitation of the courageous and persistent activists in the interfaith peace movement of northern Uganda to sit together around a fire circle that spans the oceans, in order to learn from their example of locally grounded, collaborative, and many-dimensional healing after conflict.

Notes

1. "Jiggers," or "chigoe fleas," are parasitic insects native to the tropical regions of the New World that were inadvertently introduced to sub-Saharan Africa. They burrow into exposed skin on victims' feet, where they lay eggs that produce painful lesions and loss of toenails or toes. Untreated infections that result may be fatal. These parasites, species *Tunga penetrans,* are unrelated, despite their similar behavior and similar common name, to the "chiggers" of temperate zones, including North America. The latter are species of the genus *Trombiculidae,* small mites that also produce irritation in their hosts by penetrating the skin and laying eggs, but the result is nothing worse than a short-lived itchy rash.
2. CARE, based in Atlanta, works globally to alleviate problems caused by poverty and lobby for more equitable laws and policies. Originally the "Cooperative for American Remittances to Europe," it sent "CARE packages" to aid those who lost homes and family members in the Second World War. Later it became the "Cooperative for Assistance and Relief Everywhere," and eventually it was decided to employ what was formerly an acronym simply as an organization name (CARE n.d.).

8

Healing Conflict and Building Community

*Many international organizations started pulling away, thinking that peace
had returned to northern Uganda. It was a huge challenge, coupled with the
international financial crisis—money became very thin and we had to cut
back on our activities. But resettlement and rehabilitation is a time when we
need a lot of support. So many of them said, no, we are withdrawing, there is
relative peace. For us it was a big challenge . . . .*

*It's not only during the emergency that the need is there, but we need support
after the conflict is over, because that is when people need to rebuild their lives,
rebuild their homes, and come back to that sense of just being a human being,
providing what they need not just physically but psychologically, helping people
to overcome conflicts [family conflicts, land disputes, etc.], showing that there is
hope for the future. That is what the religious leaders are doing.*

—John Bosco Komanech
(J. B. Komanech 2014)

*It is not just a matter of the guns' silence, but what the gun has done to the
people.*

There are deep wounds to the mind and the heart that politics cannot heal.

—Monsignor Matthew Odong
(Odong 2016)

A STORY RELATED ON my most recent visit to Uganda by two people
who have lent invaluable assistance to me in this project, Dr. Margaret
Angucia and Sister Lucy Dora Akello, calls attention to several unusual
features of the civil war in northern Uganda and its aftermath. I recount

it here to set the tone for this final chapter in which we will explore the significance of the interfaith activism of ARLPI and the lessons that can be learned from its work in seeking a better understanding of structures and systems of consent and accountability in societies under stress.

Both Margaret and Lucy were young novices in a Catholic order, the Little Sisters of St. Francis, in Gulu during some of the worst years of the LRA occupation in the 1990s. Both lost family members and friends to LRA abduction or raids, but they were not themselves the victims of such violence. All this I knew from many previous conversations. But when we met once again in 2016, the two women related a story from that period that I had not heard before, with a startling postscript.

One night, they recalled, all the novices were awakened by gunshots and shouting in the school compound. Soldiers had broken the gate open to raid the novitiate for supplies. The Mother Superior and her colleagues offered no resistance. They met the soldiers in the yard of the compound and asked what they were seeking. Now go back to your lodgings, the sisters told them, and the items you have asked for will be brought to you. The soldiers complied.

The more senior members of the order went to the dormitory where the young women slept and told them to dress quickly and then gather up the items that the soldiers had demanded: mattresses, blankets, soap and food supplies. The novices left the compound in a group and carried their loads to the soldiers' place of lodging—not stopping along the way, or taking an indirect route, for fear the soldiers would observe this and attack them. When they arrived. they were instructed to leave all the materials outside in a designated place, from which the soldiers would fetch them. They did as they were told, completed their errand, returned to their dormitory, and tried to sleep.

The novices could not tell whether the soldiers were from the LRA or from the national army, Margaret and Lucy added. Their uniforms were very similar, as we have noted above. This was what made it possible for Moses Okello to walk past a UPDF army outpost in his LRA officers' uniform when he made his escape. And in this instance, after all, it was the dead of night. Their experience was not unique: in many instances, the victims of attacks during the 20-year conflict could not be sure whether the soldiers who were firing at them and kidnapping children were agents of the government or of the rebels.

Just a few years ago, Margaret related, she met a man who had served in the Ugandan army in the north who told her that he remembered having taken part in activities of this kind. When she described the nighttime raid on her convent, he said, yes, he remembered it as one of the actions of his unit. He had been part of the group that came to the novitiate to demand mattresses and food.

Why, asked Margaret, did you do this? Because the government was not paying us our salary, he said, or providing for us in any way. We were told that if we wanted food and supplies we must go and get them for ourselves. So we had no choice but to use the threat of our guns to obtain them. Today, retired from military service, he lives in the community among former soldiers, former rebels, and victims of their attacks. Today, he said—like every other resident of northern Uganda—he simply wants to live in peace.

The Results of the Northern Uganda Experiment

In the preceding chapters we have looked closely at what I have called an extended experiment in practical political philosophy, a venture in which community leaders facing seemingly insoluble problems of civil war undertook to restore order, when those entrusted with public office in their nation and in their region had utterly failed to do so. The emergence of ARLPI and its effectiveness in both disseminating accurate information about the conflict and working toward its resolution provide a remarkable field study in the relationship between political power, moral authority, and credibility in a community.

The response of the government of Uganda and its armed forces to the challenge of a northern rebellion, one that initially described itself as a movement for spiritual renewal, was to dispatch a military force to crush the insurgents. Against Alice Lakwena and her Holy Spirit Mobile Force, this strategy achieved a quick and resounding success. The small rebel army approaching Kampala was surrounded, defeated, and dispersed. Against Joseph Kony's Lord's Resistance Army, however, the same tactics produced a 20-year stalemate.

It was the worst possible sort of stalemate, one marked by frequent outbursts of violence. Sympathy for the cause of the rebels only grew stronger when undisciplined government soldiers took out their frustrations on the residents of the north, using tactics as brutal as those of their opponents. Even after peace talks had at last begun in Juba in 2004, the president of Uganda still insisted, in a conversation with a UN representative, that "there will only be a military solution" (BSN 2008).

As the actions of the Museveni regime eroded public confidence in its commitment and its ability to restore peace, the war raged on, and northern Ugandans sank deeper into poverty and isolation. Political leadership in the Acholi sub-region was not very effective, either: members of Parliament representing the areas most affected by LRA depredations were mostly silent, unwilling to take a forthright stand on behalf of their constituents and risk appearing to side with the rebels. But when they avoided direct confrontation with the Museveni administration and failed to challenge its misleading claims about imminent victory, they seemed to be ignoring the suffering of the people.

A study commissioned by the United States Agency for International Development in 2001 came to the conclusion that, during the period of the conflict, there had been a "leadership vacuum" that was "heightened by the fragmentation within the Acholi community," which prevented the elected representatives from speaking with a consistent voice or representing their peoples' interests effectively. Until 1995 there were no opposition parties in Uganda, as has been noted above. After that date other parties were permitted, but the ruling party, the National Resistance Movement, took steps to maintain closer control than ever over Uganda's political life.

A review of the political and economic situation in Uganda by a distinguished American political scientist, the late Joel Barkan, offered a trenchant assessment of the deterioration of democracy in Uganda in a 2009 article. In Tanzania, he noted, there is a de facto ruling party: the Chama cha Mapundizi party has won at least a 70 percent majority in every multi-party election since 1995. Its party structure and practices are collaborative, however, and government policies usually benefit from discussion and intense debate among party leaders.[1]

In marked contrast, Uganda has evolved into a one-party-dominant system in which all major decisions are made by Museveni. Politics has degenerated into a system of neopatrimonial rule reminiscent of Africa prior to the 1990s. Once hailed as one of the new leaders of Africa, Museveni governs Uganda as Daniel arap Moi and Mobuto Sese Seko governed Kenya and Zaire at the height of their power: through patronage and kleptocracy. There is, however, an important difference. Whereas Moi and Mobutu paid no heed to the laws of economics and resisted macroeconomic reform, Museveni has continued to embrace them to ensure continued inflows of donor assistance, especially budget support. (Barkan 2009, 81)

The dysfunction and autocracy that had emerged in Kampala undermined democratic institutions in regional government as well. The door had been opened to opposition parties by the 1995 Constitution, generating favorable publicity with foreign donors, but the opening was never wide enough for any credible challenge to the NRM regime to pass through. In effect, the political institutions of Uganda had failed to keep faith with the promises of its constitution—that government would be truly representative of the people and responsive to their needs. Nongovernmental institutions stepped in and sought to do the work the government was not doing.

Recall that in 1998 Uganda's star was rising rapidly in the eyes of the West. It was in that year that President Clinton hailed President Museveni for his contributions to the "African Renaissance," and Secretary of State Madeleine Albright cited him as "a beacon of hope" for the continent. But US observers had little knowledge of, and little concern for, the depredations undergone by the people of the north. In 2001 a report for USAID confirmed that, where government had failed, other nonpolitical organizations were seeking to raise awareness and bring resolution.

As the NRM gradually allowed the resumption of political activities, a deep gulf emerged between Acholi elected members of parliament and government ministers and local state agencies. In the absence of clear leadership, the ARLPI seemed ready to fill the vacuum as a locus of community leadership and a bridge-builder between the Acholi and central government. (Khadialaga 2001, 3–4)

How did ARLPI come to occupy this role, that of the principal channel for communication between the government of Uganda and the people of the Acholi region? Not through the processes or institutions of politics, certainly. There were no public debates, declarations of candidacy for office, or elections that validated the role of ARLPI as advocate of the people or intermediary with the national government. Certainly its leaders never sought legislative or executive powers of any kind, nor did they request or receive financial support from the national or local government. From the beginning, their aim was simply to initiate dialogue and facilitate reconciliation.

In the absence of an effective local government, faced with an insensitive and sometimes openly repressive and abusive national government, ARLPI emerged as the most effective agent in advancing common goals, in effect taking the place of elected and appointed government officials who had failed to fulfill their responsibilities. The respect they received from residents, and the cooperation they eventually obtained, at great risk, from both rebel leaders and government officials, were not bestowed through either ballots or appointment letters. Rather, they were earned by concerted and courageous action. It is evident, moreover, that the interfaith character of the organization greatly enhanced the credibility and the influence of its work.

In the introduction to this study we posed four broad questions about the functioning of political and social structures—four questions that the "experiment" of ARLPI can help us to answer. Let us return to them now, and then reflect, in closing, on some of the factors that have made it possible for the organization to achieve as much as it has.

Can the divisions and power imbalances of colonialism be overcome after independence?

This was the first question asked earlier. The historical sketch of the British protectorate and its emergence as an independent nation provided in Chapter 2 suggests the answer: neither an unqualified yes nor an unqualified no. The history of Uganda, like that of many other former colonies, shows that the transition from colonial rule to independence may bring fewer changes than anticipated. Too much power entrusted to a centralized administration, too many key administrative positions dispensed on the basis of personal loyalty rather than capability, and exploitation of ethnic divisions in ways that reward some and penalize others—all of these familiar features of colonial regimes remain evident in many independent African nations today. New constitutions that mandate an open and democratic polity often prove to be more aspiration than reality.

Needless to say, this is not a problem unique to Africa. Such distortions and abuses are common in every sort of social and political order, on every continent, in every age. Indeed, some of the traditional kingdoms that predated colonial rule in Africa were even more autocratic than the European governors who displaced them; and where nepotism is usually considered a defect in a modern government, it is a defining characteristic of delegated authority under a ruling clan. Other traditional forms of rule across the continent, on the other hand, incorporated systems of debate and requirements for consensus that adhere closely to the guiding principles of liberal democracy.

Whatever the preexisting structures of community governance, colonial rulers imposed more centralized control, acting as agents of a king or parliament a continent away. Colonizers believed they were entitled to their authority, as the representatives of progress, science, and European civilization. Such claims were no longer credible by the mid-twentieth century—whether they came from the mouths of Europeans or those of emerging African leaders—but the pattern of authoritarian rule often outlived its onetime rationalization.

Yet colonial rule did come to an end, and African nations achieved their independence. For the past half-century, they have set their own course. In Uganda and elsewhere, neocolonial influences remain strong: patterns of international trade, opportunities for higher education, ties of literature and culture, and the national language all link the region that was once part of British East Africa with the United Kingdom today. The conditions of other former colonies, whether they were British or French or Portuguese, exhibit similar continuities.

But the laws of Uganda today have been drafted and enacted by Ugandans, its institutions built and maintained by citizens of an independent nation. The people of Uganda's dozens of ethnic communities who lived within the boundaries of the former protectorate work today alongside immigrants from Europe and Asia, none having superior status under the law, all entitled to basic constitutional rights. In business enterprises Africans report to European supervisors and vice versa; in churches Europeans look for guidance to African priests and pastors and vice versa. Traces of colonial patterns and divisions remain discernible, but they no longer dominate the cultural or political life of African nations such as Uganda. So our answer to the first question must be a qualified yes. The patterns of colonial division are not ineradicable.

Can ethnic divisions and the resulting mistrust be overcome to achieve common goals?

This question highlights one of the most persistent challenges to democratic institutions across many regions of Africa, Uganda included. As we have seen, the LRA movement arose and gained support as a result of longstanding patterns of neglect and hostility directed by southern ethnic groups, who had won control of the national government, toward the Acholi, Lango, Teso, and other northern groups. The history of the Ugandan military, in particular, demonstrates again and again the dangers that arise when army officers and soldiers are drawn primarily from one ethnic group. A powerful instrument of state control is likely to become a vehicle for repression of other groups that are perceived as enemies or rivals.

Ethnic differences often coincide with political as well as geographic divisions, as is evident in the poor showing of the candidates of Museveni's NRM party in parliamentary elections in the north. Even while the NRM has put itself forward as the party of all Ugandans, regardless of ethnicity and religion, its leaders have slipped into ethnic abuse from time to time, for example by describing the Acholi as an inherently violent people. Comparing a particular group of voters to cannibalistic grasshoppers trapped in a bottle is not an effective way to win their trust. Yet in Uganda these conflicts have never led to ethnic wars of the sort that its neighbors such as the DRC and Rwanda have witnessed in recent decades.

An important example of the possibility of overcoming these differences can be found precisely in the work of ARLPI, which has succeeded in building bridges across political, religious, and ethnic lines.

Its core constituency is among the Acholi, to be sure, and its principal aim is to improve their lives and bring healing to their communities. Both the Kampala government and the members of neighboring ethnic groups have viewed it with suspicion because of this alignment. But in its activities ARLPI has shown that its concern extends far beyond the welfare of the Acholi alone. Its patient work of advocacy and direct assistance, directed not simply to helping the Acholi but to bringing healing to the nation, have earned the respect and cooperation of others both within Uganda and abroad.

Two other questions posed in the introduction remain to be discussed:

Can competing religious communities find common ground against conflict?

What do "consent" and "accountability" mean in religious and ethnic communities, and what do they mean under an autocratic regime?

Of these two, the first question was answered unambiguously in the affirmative by the "experiment" that has been the focus of this entire study, the formation of ARLPI. We will return to this question below, in the closing section of this chapter: there we will take note of the ways in which an organization with no precedent in modern Ugandan history, having few resources, faced with suspicion and mistrust on all sides, nevertheless succeeded in helping advance its goals of peace and reconciliation.

The fourth question is a complex and difficult one. But we have already discussed briefly a particular objective of ARLPI work, one that was identified as a priority from its founding, that can bring this question into clearer focus. This is the amnesty provision, which did not initially have broad public support but which proved indispensable to the resolution of the conflict. In this example we see some of the ways in which nongovernment agents can sometimes do the work that government has been unable to do, thus earning a public legitimacy that is grounded more in the social and moral than in the political realm. This element in the resolution of the LRA conflict warrants further attention in this closing chapter before we sum up the accomplishments of ARLPI.

Questions of Justice and the Amnesty Law

Recall that in 1999–2000, when ARLPI helped to persuade president and parliament to enact a general amnesty, the civil war had already raged for more than a decade, and previous efforts to bring about a resolution had ended in complete failure and renewed violence. The difficulties that ARLPI leaders faced in advocating both for amnesty and for direct negotiations were daunting.

For decades, indeed for centuries, communication between the Christian and Muslim communities in Uganda had been infrequent, and mistrust had been prevalent. The interfaith organization struggled first of all to win the support of its leaders' own congregations. From the standpoint of the opposing sides of the civil war, there was widespread suspicion that the religious leaders were only pretending to be neutral. The Museveni government and its military officers, reflecting centuries of ethnic division between south and north, suspected that the religious leaders' loyalty to the Acholi people made them rebel sympathizers. Officers of the LRA, on the other hand, feared that, in conveying peace overtures from the UPDF, pastors and imams were either the willing agents or the unwitting dupes of the government, and in either case were aiding its military campaign against them. Ceasefires and peace talks, after all, might be ruses intended to put them off their guard and enable the government soldiers to find their camps. Both sides had agreed on ceasefires before, and each side had, on one occasion or another, been the first to violate them.

The work of ARLPI offers an instructive case study in how to bring about significant change in the life of a community against overwhelming odds. It is, in effect, an example of how ideals of justice and peace can be translated into reality even when reality is stubbornly uncooperative. What we witness in the work of ARLPI leaders is a bold and creative application of a practical sort of philosophy and theology to a situation in which all the parties involved appeared to be bent on a destructive course of action they had pursued for decades.

But what sort of resolution, we may wonder, should they seek? What would be a just and fair solution to the conflict? In a situation where a region and a nation are struggling to restore peace after a protracted conflict, it is very difficult to discern just what justice demands. The questions that arise cannot be resolved by invoking simple principles of fairness. Debate over amnesty brought these questions to public attention and provoked contentious debate.

Should the former commanders of a rapacious rebel force like the LRA be brought to trial, first of all, rather than granted amnesty? If an offer of amnesty is judged to be essential for hastening a return to normal life, should it be given to the formerly abducted but withheld from individuals who joined the LRA voluntarily? Should amnesty be refused to anyone who ordered or supervised war crimes, or only to senior commanders?

Equally difficult questions—moral rather than legal—carry right into homes disrupted by war. What is the obligation of family members who bear lasting scars from LRA violence to young men returning from a decade or more in Kony's remote military camps? Can siblings and parents and extended family members be expected to extend a welcome today to those who carried out unspeakable crimes as soldiers in Kony's rebel army, having been abducted as children and separated from their families for decades? Do these returnees deserve equal consideration with others in matters of land tenure, agricultural assistance, and education? Should they receive an additional measure of help, given the harsh circumstances under which they lived? Or should they take second place behind those who were their victims during the war?

These questions continue to be debated on every level of Ugandan society even today, from the halls of parliament to the family compound. They raise intractable questions of fairness and give rise to competing claims for social resources today. On the one hand, justice demands that those responsible for heinous crimes be held accountable for what they have done. On the other hand, rebuilding communities after a quarter-century of conflict requires unusual and sometimes unpopular initiatives in reconciliation and bridge building.

The amnesty law enacted by the Ugandan Parliament and signed by its president, taking effect in 2000, granted immunity from prosecution for acts dating back to 1986. It was highly controversial, as we have noted earlier. After assisting tens of thousands from LRA camps to return home, the law was allowed to expire. This was one of the reasons why former LRA commander Thomas Kwoyelo still faces criminal charges in a Uganda court: when he was apprehended the amnesty law was not in effect. But then a renewal was enacted, and allowed to expire, and reenacted. An amnesty provision remains in effect today, although the flow of former soldiers requesting it has slowed to a trickle.

Given the poor communication lines between the remaining Kony forces in the bush and the towns of the region in the years when the amnesty provision was in effect, it was difficult for anyone considering a return home to be certain that he would not be subject to criminal charges, in Uganda or in an international tribunal. Moreover, the changes and uncertainties of the amnesty law lent credibility to the warnings of LRA leaders that the amnesty offer was a sham. Anyone lured by the government's deceptions to return home, they warned, would only be thrown into prison to await trial—or, worse yet, would be the object of summary justice meted out by residents who lacked the patience to wait for the courts to act.

Nevertheless, from the late 1990s, when they began pressing Parliament to enact an amnesty offer, down to the present day, the religious leaders of the Acholi region joined hands across longstanding religious barriers and conveyed a consistent message to both of the warring parties, at great risk to themselves and to their supporting communities. The message was stated in slightly different ways by most of the individuals whom I interviewed. Paul Rubangakene put it this way:

> One very important activity has been peace building, or what we call fostering reconciliation. About 93 percent of our population is affected by this war. There are people who were abducted and they know their abductors.
>
> Some people have come back, and some still have not. If I know that it was Sister [pointing to Sister Lucy] who abducted my children, and she is back, but my children are not yet back, definitely my family will cause problems to Sister.
>
> But the church played a very great role in fostering reconciliation so that people could accept the situation, because Jesus has taught us to forgive. And if you ask yourself how long you should keep forgiving, Jesus gave the answer, and that is "70 times 7 times." So that must be a part of our life.

One initiative taken by the religious leaders after the LRA withdrawal, he added, was to go to places where many had died during the conflict and invite members of all religious groups to join in mourning the losses they had suffered and in praying for healing.

> And this is where the church played a powerful role making sure that the people all see themselves as human beings, by these prayers and by doing charity and other activities. In this way . . . we were bringing the people together, working together regardless of your religious denomination, which was a very good thing for us. (Rubangakane 2014)

John Bosco Komanech emphasized that reconciliation is achieved in a very different way in traditional African communities than in the West. When someone in Europe or North American is wronged by someone else, he observed, if you cannot work out your differences person to person you are likely to appeal to the legal system to resolve the dispute. In the West, he said, this is the normal practice: an impartial arbitrator who has no connection with the parties will listen to the arguments of each party, render a judgment, and expect everyone to comply. In Uganda, he said, conflicts are resolved very differently.

> When I do something wrong to you, we do not go for a legal procedure. There is a process, and it does not involve me and you only. It brings in the clan heads and the people, so that we can sort out the problem together and learn what is needed to live together. Maybe in the end we say, "okay, fine—your clan and my clan can intermarry so that we forget the past." (J. B. Komanech 2014)

This is how reconciliation can be achieved, he said: through a process in which community leaders and community members come to agreement on how to go forward. "Reconciliation is a very strong and powerful tool for bringing us back together," he added.

Issa Mubarak, a Muslim man who spent four years in LRA captivity, made the same point with a personal example and a reference to his sacred scriptures. He is married to a woman who had been forced to bear Joseph Kony's children, now being raised as part of one family along with Issa's child.

She is reading and studying, and she is leading a normal life, and
I have told her: you know what problems I have had, and I know
what problems you have had, and it is better that we live together now
without any conflict. And when I look at those children [fathered by
Kony], I know for certain that they are my children. They are here
because this is what God has planned for us.

Issa related a story from the Qur'an of someone who welcomed a
stranger to his home, gave him water, fed him, and gave him supplies
for his journey onward.

Then the Prophet Mohammed told him, "Do you know that you
were caring for the angels of Allah? So I tell you that from today you
are blessed." This is the teaching of the Qur'an, that you must care
for anyone who is in need. If you do not help, or you hurt someone,
you are an enemy of God. (Mubarak 2014)

Sheik Musa Khalil, leader of the Gulu Muslim community, emphasized
how critical it was that all of the religious communities join together
after the LRA withdrawal and support each other in proclaiming the
same central message: it is time now to forgive. To the representatives of government, foreign NGO staff, and members of their own
communities, the leaders of ARLPI insisted, "We must forgive ninety
times, or is it one hundred times . . ." Are you thinking of the saying of
Jesus, I asked, that we should forgive seventy times seven? "Yes! That is
it! In the Qur'an it is ninety times, and in the Bible it is seventy times
seven." Listening to a Muslim leader trying to remember whether he
was quoting the New Testament or the Qur'an was a startling confirmation of the close ties that have been formed between formerly divided religious communities as they work together to heal the wounds
of war (Khalil 2014).

Christian and Muslim leaders came together out of a common conviction that the military solution to the LRA insurgency, which had
been pursued with very little effect except to compound the suffering
of the people, would never bring peace, to say nothing of healing and
reconciliation. In no way did this amount to regarding the two warring
parties as equally for fault in the conflict. Without question, it was

Joseph Kony, following in the footsteps of Alice Lakwena, who bore the greatest responsibility for the abductions, maimings, and killings that had tormented the people of northern Uganda and driven them from their homes for nearly a quarter of a century. Kony's initial claim to be standing up for the rights of the Acholi against a repressive central government enhanced his credibility at the beginning of his insurrection, to be sure; and the harsh countermeasures taken by the national army only gave the residents of the region additional reasons to believe these claims. Yet it was Kony who decided within a few years to augment his forces through kidnapping and to turn young boys into merciless killers through misinformation and indoctrination. At no point did any of the leaders of ARLPI suggest that there was a moral equivalence between the depredations of the LRA and the abuses committed by the government. They simply asked that the violence committed by both parties be acknowledged—and then renounced, through a process that would lead to healing and renewal.

LRA leaders continued to see the religious leaders' demand for dialogue and a peace agreement as a cover for their complicity with the government. Military leaders in the UPDF saw the same initiatives as evidence that the loyalties of the priests, pastors and imams were with their Acholi ethnic group, not the nation of Uganda. Overcoming these misperceptions and the resulting mistrust was a challenging task. But ARLPI continued its work in the conviction that the crimes committed by both sides would come to an end only through dialogue and negotiation, not a continuation of the clash of army against army. Amnesty for LRA soldiers and commanders was a necessary step toward this resolution.

A blanket amnesty had already been effectively granted, after all, to commanders and soldiers of the UPDF who were guilty of abduction, rape, and killing—not in explicit legislation but simply in the government's rationalization that its forces' unfortunate excesses were provoked by the enemy's misconduct. UPDF soldiers' undisciplined behavior in government-directed campaigns, and their readiness to label anyone in an LRA-controlled area a rebel sympathizer, would never be acknowledged, let alone punished. Government reports, relayed to the world with few questions asked by international media, depicted the conflict as pitting a legitimate and disciplined national army against an unprincipled band of rebels. Many Ugandans knew better. Yet they also knew that only after immunity was offered to LRA soldiers could a cessation of hostilities be discussed.

What Brought Christians and Muslims Together

When Catholic, Protestant, and Muslim leaders joined together in 1997 and created an interfaith organization, ARLPI, they were moved to act by the suffering endured by all of the residents of the region as the LRA conflict dragged on into its second decade, with no prospect of peace in sight. Also essential to this remarkable venture in bridge building were the courage and the vision of individual religious leaders who reached out to each other for advice and assistance. To understand how this was possible, we will return briefly to some of the narratives I heard from participants in the work of the organization when I asked how its formation was possible.

ARLPI project officer Abdalah Latif Nasur, who joined the organization's staff many years after its beginnings, recalled the welcome that was extended to members of his Muslim community by Christians when they began organizing on the local level. Initially, he said, the barriers were high. After all, Catholics had come to Uganda as missionaries and established schools and clinics to serve fellow Catholics. Anglicans had done the same. Neither of the major Christian groups reached out to Muslims, except as prospects for conversion, and they had very little interaction with their neighboring Muslim communities. But when peace committees were organized at the sub-county level, he said, they included members of all of these communities.

> You will find that sometimes people are very rigid. But it is just a matter of making people to understand: we are the same tribe, we are the same color, we are all Africans, we are all northern Ugandans. So you are my brother. Sometimes we may be sons of the same father and you are Catholic and I am Muslim. But I respect your practice and you respect my practice.
>
> There has always been bias in the way [non-Muslim] people talk about Muslims. They have fixed ideas, maybe because of the preaching

that they hear, or the way religion was embraced in Uganda. But in northern Uganda, people have opened up to understand. Christians have opened up, and Muslims have opened up.

When the LRA was coming, it didn't matter whether you are a Protestant or a Muslim or a Catholic! And the religious leaders played a key role in bringing understanding. They moved away from their differences of belief and said, we are one people, we are for peace, we are for all of our people. They were sitting together, eating, chatting. At the beginning it was not easy for people to accept, and there was a lot of resistance from congregations, but over time they came to accept that this is how we must do our work. (Nasur 2014)

Monsignor Matthew Odong, one of those involved in the earliest activities of the organization, remembered that it was created during one of the darkest periods of the insurgency. His comments, quoted in part in an earlier chapter, identify several of the factors that brought the organizers together.

The conflict began way back in 1986, and then in the early 1990s it intensified. In 1997 we came together as religious leaders in the Acholi region. We took the name Acholi Religious Leaders Peace Initiative, as an interfaith group comprising Catholic, Anglican, Muslim, Orthodox, and, later, other denominations.

Now why did we come together? Because of the suffering of the people. The war forced people out of their homes into internal displacement camps. There were abductions into captivity, there were killings, rapes, and all forms of human rights violations. As religious leaders we saw people dying, and government was not doing much to end the war at that time.

Then we said: let us be the voice of the voiceless. We have to let the world know about the problems of northern Uganda. So we started doing several things. The pillars of our activities were, number one, advocacy, and number two, dialogue. We were opposed to military action as a solution to the conflict. Number three, we called for reconciliation as a means to end this war. And of course—number four—we offered humanitarian support.

We raised our voices far and wide to inform people of the problems here and to ask, can you come and help?

We will return below to the "four pillars" of ARLPI activity that Odong identifies here.

The United Nations was created, Odong observed, to protect human dignity around the world. But it paid no attention to what was happening in the Acholi region.

Where was the UN? Where was the African Union? From time to time you would hear that a Briton or an American or another individual from the West had been captured, and that was news. It would be on the BBC, it would be on CNN, the world would be talking about it. But then 100 of our people here would be killed, 200 people would be burned in their homes, and nobody would talk about it. Is our human dignity different from your human dignity? For twenty years that is what we observed. (Odong 2014)

Odong's bleak assessment of the failure of both national and international authorities to take measures to resolve the conflict, or even to acknowledge its seriousness, is corroborated in many studies of the contemporary history of Uganda. Political scientist Aili Marie Tripp, whose characterization of Uganda as an "authoritarian democracy" has been cited earlier, has this to say about the LRA conflict:

Nowhere has the Museveni regime failed its own people as much as in the north and northeast from 1986 to the present. The lack of serious effort to resolve the crisis in the north despite ample opportunities – not to mention the active sabotage of some of the peace talks – left the northerners feeling that they were being punished for the actions of previous governments, armies and armed groups.
    Most of the international community similarly failed Uganda . . . .
(Tripp 2010, 159)

Sheik Musa Khalil represented the Muslim community from the earliest stages of ARLPI advocacy and assistance. In our interview he recalled the failure of earlier efforts at negotiation and the setbacks that had impeded any attempt to restart them.

> The war dragged on [in the early 1990s] and the Muslim community was suffering, along with our Christian brothers, from abduction, maiming, and killing. During the 1994 peace dialogue that was led by [Member of Parliament] Betty Bigombe, our Muslim representative was part of the dialogue.

These negotiations, described in an earlier chapter, collapsed when the government abruptly demanded LRA surrender, and the rebels responded with renewed raids. Khalil picked up the story a few years later.

> Two of our elders were killed in 1996. Before this the cultural institutions tried to play a role in dialogue and mediation, but after the death of these two leaders they pulled out and there was a lull. There was no participation by any group in dialogue.
>
> Then in 1998 the religious leaders took courage and started playing a mediating role. We approached the government, and we met with President Museveni. He blessed our initiative and allowed us to try to mitigate the conflict. We played the role of bridge between the two fighting forces.
>
> We sustained the community with the one important weapon of forgiveness. We preached this seriously from sub-county to sub-county, from community to community. And we preached forgiveness from both the Bible and the Qur'an.
>
> We started working with the cultural institutions and the local leaders, and members of parliament became involved. We organized seminars that included all stakeholders, including the international community. We worked hand in hand with *Kacoke Madit* and with members of our community in the diaspora.

Kacoke Madit is the organization of expatriate Acholi residing in Europe and North America that has been mentioned earlier. It began meeting in London in 1997, and at its second meeting ARLPI representatives were invited to present the recommendations of their consultations with the people of the Acholi region. When it was formed, a significant number of Ugandans living abroad still regarded the LRA as a movement of freedom fighters who would help oust President Museveni. Some were secretly providing financial support to the LRA. ARLPI reports helped open their eyes to the atrocities that were being committed, out of sight of observers abroad. As a result, expatriate support for the LRA quickly dissolved, and the London conferences gave their support to ARLPI efforts for a negotiated settlement.

Khalil continued:

We did a lot of advocacy and lobbying. We traveled to the United States in 1999, as religious leaders of the northern region, and we met the Commissioner of African Affairs at the United Nations. We also met with Senators and members of Congress.

When we came back many international organizations began visiting and offering support for the pacification of the region. I thank God that we organized several consultative meetings with the rebel leaders, in the bush. And finally God made it possible for us to bring the government to talk with the rebels. (Khalil 2014)

ARLPI leaders also looked for ways of making the suffering of the people of the region more visible, countering the impression of many in Uganda and abroad that it was nothing more than a quarrel among the Acholi people that outsiders should ignore. We have taken note already of the columns of "night commuters," children who walked many miles each night from their villages to sleep in the safety that the towns afforded, and the decision of ARLPI leaders to join them. Monsignor Odong, who observed the effects of this gesture of solidarity, commented wryly: "The world did not seem to be listening to us, so we had to do some stupid things to draw attention to the suffering of the people. . . . And soon the media started reporting on the situation in northern Uganda—BBC was there, CNN was there, and then the rest." (Odong 2014).

Yet attacks on towns and villages continued. From the Seminary of the Sacred Heart, where Odong continues to serve as rector, 41 seminarians were abducted in May 2003. ("Seminarians" in this context refers to secondary-school students who are beginning a course of study with a view to eventual ordination to the priesthood, not students in post-secondary theological study.)

> After weeks, months, years, 30 of them returned—not all on the same day, but depending on their circumstances and their luck. Some escaped during a confrontation between the LRA and government troops; 11 are still not accounted for today. (Odong 2014)

ARLPI efforts to draw media attention were coordinated with advocacy work seeking to bring the two sides together for negotiations. Anyone who might be in a position to influence the Ugandan government was approached. "We were going and knocking on the doors of embassies" in Kampala, said Odong, hoping to persuade donor nations to hold the Ugandan government to account for its contribution to the violence. When the evidence mounted that the LRA was being supported and supplied by other nations, particularly Sudan, ARLPI leaders called for an international arms embargo to be imposed on that country until the conflict was resolved. The organization's leaders also made another advocacy trip abroad in 2003 to share information about the conflict, this time visiting Canada and several European countries as well as the United States.

Back home in Uganda, ARLPI leaders arranged meetings with President Museveni, as Khalil has described. Odong describes the message they conveyed.

> We met the president several times in the barracks [in Gulu] and also went to his home. We said, Your Excellency, you were once a guerrilla leader, and you understand the difficulty of a guerrilla war. We are sitting in an office like this, three of us, and someone is there who we do not see, and suddenly boom! We are gone. That is the nature of guerrilla war.
>
> At first the president undermined our movement against the insurrection, because he underestimated the strength of the rebels and said that they would be quickly defeated. But then it was proved beyond doubt that Sudan was behind the rebels, because Uganda had supported the SPLA (the Sudanese People's Liberation Army) against Sudan, so they supported the LRA as a form of retaliation.

We continued our advocacy. We had to do as Jesus says: don't come in, pray, pray, pray without getting tired. And we never got tired. We knew that the president had the power to open the door for dialogue, and finally we succeeded. He gave us permission to contact the leadership of the LRA and to initiate that dialogue. So we would go into the bush and meet them, but before going we would inform the military of where we are going—please don't send soldiers there, or our lives will be at risk. That was the agreement, and after several contacts with the rebels we finally managed to have new peace talks.

The united witness of leaders of all the major religious communities still did not persuade the government or the army to work toward a resolution rather than continue to press for victory. Recall the massive joint military campaign of 2002–2003 called Operation Iron Fist, billed as a final assault leading to defeat of the LRA but instead provoking renewed raids and reprisals. Even when peace talks were at last underway in Juba, according to UN observer Jan Egeland, President Museveni continued to insist that they could not succeed. "Let me be categorical—there will only be a military solution to this problem," he is reported to have told Egeland in 2004 (BSN 2008).

Yet the leaders of the religious communities held fast to their position: only a negotiated ceasefire followed by withdrawal and demobilization, according to terms acceptable to both sides, could bring an end to the suffering that had been inflicted on the people. Odong summed up the motivation for ARLPI advocacy and mediation: "Nobody is stopping this conflict, so we will try!" The difficulties were overwhelming, but inaction was not an option, said Odong, in words we have quoted earlier:

We had to build trust, and we did not take sides. We tried to be completely neutral in talking to both sides, first the government and then the rebels. You know when two elephants are fighting, it is the grass that suffers. The government and the LRA, of course, are the two elephants, and the people are the grass. And the grass is crying out, "I am innocent! I am innocent!" And we are the voice of this grass. (Odong 2014)

Four Pillars of ARLPI Efforts

In the interview excerpt quoted earlier, Odong pointed to four "pillars" of ARLPI's efforts: advocacy, dialogue, reconciliation, and humanitarian support. Each of these was critical, and keeping all in focus helped win respect for the group's work and advance its goals. We will review them briefly in turn.

Advocacy was the most public dimension of the work of ARLPI. In the first years after its founding, its leaders sought to draw attention to a largely unknown war through communication with members of their respective religious communities in other regions of Uganda and abroad. Later they undertook to show their support for the victims of the war by joining the "night commuters" and sleeping in the bus parks. As national and international media began to take notice, and the suffering of the Acholi people became more visible to outsiders, ARLPI leaders traveled to North America and Europe on two occasions. Meeting with church leaders and government representatives, they asked them to put pressure on the Ugandan government to seek a genuine solution to the conflict rather than continue its destructive but ineffective military efforts.

By speaking on behalf of Christians and Muslims alike, the witness of ARLPI gained greater credibility. Across many regions of Africa, Christian–Muslim tensions simmer, breaking out from time to time in overt violence, and cooperation among the two major religious communities is scarce. Western observers were amazed to see them come together to advocate for resolution of the LRA conflict.

Dialogue was a second common element in each of ARLPI's initiatives, with the goal of promoting **mediation and negotiation.** This was perhaps the least visible dimension of its work to outsiders, given the enormous difficulty of winning the trust of both government and LRA representatives. Of necessity nearly all of this work was done in secrecy.

Government representatives construed the efforts of religious leaders to open dialogue with LRA representatives as evidence of their covert support for the rebel cause and a sign that ethnic loyalty to other Acholi was stronger than loyalty to the elected national government. Only with great difficulty was it possible for ARLPI representatives to obtain an agreement that, when meetings with LRA leaders were arranged in remote locations in the bush, government troops would not follow and try to take them prisoner.

LRA representatives for their part harbored deep suspicions of the motives and allegiances of Christian and Muslim leaders who sought to meet with them. Time after time, meetings were scheduled; ARLPI representatives reported to remote sites far from any town and, more important, from any military outpost—and then the LRA negotiators stayed away, citing fears for their safety. Agreements for temporary cessation of hostilities were sometimes overridden by more senior commanders, who had seen how often the government had offered a ceasefire and then failed to honor it.

After many attempts, however, involving great personal risk for ARLPI representatives who ventured far into remote regions of northern Uganda without military or police protection, dialogue began at last. The agreements that were drafted in 2006, leading to final LRA withdrawal in the two years that followed, were not primarily the work of ARLPI representatives. Their terms were drawn up by representatives of the South Sudanese government, under the direction of Riek Machar, with assistance from the Community of Sant'Egidio. But these steps would not have occurred had they not followed years of tireless and fearless efforts by ARLPI leaders to bring the warring parties to the negotiating table.

The third goal that ARLPI leaders upheld for their own communities, from the beginning, was that of **reconciliation.** Violence breeds violence, they stressed, and every act of aggression plants the seeds for retaliatory aggression. So long as each party to the conflict was determined to settle scores, the war would never end. Resolution was possible only if the cycle could be broken, and for this reason ARLPI leaders lobbied successfully for the enactment of the 2000 Amnesty Law. When LRA combatants escaped, or were released to return home, leaders of churches and mosques helped to organize programs of rehabilitation and reentry into society. Even more important than practical support for such programs was the moral authority of religious leaders when they told their congregations, month after month and year after year, that those who lay down arms and seek to resume civilian life deserve a welcome and a helping hand, not ostracism or punishment.

The barriers to reconciliation were formidable. In my interviews, and in numerous accounts of the conflict and its aftermath, I encountered many stories of parents who had watched their own children hack their neighbors' limbs off in LRA attacks, then did not see them again for many years until they returned from the bush and sought to rejoin their families. Women returned with children fathered by their assigned LRA "husbands" and sought to resume normal life, including a genuine marriage entered into freely. Children grew up knowing that the father with whom they lived was not their biological father, and they sometimes faced prejudice and hostility from others who were also aware of their origins. In any war, postwar reconciliation poses great difficulties, as past hostility must be set aside in order to work together. But in very few wars have the deepest lines of division fallen, in so many cases, within a single family.

ARLPI staff are aware that the work of reconciliation is far from completed today, even when there are no more LRA forces in Uganda and hardly any soldiers returning from the bush. That is the reason for organizing peace committees in every town and village in the region, as has been mentioned above, and for ensuring that each such committee bridges the divisions between Christian and Muslim, between those who participated in LRA attacks and those who suffered their effects.

ARLPI leaders told me that when their efforts to bring healing were ineffective the cause could often be traced to too much top-down direction and too little involvement by grass-roots Christians and Muslims. In order to achieve their purposes, the leaders realized, they must transfer leadership to groups whose leaders and members are selected within each community. Then there will be a higher level of trust, a greater expectation of accountability, and a far higher likelihood that the community will address its challenges in a unified and coordinated way.

The fourth "pillar" of ARLPI work identified by Odong is that of **humanitarian support**, which involved soliciting donations from local and international religious bodies, nonprofit agencies, and government to meet urgent needs food, shelter, and medical care. This was an especially high priority during the period when LRA raids destroyed fields and homes and seized crops. It became even more critical after the Ugandan government forced the population into IDP camps, where they were completely dependent on relief supplies for their daily diet.

It remains important today, when families are struggling to regain access to their former lands from those who occupy them illegally, to rebuild homes razed by either LRA or government troops, and to obtain the seeds and agricultural tools that will enable them to become self-sufficient once again.

Given its small staff and limited resources, ARLPI has served primarily as an advocate for humanitarian aid, not a principal provider. Within local religious communities, however, families and individuals in need regularly receive assistance. In this the people of northern Uganda reflect the strength of African traditions of hospitality, which make it unthinkable to allow a neighbor to go hungry if there is food that could be shared. I heard relatively few specific accounts of assistance within communities, in my interviews with ARLPI leaders and others affected by the conflict, probably because, in the African context, such assistance is simply something each person can expect to receive from others. Forms of assistance that in North American and European societies would be regarded as exceptionally generous, deserving thanks and commendation, often go unnoticed and unremarked in the cultural contexts of West and East Africa.

Several of the staff members of ARLPI whom I interviewed pointed to an area of particular concern today: the level of domestic violence in families. Priests, pastors and imams have emphasized in their preaching that the reticence of outsiders to speak up for an abused wife or child must be overcome, in order to uphold the dignity and the rights of all. ARLPI program coordinator Frances Lakweya named this area in our interview as one of the most important contributions of ARLPI community efforts today, along with addressing land tenure issues and creating better options for economic livelihood (Lakweya 2016). This is among several areas that have emerged as priorities in the organization's work of fostering dialogue and reconciliation, not just between opposing armies but within communities.

In a wide-ranging review of programs undertaken by the Department for International Development (DFID) of the British government, written in 2006, the comparative contribution of various local, national, and international agents to the resolution of the LRA conflict was carefully assessed. Writing at a time when the Juba accords were still unratified but were being honored in practice, and the LRA presence in Uganda was at last on the wane, Jeremy Ginifer, principal author of the DFID review, observed how little had been contributed by military efforts.

> The situation in Uganda suggests the lesson that a heavy reliance on narrow "military solutions" such as Operation Iron Fist often have only limited utility in bringing conflict to an end even when the threat in military terms is small. Even though the GoU [Government of Uganda] has intermittently engaged in peace efforts, a lesson that might be learnt here is that multi-dimensional approaches that acknowledge and address the wider political, social, and cultural issues including reconciliation, human rights and protection, offer the best chance of reducing violent conflict in the long-term. They also have the capacity to deal with the root, structural and trigger factors that lead to violent conflict. The lack of engagement of the GoU in promoting reconciliation, national recovery and development is an area of concern. (Ginifer 2006, xiv)

British government involvement in efforts to end the LRA conflict, the report notes, date back to 1999. The goals of its involvement were identified as supporting "conflict resolution and resolution interventions" and coordinating the efforts of international agencies with local and national governments.

> Between 2001–2005, the UK has allocated approximately £2.7 million in support of conflict reduction and peace-building in Uganda. DFID's approach has been to work closely with local institutions and the GoU to bring about these changes. This support has been directed at three core areas: the development of closer coordination arrangements, common understandings, and approaches; the promotion of human rights, international humanitarian law, accurate information and the role of civil society; [and] the targeted support to reconciliation and stabilization processes with an emphasis on locally-driven initiatives. (Ginifer 2006, 9)

The report then lists the agencies that have contributed most significantly to conflict resolution during the period surveyed. In the second category of upholding human rights and enforcing international humanitarian law, international organizations such as UNICEF and Save the Children Uganda are given credit for their work in advocacy for and protection of children. In the third category, organizations that promote local initiatives promoting reconciliation and stabilization, several organizations are listed, including the government-established Amnesty Commission and the expatriate group *Kacoke Madit*. The only Uganda-based nongovernment agency listed is ARLPI, whose work is described in this way:

> ARLPI has been supported by DFID since mid-2001 in terms of capacity-building and support to advocacy and peace initiatives. ARPLI is perhaps best known for the role it played in facilitating peace contacts between the LRA and the GoU. However, ARLPI has also undertaken: training and capacity-building in negotiation, mediation, arbitration and reconciliation processes; education in justice, peace and human rights; lobbying on social justice and transformation, and development issues; mediation between communities; and exchange visits and relationship-building. (Ginifer 2006, 10–11)

A British foreign aid officer has here summed up the work of ARLPI in terms that mirror Monsignor Odong's "four pillars": it has been a policy advocate, a facilitator of dialogue and mediation, an agent of reconciliation, and a contributor to development aid. Few other organizations in East Africa or elsewhere have undertaken such comprehensive measures to heal the wounds of war.

Learning from Uganda's Example

In Chapter 1 we considered the way Uganda is seen by people around the world who have been exposed to the Invisible Children video, "Kony 2012." A hundred million viewers around the world saw Uganda as a battleground between the forces of good, represented by the defenseless people of Uganda and the courageous young volunteers from the United States who became their advocates, and the forces of evil, represented by the diminished but still potent Lord's Resistance Army. The solution put forward to solve the problem was to continue, and escalate, military efforts to bring about Kony's capture and defeat. Only a military solution, the Invisible Children organization insisted in this video and in its continuing support for U.S. military assistance, could ever close the book on the LRA conflict.

Outside agencies and foreign governments seldom challenged the Ugandan government's claims that its military effort to defeat the LRA would soon force it to surrender and disband. Invisible Children endorsed the call for more effective military action even while it discounted the government's claims of progress. Leaders of ARLPI, in contrast, insisted from early in the conflict that no military solution could be a genuine solution. History gives us reason to favor the second view.

More than two decades of repeated and often rapacious military action by Ugandan government forces failed to defeat Kony's forces. Limited successes that were attained—driving most of the LRA troops out of Uganda into Sudan, for example—were only temporary. The national army's conduct of the war in northern Uganda fueled perceptions that the Museveni government was using the LRA conflict as a pretext for repression of the Acholi people, who had not supported Museveni in presidential elections and had supported the government he ousted in 1986.

What the example of ARLPI demonstrates dramatically is that cooperation and collaboration among religious leaders can achieve seemingly impossible goals. Across Africa, examples can readily be found of conflicts in which religious differences compound other sources of mistrust and lead to violent conflict. In the eyes of many Western observers—including many who regard themselves as humanitarian benefactors—this is just the way Africans are. "They" think in terms of my religion against your religion, my tribe against your tribe, it is said, and the LRA conflict is just another example of the pervasive nature of the violence. Alex Perry sums up the prevailing view of many of Africa's self-proclaimed rescuers in ironic language:

"TIA" – this is Africa. This Africa is a place without history, where wars erupt out of nowhere, over nothing, and Africans fight and die all the time, for no good reason. War just is, because Africans are. The more incomprehensible and ceaseless the dying, the more heroic the effort to help. (Perry 2012, 118)

The work of ARLPI offers a dramatic refutation of such misconceptions. Divisions can be overcome to achieve common purposes. Religious differences are deep and important but need not be a source of crippling or violent conflict. Indeed, its example demonstrates, Ugandans themselves have the vision and the capacity to work together, across religious boundaries, for the good of their people.

Mistrust of Christians among Muslims, and of Muslims among Christians, is pervasive in many regions of Africa. Uganda is unfortunately not an exception. But courageous leaders in the Catholic, Protestant, and Muslim communities recognized, in the midst of a protracted civil war, that by working together and by upholding the power of dialogue and reconciliation to defeat the weapons of war, they could lead their people out of decades of brutal violence into a negotiated peace.

We can see in the work of ARLPI a beginning of the answer to the difficult question that was posed and set aside at the beginning of this chapter: what does "consent" mean in religious and ethnic communities, and what does it mean under an autocratic regime, a regime that a political scientist has characterized as an "authoritarian democracy"? It is evident, first of all, that although Uganda as a nation has created and maintained democratic practices and institutions, this has not translated into either credibility or accountability in regions such as the north, where the NRM government has done little to advance either economic development or peace in the past three decades. The Museveni government holds claim to the presidency and to a parliamentary majority, having won solid majorities in several national elections. Nominally, these are elections open to all: opposition parties were legalized in 1995, after all. But in fact each election has been preceded by harassment of opposition candidates, and neither Ugandans nor international observers have been willing to affirm the integrity of vote-counting procedures. Moreover, voting in the north has been overwhelmingly against the ruling party. In the government's policies and practices, what the Acholi and neighboring sub-regions see is not open and effective democratic rule grounded in consent but a desire to punish them for their lack of support.

The people of northern Uganda, then, can hardly be said to be united in support of their national government. Regional representatives to parliament, and local government officials, have inevitably been tarred with the same brush as the national government: to the extent that they play a role in national policy, they too come under suspicion. Occasionally representatives of the region have taken courageous action to advocate for the welfare of the people and to seek a resolution of the LRA conflict. A noteworthy example was the peace initiative pursued by parliamentarian Betty Bigombe in the early 1990s. The response of the Museveni government, on that occasion and others, has been to distance itself from such efforts—and even to sabotage them by failing to honor provisional ceasefires.

In the years since the withdrawal of the LRA, it should be added, the Kampala government has greatly increased its efforts to rebuild the northern region. One important step, bringing both expertise and educational opportunities to the region, was the establishment of a new national university in Gulu in 2002. Housed on the grounds of a former agricultural college, the new university was initially named Gulu University of Agriculture and Environmental Science, but as additional programs in law, medicine, development studies, and peace and strategic studies were added the name was changed: today it is the Gulu University for Community Development (Gulu University n.d.).

Enrollment has grown from about 800 students in its first few years to 3,700 students today, enrolled in B.A. and diploma programs in several dozen fields of natural science, social science, humanities, and professions (Langole 2016). Confirmation of the potential of this institution to contribute to the future of the region came with the 2017 award of a UNESCO chair to be held by an appointee to its faculty (UNESCO 2017).

The consent of the governed, the foundation of democratic polity, must be earned, not conferred. The new university is an important sign that the central government recognizes its responsibility to rebuild the society and the economy of the north, providing evidence that it no longer intends to punish its residents but rather seeks to earn their support. Major improvements have also been made in essential institutions and services. Roads long neglected have been repaired, electricity grids are being extended, and schools have been rebuilt and more adequately staffed. "Today the infrastructure is better than in most of the areas where there was no war," an ARLPI staff member told me: "Northern

Uganda now has the best roads, the best water systems, and the best primary schools in Uganda." But, he added, "People still do not trust the government." Overcoming longstanding mistrust is a slow process (Nasur 2014).

The question of what consent means in the context of religious communities is an especially difficult one. Religious leaders come to hold their positions by appointment or by election within their own communities, not by public ballot. Their qualifications for office are gained through institutions and processes internal to each community: training in seminaries or Islamic schools, experience in working with local congregations, and demonstrated organizational ability are among them. The offices they hold—bishop, archbishop, vicar general, *khadhi*—are part of each religious community's institutional governance structure, and their duties and responsibilities may appear to be defined simply by their place in a hierarchy. In many cases religious leaders are placed over their people, not selected by them.

But the emergence of ARLPI in northern Uganda puts the authority of religious leaders in a different light. When they came together in 1997 to bridge the gulf between their communities and work together for peace, they were acting on their own initiative, drawn together by the desire to relieve the suffering they saw all around them. Those who initiated these contacts on behalf of the Catholic Church were questioned by their superiors, who doubted that any good could come from such interfaith outreach and also feared for their safety. Members of the leaders' congregations had similar doubts.

But as the work of ARLPI advanced, and it achieved some remarkable victories—the passage of the amnesty law, several rounds of talks with both sides of the conflict—the organization in effect earned a resounding mandate both from above and from below. The leaders of national religious organizations listened to their recommendations and offered their support. Members of the Christian and Muslim congregations saw that the potential benefits of their leaders' efforts at resolving the conflict were more than worth the risks they were undertaking. In effect, through advocacy, dialogue, and more accurate reports on the conflict, the religious leaders earned the support and the consent of their communities—both those to whom they reported in their religious institutions and those who looked to them for guidance from the churches and mosques.

Earlier we took note of the many ways in which religion is entwined with public life in Africa, in contrast to Europe and North America. The prominent role of religious leaders in bringing the LRA insurrection to a resolution offers one more example: it was taken for granted that when archbishops, pastors, and *khadhis* seek resolution of a longstanding situation of civil war, the public and the government will listen and their recommendations will be taken seriously. This may seem inconceivable in the more secular context of the developed world, in which religion and politics are wholly separate realms, best kept out of each other's way. But a striking parallel to the role of ARLPI in resolving the LRA conflict can be found in recent American history: the role of religious leaders in the Freedom Movement of the 1950s and 1960s, which challenged the Jim Crow laws of the American South.

The Freedom Movement (or Civil Rights Movement) achieved its major results, including the Voting Rights Act of 1965, through patient and concerted efforts that anticipated the work of ARLPI in several respects: advocacy for legal equality, dialogue with politicians who had been afraid to name or challenge the racism enshrined in state and local statutes, and dissemination of accurate information about persistent practices of racial discrimination. In other respects the two movements were very different. Where ARLPI's work was mostly conducted out of the public eye, the Freedom Movement coordinated public protests across the southern states. The coalition that succeeded in enacting federal laws against racial discrimination included Christian pastors, Jewish leaders, civil rights lawyers, and members of Congress. Moreover, the campaign to dismantle discriminatory laws met determined and sometimes violent resistance from many pastors and church members in the South, which regarded the entire movement as an attempt to discredit and dismantle the fabric of southern life. The protesters who sat at lunch counters, boarded buses, and linked arms as a symbol of racial equality included Christians, Jews, Muslims, agnostics, and atheists alike. But without the public visibility and moral leadership provided by religious leaders such as Rev. Martin Luther King, Jr. and Rev. Ralph Abernathy, it is unlikely that the movement would have achieved as much as it did.[2]

Both in removing discriminatory laws from the books in the United States and in facilitating the end of a twenty-year civil war in Uganda, we can observe the ways in which leaders of religious communities can earn support and respect beyond the lines that have divided their communities historically. This is especially important when—as in Uganda, but not in the American South—the lines of division are a frequent occasion for conflict, as between Christians and Muslims. In many regions of the world, Christians and Muslims view each other with mistrust, and in some circumstances they have a justifiable fear that mistrust will issue in violence.

How was it possible for this remarkable interfaith coalition to come into existence and to advance the resolution of the northern Uganda conflict? What brought ARLPI organizers such as Archbishop John Baptist Odama, Sheik Musa Khalil, Bishop MacLeod Baker Ochala, and their Orthodox and Evangelical counterparts together, despite the wide divisions between their communities in the history of Uganda and their theological as well as cultural differences?

It is evident that the personal convictions and remarkable courage of the original organizers played a critical role. Those who came together to form ARLPI won respect beyond their own religious communities by emphasizing the common humanity of all people and the necessity of mutual assistance more than preservation and protection of their respective religious communities. This was not stated directly by the individuals whom I interviewed. They were too modest to give themselves this much credit. Nor is it emphasized in ARLPI statements. Yet it was readily apparent in the way that Catholic leaders discussed the work of their Muslim colleagues, and Muslim leaders described initiatives of the Anglicans.

More than personal appeal was necessary, however, to create an effective interfaith peace initiative. The key to ARLPI's success, I believe, lies primarily in its balanced and integrative approach to the challenges that the people of northern Uganda faced as they suffered under decades of civil war.

The government had proclaimed from the earliest stages of the insurgency that it would soon bring the LRA to its knees, arrest its leaders, and restore peace in the region. But the tactics it employed—periodic

military campaigns, stationing government troops in major towns—
had very little effect.

The government's supposed solution to the rebellion was simply to
crush it with superior force. Attempts to do so brought some temporary
and limited successes, but these were soon followed by harsh retaliation
from the LRA. And the egregious misbehavior of government troops
and administrators only exacerbated the Acholi people's sense that they
were unimportant pawns in a contest for power between two cruel and
unprincipled antagonists.

International agencies such as the United Nations, and donor nations including the United States and Great Britain, provided extensive
humanitarian aid. This was especially critical during the period when
the rural Acholi population had been herded into IDP camps where
they could no longer provide for themselves. Important as this assistance was in preventing mass starvation, it did not address the causes
of the conflict or advance its resolution. It offered little more than pal-
liative aid to a people cut off from their land and livelihood, facing the
constant threat of violence.

When Catholic, Protestant, and Muslim leaders came together in
1997 to create the Acholi Religious Leaders Peace Initiative, they could
not predict what effect their work might have in alleviating the suffering of the people or in facilitating a resolution of the conflict. Few
outside the northern region of Uganda knew anything about the reign
of terror under which their people had suffered for the past decade.
The religious leaders had no international NGO backing their efforts,
no support from the Ugandan government, and no assurance that they
would ever be able to win the trust and cooperation of either of the
warring parties.

Yet they moved forward in the shared conviction that cooperation and dialogue would in the end prove stronger than the weapons
of war. Without denying their theological differences, maintaining
their role as leaders of communities that had traditionally had little
to do with each other, they forged a new kind of community across
religious lines. Their example is important not only in Uganda,
not only in Africa, but for religiously diverse communities around
the globe.

If Christians and Muslims can join together and help bring about the resolution of one of the longest and most destructive civil conflicts of the past half-century, we may hope, they can reach out to each other in London, in Brussels, and in the cities of the United States as well. Against the fears and misrepresentations of those who depict Muslims as the enemies of Christianity, or who see Christianity as devoted to the destruction of Islam, they can help their respective communities find common ground to advance the common good.

Why has Uganda escaped from the cycles of Christian–Muslim violence that have engulfed northeastern Nigeria, the eastern regions of the Central African Republic, and too many other regions in Africa and elsewhere? The example of ARLPI—this extended experiment in politics and public life catalyzed by clerics—shows that major changes can occur, overcoming decades of violence and government neglect, when leaders emerge who win the support and consent of the people and serve as their voice. Eventually, despite grave defects in the formal institutions of democratic governance and accountability, political authorities listened and acted. Without explicit authorization in their own religious institutions, without any prior assurance that their efforts would win support from their own communities, a small band of Catholic, Protestant, and Muslim clerics and community leaders in Kitgum and Gulu came together to envision, and after many years of patient effort to bring about, an end to war and a restored community. At last, after a quarter-century of trampling the people of the region underfoot, the elephants, the national army and the rebel army, stopped fighting. And they listened to what the grass had been trying to say.

The last word belongs to Julius Omony, a member of the Peace and Justice Commission, when I asked him what were the most important lessons to be learned from the history of the LRA civil war. He replied:

> What I learned is that peace is the best gift you can receive. In the absence of peace, everything will be destroyed. All human interests and human aspirations will fail. Peace is a gift, and it is something that all humanity prays for. (Omony 2014)

Notes

1. Unfortunately Barkan's optimistic assessment of the political future of Tanzania has proven to be unfounded, as the president elected in 2015, John Magufuli, has relentlessly tightened his control over the country by banning opposition parties, closing newspapers, sacking government ministers who criticize his policies, and worse. "Mr Magufuli is fast transforming Tanzania from a flawed democracy into one of Africa's more brutal dictatorships. It is a lesson in how easily weak institutions can be hijacked and how quickly democratic progress can be undone," wrote a reporter for *The Economist* in March 2018 (Economist 2018).

2. Among dozens of historical studies of this important period two can be cited as representative: David Garrow's study of King and the Southern Christian Leadership Conference (Garrow 1987) and the three-volume account of the King years by Taylor Branch (Branch 1988) (Branch 1999) (Branch 2007)

REFERENCES

———◦✦◦———

Adjaye Associates. 2018. "Ghanaian President Unveils Adjaye Associates'
   Design for New Ghana National Cathedral in Accra." *www.adjaye.com*.
   Mar. 6. Accessed Apr. 18, 2018. http://www.adjaye.com/news/appointments/
   ghanaian-president-unveils-adjaye-associates-design-for-new-ghana-national-
   cathedral-in-accra/.
Aeko, Jessica (Member, Peace and Justice Commission, Diocese of Gulu),
   interview by David Hoekema. 2014. (Jan. 28).
Afako, Barney. 2006. "Traditional Drink Unites Africans." *BBC Focus on Africa*,
   Sept. Accessed May 23, 2016. http://news.bbc.co.uk/2/hi/africa/5382816.stm.
Al-Jazeera. 2003. "Uganda War 'Worst Forgotten Crisis'." Nov. 11. Accessed Mar.
   31, 2018. https://www.aljazeera.com/archive/2003/11/2008410151518420888.
   html.
Allen, Tim. 2006. *Trial Justice: The International Criminal Court and the Lord's
   Resistance Army*. London: Zeb Books.
Allen, Tim. 2010. "Bitter Roots: The 'Invention' of Acholi Traditional Justice." In
   The Lord's Resistance Army: Myth and Reality, edited by Tim Allen and Koen
   Vlassenroot, 242–261. New York: Zed Books.
Allen, Tim, and Koen Vlassenroot. 2010. *The Lord's Resistance Army: Myth and
   Reality*. London: Zed Books.
Amony, Evelyn. 2015. *I am Evelyn Amony: Reclaiming My Life from the Lord's
   Resistance Army*. Madison, WI: University of Wisconsin Press.
Anderson, David. 2005. *Histories of the Hanged: The Dirty War in Kenya and the
   End of Empire*. London: Weidenfeld and Nicolson.

Angucia, Margaret. 2010. *Broken Citizenship: Formerly Abducted Children and Their Social Reintegration in Northern Uganda.* Amsterdam: Rozenberg Publishers.

ARLPI. 2003. *War of Words: An Analysis of Newspaper Coverage of Military Operations in Northern Uganda from January 2002 to 2003.* Acholi Religious Leaders Peace Initiative and Justice Resources. Accessed Sept. 12, 2017. https://docs.google.com/a/arlpi.org/viewer?a=v&pid=sites&srcid=YXJscGkub 3JnfHd3d3xneDo3ZTZiMjNiMDlkNTZhZmU3.

ARLPI. 2009. "ARLPI's Position on the International Criminal Court." Accessed Apr. 29, 2016. http://www.arlpi.org/international-criminal-court-s-icc-uganda.

ARLPI. 2011. *"Together for Peace:" Annual Report.* Gulu: Acholi Religious Leaders Peace Initiative. ARLPI_OAR_2011.pdf www.arlpi.org/about-us.

ARLPI. 2016. "ARLPI Religious Leaders Biographies." Accessed Apr. 30, 2016. http://www.arlpi.org/arlpi-religious-leaders-biographies.

AVSI. 2009. *A Time Between: Moving On From Internal Displacement in Uganda.* Association of Volunteers in International Service. Accessed May 6, 2016. http://www.unhcr.org/4baaofd86.html.

Baines, Erin, Eric Stover, and Marieke Wierda. 2006. *War-Affected Children and Youth in Northern Uganda: Toward a Brighter Future.* Chicago: John D. and Catherine T. MacArthur Foundation.

Baker Ochola, MacLeod. 2004. "Hope in the Storm: The Experience of ARLPI in Conflict Resolution." Conference paper, Uppsala. Sweden. Accessed Apr. 27, 2016. http://www.rel-med.net/fitxer/494/escrit_bisbe_ochola_ENG.pdf.

Barkan, Joel. 2009. "Rethinking Budget Support for Africa: A Political Economy Perspective." In *Smart Aid for African Development*, edited by Richard Joseph and Alexandra Gillies, 67–86. Boulder, CO: Lynn Rienner.

BBC. 2012. "ICC Finds Congo Warlord Thomas Lubanga Guilty." Mar. 14. Accessed Apr. 29, 2016. http://www.bbc.com/news/world-africa-17364988.

BBC. 2015. "Profile: Dominic Ongwen of Uganda's LRA." Jan. 16. Accessed Apr. 29, 2016. http://www.bbc.com/news/world-africa-30709581.

BBC. 2018. "As It Happens: Mugabe Resigns." Nov. 21. Accessed Mar. 31, 2018. http://www.bbc.com/news/live/world-africa-42063744.

Bediako, Kwame. 2004. *Jesus and the Gospel in Africa: History and Experience.* New York: Orbis.

Behrend, Heike. 1999. *Alice Lakwena and the Holy Spirits: War in Northern Uganda 1985–97* (tr. Mitch Cohen). Oxford: James Currey.

Bellamy, Carol. 2004. "Uganda's Night Walkers." *International Herald Tribune*, July 16. Accessed Apr. 26, 2016. http://www.unicef.org/media/media_22368.html.

Boraine, Alex. 2000. *A Country Unmasked.* Cape Town: Oxford University Press.

Branch, Taylor. 1988. *Parting the Waters: America in the King Years, 1954–1963.* New York: Simon and Schuster.

Branch, Taylor. 1999. *Pillar of Fire: America in the King Years 1963–65.* New York: Simon and Schuster.

Branch, Taylor. 2007. *At Canaan's Edge: America in the King Years, 1965–68.* New York: Simon and Schuster.

Bronner, Ethan. 2003. "The Obscenely Easy Exile of Idi Amin." *New York Times*, Aug, 19. https://www.nytimes.com/2003/08/19/opinion/editorial-notebook-the-obscenely-easy-exile-of-idi-amin.html

BSN. 2008. "Jan Egeland Book Raises Doubts about Uganda Commitment to Peace Talks." *Black Star News*, May 12. Accessed May 3, 2016. http://www.blackstarnews.com/global-politics/others/jan-egeland-book-raise-doubts-about-uganda-commitment-to-peace-talks.html.

Burke, Jason. 2017. "Trial of Ex-Child Soldier Dominic Ongwen to Hear Prosecution Case." *Guardian*, Jan. 16. Accessed Apr. 2, 2018. https://www.theguardian.com/law/2017/jan/16/trial-ex-child-soldier-dominic-ongwen-to-hear-prosecution-case-icc-uganda.

CARE. n.d. *About CARE.* Accessed June 3, 2016. http://care.org/about/faqs.

CBS. 2017. *100 Said Killed as Christian Militia, Muslim Rebels Clash.* June 21. Accessed Sept. 3, 2017. https://www.cbsnews.com/news/central-african-republic-christian-anti-balaka-militia-seleka-muslim-rebels/.

Chan, Melissa. 2015. "White House Says It Won't Declare Muslim National Holiday." *Time*, Dec. 12. Accessed June 6, 2016. http://time.com/4146780/eid-al-fitr-muslim-holiday-white-house/.

Cisternino, Mario. 2004. *Passion for Africa: Missionary and Imperial Papers on the Evangelization of Uganda and Sudan, 1848–1923.* Kampala, Uganda: Fountain Publishers.

Cisternino, Mario. 2004. *Passion for Africa: Missionary and Imperial Papers on the Evangelization of Uganda and Sudan, 1848–1923.* Kampala, Uganda: Fountain Publishers.

Clinton, William J. 1998. "Communique: Entebbe Summit for Peace and Prosperity." *American Presidency Project.* Mar. 28. Accessed Aug. 11, 2016. http://www.presidency.ucsb.edu/ws/?pid=55678.

Coalition for the International Criminal Court. n.d. "History of the ICC." Accessed Apr. 29, 2016. http://www.iccnow.org/?mod=icchistory.

Cole, Teju. 2012. "The White-Savior Industrial Complex." *Atlantic*, Mar. 21. Accessed Aug 25, 2016. http://www.theatlantic.com/international/archive/2012/03/the-white-savior-industrial-complex/254843/.

Collier, Paul, and Ritva Reinikka. 2001. *Uganda's Recovery: The Role of Farms, Firms and Government.* Washington, DC: World Bank.

Commonwealth Secretariat. 2017. *Uganda: History.* Secretariat of the British Commonwealth. Accessed Sept. 1, 2017. http://thecommonwealth.org/our-member-countries/uganda/history.

Community of Sant'Egidio. n.d. *The Community.* Accessed Apr. 29, 2016. http://www.santegidio.org/pageID/2/langID/en/THE-COMMUNITY.html.

Conciliation Resources. 2002. *Kacoke Madit: A Diaspora Role in Promoting Peace.* London: Conciliation Resources. Accessed Aug. 23, 2017. http://www.c-r.org/accord-article/kacoke-madit-diaspora-role-promoting-peace-2002.

Conciliation Resources. 2015. *Conversation with Former LRA Commander Ray Apire.* London: Conciliation Resources. Accessed Aug. 26, 2017. http://www.c-r.org/accord/engaging-armed-groups-insight/box-2-conversation-former-lra-commander-captain-ray-apire.

Coupland, Douglas. 1939. *The Arab Slave Trade.* London: Faber and Faber.

Dealtry, Baron Frederick John, and Ernest L. Bentley. 1892. *British East Africa and Uganda: A Historical Record.* Edited by Baron Frederick John Dealtry and Ernest L. ed Bentley. London: Chapman and Hall.

Designboom. 2018. "David Adjaye Presents Plans for Ghana's New National Cathedral in Accra." *DEsignboom*, Mar. 6. Accessed Apr. 18, 2018. https://www.designboom.com/architecture/david-adjaye-ghana-national-cathedral-accra-03-06-2018/.

DeYoung, Karen. 2014. "On the Hunt for Joseph Kony." *Washington Post*, Mar. 23. Accessed May 5, 2016. http://wpo.st/A7Ss1.

Downie, Richard. 2011. *The Lord's Resistance Army.* Center for Strategic and International Studies. Accessed May 5, 2016. http://csis.org/publication/lords-resistance-army.

Dunson, Donald H. 2008. *Child, Victim, Soldier: The Loss of Innocence in Uganda.* New York: Orbis Books.

Economist. 2007. "Alice Lakwena (obituary)." *Economist*, Jan. 17. Accessed Aug. 21, 2017. http://www.economist.com/node/8584604.

Economist. 2017. "Why Uganda's Politics Are Failing its People." *Economist*, Oct. 3. Accessed Mar. 31, 2018. https://www.economist.com/blogs/economist-explains/2017/10/economist-explains-3?zid=304&ah=e5690753dc78ce9190908 3042ad12e30.

Economist. 2018. "Democracy Under Assault: Tanzania's Rogue President." *Economist*, Mar. 15. Accessed Apr. 2, 2018. https://www.economist.com/news/middle-east-and-africa/21738919-strong-constitutions-matter-tanzanias-rogue-president.

Egeland, Jan. 2008. *A Billion Lives: An Eyewitness Report From the Frontlines of Humanity.* New York: Simon and Schuster.

Fahs, Sophia Lyon. 1907. *Uganda's White Man of Work: A Story of Alexander M. Mackay.* New York: Missionary Education Movement of the US and Canada.

Faupel, J. F. 1962. *African Holocaust: The Story of the Uganda Martyrs.* New York: P. J. Kenedy and Sons.

Finnegan, Amy. 2010. "Forging Forgiveness: Collective Efforts Amidst War in Northern Uganda." *Sociological Inquiry* 80 (3): 424–447.

Finnström, Sverker. 2008. *Living With Bad Surroundings: War, History and Everyday Moments in Northern Uganda.* Durham, NC: Duke University Press.

Foden, Giles. 1999. *The Last King of Scotland.* New York: Vintage Books.

Garrow, David. 1987. *Martin Luther King, Jr., and the Southern Christian Leadership Conference.* New York: Harper Collins.

Gates, Henry Louis, and Anthony Appiah. 2005. *Africana: The Encyclopedia of the African and African-American Experience, 2d ed.* Oxford: Oxford University Press.

Geria, Samson Ayub. 1973. *A Traditional History of the North- Western Lugbara of Uganda.* Kampala: BA Dissertation, Makerere University.

Gersony, Richard. 1997. *The Anguish of Northern Uganda: Results of a Field-Based Assessment of Civil Conflicts in Uganda.* Report commissioned by US and USAID, Kampala, Uganda: Embassy of the United States.

Gettleman, Jeffrey, and Eric Schmitt. 2009. "U. S. Aided a Failed Plan to Rout Ugandan Rebels." *New York Times*, Feb. 6. Accessed May 5, 2016. http://nyti.ms/1JLdCcw.

Ginifer, Jeremy. 2006. "Internal Review of DFID's Engagement with the Conflict in Northern Uganda." Department for International Development (UK), Feb. Accessed June 10, 2016. http://www.oecd.org/countries/uganda/36503954.pdf.

Green, Matthew. 2009. *The Wizard of the Nile: The Hunt for Africa's Most Wanted.* Northampton, MA: Olive Branch Press.

Grossman, Samantha. 2012. ""Kony 2012" Documentary Becomes Most Viral Video in History." *Time*, Mar. 12. newsfeed.time.com/2012/03/12/kony-2012-documentary-becomes-most-viral-video-in-history/.

Gulu University. n.d. *Historical Background of Gulu University.* Accessed Sept. 1, 2017. http://gu.ac.ug/historical-background/.

Hoad, Neville. 2007. *African Intimacies.* Minneapolis: University of Minnesota Press.

Hoekema, David. 2010. "Religious rights: Christians and Muslims in Kenya." *The Christian Century*, June 15: 10–11.

Hoekema, David. 2013. "African Politics and Moral Vision." *Soundings: An Interdisciplinary Journal* 96 (4): 121–144.

Hoekema, David. 2015. "Captives of the Prophet." *Books and Culture*, Jul.-Aug. Accessed Mar. 31, 2018. http://www.booksandculture.com/articles/2015/julaug/captives-of-prophet.html.

Human Rights Watch. 1997. *The Scars of Death: Children Abducted by the Lord's Resistance Army in Uganda.* New York: Human Rights Watch.

Information for Youth Empowerment Program. n.d. Uganda Action Movement. Accessed June 3, 2016. http://students.brown.edu/Uganda_Action_Movement/IYEP.htm.

International Court of Justice. 2005. "Armed Activities on the Territory of the Congo (Democratic Republic of the Congo vs. Uganda)." Press release. http://www.icj-cij.org/docket/files/116/10521.pdf.

International Criminal Court. 2005. "Warrant of Arrest for Dominic Ongwen." Criminal indictment, The Hague. Accessed Apr. 29, 2016. https://www.icc-cpi.int/iccdocs/doc/doc97201.PDF.

International Criminal Court. 2017. *Ongwen Case: The Prosecutor vs. Dominic Ongwen*. Hague: ICC. Accessed Apr. 2, 2018. https://www.icc-cpi.int/uganda/ongwen.

Invisible Children. 2016. *Obama and Uganda* (blog). Accessed May 5, 2016. http://invisiblechildren.com/blog/tag/obama/.

Invisible Children. 2017. *LRA Crisis Tracker*. Accessed Aug. 25, 2017. https://lracrisistracker.com/.

IRIN. 2004. "Row Over Fire and Arrests of "Rebels" in IDP Camp." Accessed Apr. 26, 2016. http://www.irinnews.org/report/48403/uganda-row-over-fire-and-arrests-rebels-idp-camp.

IRIN. 2006. "Fewer 'Night Commuters' But Children Still Vulnerable." Accessed June 20, 2016. http://www.irinnews.org/report/60084/uganda-fewer-night-commuters-children-still-vulnerable.

IRIN. 2012. "Amnesty or Prosecution for War Criminals." Accessed Mar. 31, 2018. http://www.irinnews.org/report/95476/uganda-amnesty-or-prosecution-war-criminals.

IRIN. 2015. "Forgive and Forget? Amnesty Dilemma Haunts Uganda." Accessed Aug. 23, 2017. http://www.irinnews.org/report/101625/forgive-and-forget-amnesty-dilemma-haunts-uganda.

Jagielski, Wojciech. 2012. *The Night Wanderers: Uganda's Children and the Lord's Resistance Army.* Translated by Antonia Lloyd-Jones. New York: Seven Stories Press.

Justice and Reconciliation Project. 2009. "Kill Every Living Thing: The Bunyoro Massacre." Accessed Aug. 25, 2017. http://justiceandreconciliation.com/wp-content/uploads/2009/02/JRP_FN9_Barlonyo-2009.pdf.

Kane, Ross. 2017. "Communion of Ancestors." *Christian Century*, Apr. 11: 30–33.

Katongole, Emmanuel. 2011. *The Sacrifice of Africa: A Political Theology for Africa Today.* Grand Rapids, MI: Eerdmans Publishing.

Khadialaga, Gilbert. 2001. *The Role of the Acholi Religious Leaders Peace Initative in Peace Building in Northern Uganda.* Washington, DC: Management Systems International.

Khalil, Muza (Khadhi of Gulu Muslim community), interview by David Hoekema. 2014. (Jan 30).

Kollman, Paul V. 2005. *The Evangelization of Slaves and Catholic Origins in Eastern Africa.* New York: Orbis Books.

Komanech, John Bosco (Gulu director, Caritas), interview by David Hoekema. 2014. (Jan. 27).

Krog, Antjie. 1999. *Country of My Skull.* New York: Times Books.

Kron, Josh. 2016. "Yoweri Museveni, Uganda's President, Wins a Widely Criticized Election." *New York Times*, Feb. 16.

Kyaga-Nsubuga, John. 1999. "Managing Political Change: Uganda Under Museveni." In *Civil Wars in Africa: Roots and Resolution*, edited by M. Ali Taisier M. Ali and Robert O. Matthews, 13–34. Montreal: McGill-Queen's University Press.

Ladah, George Openjuru (Deputy Vice Chancellor, Gulu University), interview by David Hoekema. 2016. (Nov. 11).

Lakweya, Frances (program coordinator, ARLPI), interview by David Hoekema. 2016. (Nov. 1).

Lambright, Gina M. S. 2011. *Decentralization in Uganda: Explaining Successes and Failures in Local Government.* Boulder, CO: First Forum Press (Lynne Rienner).

Langole, Stephen (director, Institute of Peace and Strategic Studies, Gulu University), interview by David Hoekema. 2016. (Nov. 11).

Latigo, James, and MacLeod Baker Ochola. 2015. *The Acholi Religious Leaders' Peace Initiative: Local Mediation with the Lord's Resistance Army.* London: Conciliation Resources. Accessed Aug. 26 2017. http://www.c-r.org/accord/engaging-armed-groups-insight/ northern-uganda-acholi-religious-leaders-peace-initiative-local.

Lederach, John Paul. 2010. "The long journey back to humanity: Catholic peacebuilding with armed actors." In *Peacebuilding: Catholic Theology, Ethics and Praxis*, edited by Robert J. Schreiter, R. Scott Appleby and Gerard F. Powers, 23–55. New York: Orbis Books.

Leebaw, Bronwen. 2011. *Judging State-Sponsored Violence, Imagining Political Change.* New York: Cambridge University Press.

Lehrer, Kim Jamie. 2010. *Economic Behaviour during Conflict: Education and Labour Market Participation in Internally Displace People's Camps in Northern Uganda.* Unpublished Ph.D. dissertation. Vancouver, BC: University of British Columbia. Accessed Sept. 24, 2018. https:// open.library.ubc.ca/cIRcle/collections/ubctheses/24/items/1.0071050

Leopold, Mark. 2006. "Legacies of slavery in North-West Uganda: The story of the 'One-Elevens'." *Africa: Journal of the International Africa Institute* 76 (2): 180–99.

Library of Congress. 1992. *Uganda: A Country Study.* Edited by Rita M. Byrnes. Washington, DC: U. G. Government Printing Office.

Lukwiya Ochola, Robert. 2006. *The Acholi Religious Leaders' Peace Initiative in the Battlefield of Northern Uganda.* Innsbruck: Theological Faculty of the University of Innsbruck (unpublished MA thesis).

Lumumba, Patrick (Head, Peace and Development Department, Diocese of Northern Uganda), interview by David Hoekema. 2014. (Jan. 29).

Mazrui, Ali. 1993. *General History of Africa, Vol. VIII.* New York: UNESCO.

Mbiti, John. 1969. *African Religions and Philosophy.* New York: Praeger.

Mbiti, John. 1986. *Bible and Theology in African Christianity.* Nairobi: Oxford University Press.

McEwan, P. J. M. 1968. *Readings in African History: Twentieth-Century Africa.* Oxford: Oxford University Press.

Mubarak, Issa (former LRA sergeant), interview by David Hoekema. 2014. (Jan. 29).

Muhuzuma, Rodney. 2016. "Uganda to Withdraw Troops from Central African Republic." *Associated Press*, June 10. Accessed June 20, 2016. http://bigstory. ap.org/node/12855641.

Nasur, Abdala Latif (Project Officer, Acholi Religious Leaders Peace Initiative), interview by David Hoekema. 2014. (Jan 30).

Nasur, Abdala Latif (Project Officer, Acholi Religious Leaders Peace Initiative), interview by David Hoekema. 2016. (Nov. 11).

NBC. 2005. *Dateline: Children of War in Uganda.* New York, Aug. 22. Accessed Apr. 26, 2016. http://www.nbcnews.com/id/9006024/ns/dateline_nbc/t/children-war-uganda/#.Vx5y5TArKUk.

New Vision. 1987. "Museveni Directs Final Lakwena Offensive." *New Vision,* Nov. 6.

New Vision. 2001. "Amin, Obote Were Hyenas—Museveni." *New Vision,* March 25.

New Vision. 2006. "Museveni Hails Gulu Archbishop Odama." *New Vision,* Oct. 22.

Niwano Peace Foundation. 2004. "Recipients of Niwano Peace Prize." Accessed June 20, 2016. http://www.npf.or.jp/english/peace_prize/npp_recipients/21st.html.

No Place for a Rebel. 2017. Directed by Ariadne Asamakopoulos. https://www.noplaceforarebel.com/.

Ocayo, James (assistant planning officer, Diocese of N. Uganda), interview by David Hoekema. 2014. (Jan. 29).

Odama, John Baptist. 2004. *Reconciliation Process (Mato Oput) Among the Acholi Tribe in Northern Uganda.* Tokyo: Niwano Peace Foundation. Accessed June 20, 2016. http://www.npf.or.jp/npf/index_e.html.

Odong, Matthew (Vicar General, Diocese of Northern Uganda), interview by David Hoekema. 2014. (Jan 31).

Odong, Matthew (Vicar General, Diocese of Northern Uganda), interview by David Hoekema. 2016. (Nov. 11).

Ogaba, Joseph (member, Peace and Justice Commission, Diocese of Gulu), interview by David Hoekema. 2014. (Jan. 28).

Ogora, Lino Owor. 2018. "Confirmation of Charges Hearing against Thomas Kwoyelo Postponed Again." *International Justice Monitor,* June 14. www.ijmonitor.org/2018/06/confirmation-of-charges-hearing-against-thomas-kwoyelo-postponed-again/

Okello, Moses Rubangageyo (Field Coordinator, N. Uganda Initiative for Affected Youth), interview by David Hoekema. 2014. (Jan. 28).

Okeowo, Alexis. 2012. "Thomas Kwoyelo's Troubling Trial." *New Yorker,* July 20.

Okot, Jacinto, interview by David Hoekema. 2014. (Jan. 28).

Okwarmoi, Lucy, interview by David Hoekema. 2014. (Jan. 29).

Omony, Julius (Member, Peace and Justice Commission, Diocese of Gulu), interview by David Hoekema. 2014. (Jan. 28).

Onitsi, Noremitsu. 1979. "U. S. and Africa: Unfulfilled Promises and Skepticism." *New York Times.*

Otim, Patrick William. 2009. *The Role of the Acholi Religious Leaders Peace Initiative in Uganda's Peacebuilding.* Case Study, Boulder, CO: University of Colorado Conflict Information Consortium. Accessed Apr. 25, 2016. http://www.beyondintractability.org/casestudy/otim-role.

Otonnu, Ogenda. 1998. "The Path to Genocide in Northern Uganda."
    Refuge: Canada's Journal of Refugees 17 (3): 4–13.
Parliament of the World's Religions. 2015. *Carus Award.* Accessed Aug. 25, 2017.
    https://parliamentofreligions.org/content/paul-carus-award.
Parliament of Uganda. n.d. "Amnesty Act (2000)." Accessed Mar 30, 2014.
    http://www.ulii.org/ug/legislation/consolidated-act/294.
"Patience," interview by David Hoekema and Lucy Dora Akello. 2014. (Jan. 28).
Perry, Alex. 2015. *The Rift: A New Africa Breaks Free.* New York: Little, Brown
    and Co.
Perry, Tony. 2012. "New Video Aimed at African Warlord: Invisible Children
    Plans a Rally to Urge Capture of Ugandan Joseph Kony." *Los Angeles Times*,
    Oct. 12.
Petitions 24. n.d. *Most Popular Petitions (all dates).* Accessed June 16, 2016. www.
    petitions24.com.
Pew Research Center. 2010. "Tolerance and Tension: Islam and Christianity in
    Sub-Saharan Africa." June 15. Accessed June 7, 2016. http://www.pewforum.
    org/2010/04/15/executive-summary-islam-and-christianity-in-sub-saharan-
    africa/.
Pew Research Center. 2011. "Global Christianity—A Report on the Size and
    Distribution of the World's Christian Population." Accessed June 7, 2016.
    http://www.pewforum.org/2011/12/19/global-christianity-exec/.
Pew Research Center. 2012. "Table: World Religious Population, by Numbers."
    Accessed June 7, 2016. http://www.pewforum.org/2012/12/18/table-religious-
    composition-by-country-in-numbers/.
Pew Research Center. 2012. "Table: Religious Composition by Country, in
    Percentages." Accessed June 7, 2016. http://www.pewforum.org/2012/12/18/
    table-religious-composition-by-country-in-percentages/.
Posnansky, Merrick. 1963. "Towards an Historical Geography of Uganda."
    East African Geographical Review 1 (1): 7-20. Accessed Sept. 24, 2018.
    https://www.ingentaconnect.com/content/sabinet /eagr/1963/00001963/
    00000001/art00005
Pretorius, Fransjohan. 2013. *BBC History: The Boer Wars.* Mar. 29. Accessed Sept.
    1, 2017. http://www.bbc.co.uk/history/british/victorians/boer_wars_01.shtml.
Reuters. 2017. "Christian Militias Kill up to 30 Civilians as Hundreds Seek
    Refuge Inside Mosque." *Telegraph*, May 15. Accessed Aug. 29, 2017. http://
    www.telegraph.co.uk/news/2017/05/15/central-african-republic-death-toll-
    could-reach-30-says-un/.
Rodriguez, Carlos. 2002. "Protracted Conflict, Elusive Peace: Initiatives to End
    the Violence in Northern Uganda." *Accord.* Accessed Apr 30, 2016. http://
    www.c-r.org/accord-article/role-religious-leaders-2002.
Ronan, Paul. 2017. "The Closing of The Resolve LRA Crisis Initiative and
    What's Next." *www.theresolve.org.* Jan. 31. Accessed Aug. 25, 2017. http://www.
    theresolve.org/2017/01/the-closing-of-the-resolve-lra-crisis-initiative-and-
    whats-next/.

Royal Geographical Society. 1876. *Proceedings of the Royal Geographical Society.* London: Royal Geographical Society.

Rubangakene, Paul (member, Justice and Peace Commission, Diocese of Gulu), interview by David Hoekema. 2014. (Jan. 28).

Rubongaya, Joshua B. 2007. *Regime Hegemony in Museveni's Uganda: Pax Musevica.* New York: Palgrave Macmillan.

"Sam" (U. S. Special Forces), interview by David Hoekema. 2014. Gulu, Uganda, (Jan 31).

Secure Livelihoods Research Consortium. 2012. *Livelihoods, Basic Services, and Social Protection in Northern Uganda and Karamoja.* London: Overseas Development Institute. Accessed Mar. 31, 2018. https://securelivelihoods. org/publication/livelihoods-basic-services-and-social-protection-in-northern-uganda-and-karamoja-3/.

Shorter, Aylward. 2006. *Cross and Flag in Africa: The "White Fathers" During the Colonial Scramble (1892–1914).* New York: Orbis Books.

Ssemakula, Mukasa E. n.d. *Christian Martyrs of Uganda.* Accessed June 17, 2016. http://www.buganda.com/martyrs.htm.

Tempels, Placide. 1945. *La Philosophie Bantou.* Paris: Presence Africaine.

The Last King of Scotland. 2006. Directed by Kevin MacDonald.

Tiessen, Rebecca, and Lahoma Thomas. 2014. "Gendered Insecurity and the Enduring Impacts of Sexual and Gender-Based Violence in Northern Uganda." In *Sexual Violence in Conflict and Post-Conflict Societies: International Agendas and African Contexts,* edited by Doris Buss, Joanne Lebert, Blair Rutherford, Donna Sharley, and Obijiofor Aginam, 90–135. New York: Routledge.

TRC. 2000. *Amnesty Decisions.* Pretoria: Truth and Reconciliation Commission of South Africa. Accessed Apr. 7, 2018. http://www.justice.gov.za/trc/media/pr/2000/pr001213a.htm.

Tripp, Aili Marie. 2010. *Museveni's Uganda: Paradoxes of Power in a Hybrid Regime.* Boulder, CO: Lynner Riener Publishers.

Tutu, Desmond. 2000. *No Future Without Forgiveness.* New York: Image Books.

Uganda Bureau of Statistics. 2016. *National Population and Housing Census 2014.* Kampala: Uganda Bureau of Statistics. Accessed June 7, 2016. http://www.ubos.org/onlinefiles/uploads/ubos/NPHC/2014%20National%20Census%20Main%20Report.pdf.

UNESCO. 2017. *Nederlandse Hoogleraar Benoemd op UNESCO-leerstoel in Oeganda.* Jan. 6. Accessed Sept. 1, 2017. https://www.unesco.nl/artikel/nederlandse-hoogleraar-benoemd-op-unesco-leerstoel-oeganda.

UNHCR. 2012. "UNHCR Closes Chapter on Uganda's Internally Displaced People." *Briefing Notes,* Jan. 6. Accessed May 12, 2016. http://unhcr.org/4f06e2a79.html.

UNICEF. 2004. "Children Flee their Homes to Escape Abduction." May 26. Accessed Apr. 26, 2016. http://www.unicef.org/about/structure/uganda_newsline_2.html.

United Press International. 1985. "Uganda's New Military Rulers." July 29.
    Accessed Sept. 1, 2017. http://www.upi.com/Archives/1985/07/29/Ugandas-
    new-military-rulers-today-named-army-commander-Lt/7228491457600/.
USIP. 1986. *Truth Commission: Uganda 1986.* Washington, DC: United States
    Institute of Peace. Accessed Apr. 7, 2018. https://www.usip.org/publications/
    1986/05/truth-commission-uganda-86.
USIP. 2002. *Truth Commission: South Africa.* Washington, DC: United States
    Institute of Peace. Accessed Apr. 7, 2018. https://www.usip.org/publications/
    1995/12/truth-commission-south-africa.
USIP. 2016. *Uganda's Troubled Election: On the Issues with Elizabeth Murray.*
    Washington, DC: United States Institute of Peace. Accessed June 20, 2016.
    http://www.usip.org/publications/2016/02/25/qa-uganda-s-troubled-election.
wa'Thiongo, Ngugi. 1967. *A Grain of Wheat.* London: Heinemann.
Walls, Andrew. 1987. "Primal Religious Traditions in Today's World." In *Religion
    in Today's World: The Religious Situation of the World from 1945 to the Present
    Day*, edited by Frank Whaling, 250–278. Edinburgh: T. and T. Clark.
War Dance. 2007. Directed by Sean Fine and Andrea Nix.
Whitmore, Todd D. 2010. "Peacebuilding and its Challenging Partners."
    In *Peacebuilding: Catholic Theology, Ethics and Praxis*, edited by
    Robert J. Schreitter, R. Scott Appleby and Gerard F. Powers, 155–189.
    New York: Orbis Books.
Wilson, Frances. 2004. "What Am I Bid for This Lady?" *Telegraph*, Mar 29.
    Accessed Sept. 1, 2017. http://www.telegraph.co.uk/culture/books/3614526/
    What-am-I-bid-for-this-Lady.html.
World Bank. 2016. *Uganda Overview.* New York: World Bank. Accessed June 20,
    2016. http://www.worldbank.org/en/country/uganda/overview.
World Renew. n.d. Accessed Aug. 14, 2016. www.worldrenew.net/uganda.

INDEX

abduction, 13, 85, 128, 132, 137, 157
Acholi culture, 83, 147, 205–13, 229–30
Acholi people, 28, 57, 61, 83, 146, 253
Acholi region, 13, 45, 68, 81, 158
Acholi Religious Leaders Peace Initiative. *See* ARLPI
Acholi tradition
   reconciliation rituals, 206–11
   role of clan elders, 83
Adjaye, David, 111–12
advocacy
   for amnesty law, 133, 160
   as ARLPI priority, 137, 159–60, 239, 247, 250
Africa
   European colonization, 23, 32–34, 61, 236–37
   peoples of, 2, 21–22, 25–27, 238
African National Congress. *See* ANC
African Union, 9, 181, 184
agencies, international, 96, 158, 194, 265
Akello, Lucy Dora, xxi, 19n1
Akufo-Addo, Nana Addo Dankwa (Ghanaian head of state), 112

Amin, Idi (Ugandan head of state), 44, 44–55, 62, 68
amnesty
   ARLPI advocacy for, 118, 160, 239, 254
   effects of Ugandan law, 142, 160, 195, 242
   enactment of Ugandan law, 120, 132–35, 195, 240
   offered to Lakwena militia, 74
   in South Africa (*see* TRC)
Amony, Evelyn, 89–90
ANC (African National Congress), 138
Anderson, David, 24
Anglicans. *See* Church of Uganda
Angucia, Margaret, xx, 43–44, 192, 200, 207, 212, 231
apartheid, 138–39
ARLPI (Acholi Religious Leaders Peace Initiative)
   achievements of, 164, 186, 188, 253–58
   activities of, 131–32, 159–63, 193–204, 215–19
   credibility and authority, 236, 240
   formation of, 120, 123–29
   international awards received, 175

   negotiations with LRA, 133, 167, 171–72
   negotiations with Ugandan government, 131, 134, 161, 171, 174
   reports on LRA conflict, 123, 130, 157
Atyam, Angelina, 17, 153
AVSI (Association of Volunteers in International Service), 191–92

Bacwezi Kingdom, 25
Baganda people, 23, 27–28, 36–37, 39–40
Baker, Samuel White, 22, 28, 32, 223
Baker Ochola, MacLeod, 128, 132, 159–60, 162–63, 175, 264
Bantu and Nilotic population movements in East Africa, 25–27
Bediako, Kwame, 113
Behrend, Heiko, 66, 69, 71–73, 75–78
Bellamy, Carol, 151–52
Bigombe, Betty, 60, 249, 261
Binaisa, Godfrey (Ugandan head of state), 51–52
Branch, Taylor, 267n2

Buganda kingdom, 2, 25,
    33–34, 39, 45, 107–8
  royal succession by clan, 27
Bunyoro kingdom,
    26–27, 39–41
Bush, George W., 179

CARE, 226–27, 230n2
Catholic and Protestant
    missions in Uganda, 102,
    106–7, 110, 124–25, 246
Catholic-Protestant relations
    in Uganda, 34–36, 102,
    106–7, 110, 124
Central African Republic, 55,
    105, 136, 166, 180
Christianity, rapid growth in
    Africa, 115
Christian Reformed World
    Relief Committee. See
    World Renew
Church of Uganda, 102, 110,
    116, 194, 215
Cisternino, Mario, 20, 29–31,
    36, 58, 125
Clinton, Bill, 93, 235
Cole, Teju, 12–13
colonialism, effects of,
    36, 56, 236. See also
    Africa: European
    colonization
"community dialogue
    approach," 204–5, 213
Conciliation Resources,
    128, 172–73
conflict resolution, 193, 204,
    215, 218, 257
consent, as basis of authority,
    232, 239, 260–62, 266
cotton, 3, 22, 37, 40
counseling, for formerly
    abducted, 198–99, 221–22
Coupland, Douglas, 30–31
courts
  international (see ICC; ICJ)
  Muslim, in Kenya, 106
  Ugandan, 49, 136, 177, 186

Democratic Republic of the
    Congo. See DRC
Department for International
    Development. See DFID

DFID (Department
    for International
    Development), 256–58
dialogue
  as alternative to military
    conflict, 174, 245,
    260, 265
  as ARLPI priority, 137,
    204–5, 253, 256, 262, 265
  interreligious, 104, 175
  as means of addressing land
    disputes, 201, 204
  role in traditional
    culture, 210
DP (Democratic Party of
    Uganda), 39, 43–44,
    52, 125
DRC (Democratic Republic of
    the Congo), 42, 81,
    165–69, 179–80, 182–85
  ICJ dispute with
    Uganda, 169
  as refuge for LRA, 11, 55, 136
  in regional conflict, 94, 165
  US-backed coup in, 44

economic growth, under
    Museveni, 64
Egeland, Jan, 157–58, 164,
    178, 252
elections
  in British protectorate, 38–39
  Ugandan national, 52, 63,
    65, 168, 260
Equatoria (Egyptian-British
    province), 28–29
Ethiopia, 30, 81, 92, 94,
    100, 118
ethnic groups
  British policies toward, 36, 38
  military recruitment from,
    44–45, 61, 238
  pre-colonial relations, 24–26
European governments, 4, 33,
    107, 124, 216

Fahs, Sophia Lyon, 2–3
farming
  disruption by conflict, 53,
    121, 142–44, 189, 202
  by Kenyan settlers, 24, 33
Faupel, J. F., 107–9

Finnegan, Amy, 206–7, 209–10
Finnström, Sverker, 23, 57–58,
    83–86, 96
Foden, Giles, 49
forgiveness
  as ARLPI priority, 136–38,
    167, 206, 208, 249
  facilitated by Acholi
    ritual, 208
  as goal of TRC (South
    Africa), 138
Freedom Movement
    (Civil Rights Movement),
    263, 267n2
"freedom roads," 217–19

Gaddafi, Muammar (Libyan
    head of state), 47–48,
    51, 196
Garrow, David, 267n2
Gersony, Richard, 142–44
Ghana, 100, 103–4, 111–14
Ginifer, Jeremy, 257–58
government of Uganda
  negotiations with LRA, 153,
    175, 178
  request for ICC
    indictments, 165–66, 177
  role in rehabilitation
    centers, 199
  support for Sudanese
    rebels, 122
  support from US
    government, 94, 179, 183
Great Lakes region (East
    Africa), 21, 54, 58, 101–2
Gulu (district), 143, 148, 221
Gulu (town), 148–49, 191, 225,
    232, 261
  author's interviews in,
    xxi, 129
  home of Alice
    Lakwena, 66–67
  screening of "Kony 2012," 12
  visit by British officer
    Postlethwaite (1913), 20, 22
Gulu United to Save the
    Children Organization.
    See GUSCO
GUSCO (Gulu United
    to Save the Children
    Organization), 16, 19n3

Hague. *See* ICC
history of East Africa
　Egyptian-British
　　period, 22–23
　pre-colonial, 4, 21, 23–24,
　　34, 58n1
　religious, 101, 101–6, 117
history of Uganda
　as British protectorate, 31–34,
　　37–39, 58n1, 105, 110
　post-independence, 21, 40–41,
　　58n1, 60, 110, 236
Hoima, 217
Holy Spirit Diesel Engine
　Repair, 112
Holy Spirit Mobile Force.
　See HSMF
Holy Spirit Movement, 69,
　73–74, 76, 79–81
HSMF (Holy Spirit Mobile
　Force), 67–74, 76, 80, 233
humanitarian aid
　as ARLPI priority, 247,
　　253, 255
　from foreign donors, 93,
　　164, 193
human rights
　African Charter on Human
　　and People's Rights, 93
　claimed violations, 121, 128
　Ugandan government
　　claims to uphold, 75,
　　94, 140
　Ugandan violations cited by
　　ICJ, 198
　under apartheid in South
　　Africa, 139
Human Rights Watch,
　71, 88–89

ICC (International Criminal
　Court), 164–68, 177
ICJ (International Court of
　Justice), 168–69
IDP camps
　closing of, 185, 188–89, 191,
　　213, 217
　conditions in, 97, 145–47
　forced relocation to, 53, 74,
　　121, 142
　LRA attacks on, 143,
　　146, 161

"relief mentality" instilled
　in, 218–19
　UN management of, 191–92
indirect rule, as British
　colonial policy, 32,
　34–36, 56–57
Integrated Regional
　Information Network.
　See IRIN
International Court of Justice.
　See ICJ
International Criminal Court.
　See ICC
Invisible Children (NGO),
　6–7, 12, 181–83
　advocacy for military action,
　　7, 185, 259
　videos on LRA conflict, 6,
　　11, 66, 86, 258
　Washington rally, 7–8
IRIN, 135–37, 146, 153
Islam, growth in Africa,
　101–3, 114–15
Israel, as Ugandan ally, 45–46
ivory trade in East Africa,
　31–32, 44, 46

Jagielski, Wojciech,
　90–91, 148–49
John Paul II, Pope (visit to
　Uganda), 161

kabaka (Buganda king), 23, 26,
　34–36, 39–40, 45, 106–10
Kabaka Yekka. *See* KY
Kacoke Madit ("big meeting"),
　128, 249
Kampala
　Amin militia occupation, 46
　HSMF campaign to
　　occupy, 72
　occupation by Tanzanian
　　and exile forces, 51
　Olara-Okello militia
　　occupation, 54
　terrorist attacks, 105
　US president and Secretary
　　of State visits, 93
　US Special Forces base, 11
Katongole, Emmanuel, 18, 153
Kaunda, Kenneth (Zambian
　head of state), 46

Kenya, 23–24, 38, 41, 94,
　100, 105–6
Kenyatta, Jomo (Kenyan head
　of state), 46
Khadialaga, Gilbert, 131, 235
King's African Rifles, 37, 44, 48
Kitgum (town), 128, 148
Komanech, John Bosco, 10–12,
　130, 159, 190, 194, 197–98,
　231, 243
Kony, Joseph, 8, 13, 183, 241
　abducted "wives" of, 79–80,
　　89, 243
　early support for, 77,
　　80–82, 84
　indictment by ICC, 164, 177
　lack of endorsement by clan
　　elders, 83
　refusal to sign negotiated
　　agreement, 177
　religious claims and
　　practices, 77–80, 82, 87
　as successor to Alice
　　Lakwena, 66, 74, 76, 80
"Kony 2012" (video), 6–8, 12,
　14, 66, 86, 258
Kwoyelo, Thomas, 136,
　186, 196
KY (Kabaka Yekka)
　(Ugandan political
　party), 39, 44

Ladah, George Openjuru, 147
Lakwena, Alice, 66–67,
　81–82, 245
　communication with
　　spirits, 71, 81
　exile and death in Kenya, 73
Land conflicts, 199, 201,
　203–4, 228
Langole, Stephen, 147, 202
Lango people, 39, 41, 161
　role in military forces,
　　47, 53, 74
"Last King of Scotland" (book
　and film), 49, 86
Latigo, James, 131–32, 171
Lederach, John Paul, 137–38
Leebaw, Bronwen, 141
Leopold, Mark, 32, 58
Livingstone, David, 31
Lokot, Mary Tarcisia, 137

Lord's Resistance Army.
  See LRA
LRA (Lord's Resistance Army)
  abductions, 13, 85, 128, 149,
    157, 189
  amnesty offered to,
    120, 133, 142 (see also
    amnesty: enactment of
    Ugandan law)
  depicted in viral videos, 6,
    12, 14, 66, 86
  discounting by international
    observers, 95–96, 157
  failed military campaigns
    against, 120, 123,
    156–57, 179
  failure of 1990s
    negotiations, 124
  historical background, 26,
    42, 55, 66, 77–81, 238
  ICC indictments of officers,
    165–68, 177
  increasing international
    awareness, 121, 158
  local efforts to resist,
    13, 18, 21
  NBC "Dateline"
    report, 152–53
  negotiations for withdrawal,
    14, 153, 171, 175, 178
  occupation of northern
    Uganda, 13, 81–91, 185, 188
  political manifestos, 85–86
  relationship with Sudan
    governments, 92, 122, 156,
    224, 251
  support from Ugandans in
    exile, 94, 250
  uniforms similar to UPDF,
    225, 232
  withdrawal from Uganda,
    153, 164, 180
LRA Crisis Tracker, 181–82
Lubango, Thomas, 165
Lukoya, Severino (father of
  Alice Lakwena), 75–77
Lule, Yusef (Ugandan head of
  state), 51
Lumumba, Patrice (DRC rebel
  leader), 44
Lumumba, Patrick, 213–15,
  218, 227

Magamaga, 73
martyrs. See Uganda martyrs
Mbiti, John, 113
military operations
  British campaign against the
    Buganda king, 35–36, 124
  "Operation Iron Fist"
    (2002–3), 123, 157,
    179, 252
  "Operation Lightning
    Thunder" (2008–9),
    179–80
Minot, Susan, 87–88
Mtesa (Buganda king), 1
Museveni, Yoweri (Ugandan
  head of state, 1986-present)
  coup and consolidation of
    power, 52–54, 62–63
  dismissal of nonmilitary
    solutions to LRA crisis,
    178, 252
  disparagement of Acholi,
    57, 69, 74
  effective one-party rule,
    234–35, 260
  lack of support among
    Acholi, 13, 74, 95, 144
  meeting with ARLPI
    leaders, 174, 249, 251
  proposes new constitution
    (1995), 62, 122
  relationship with foreign
    governments and
    agencies, 64–65, 93, 95,
    156, 235
  removal of term limits, 63,
    65, 168
Muslim-Christian relations in
  Uganda, 101, 104–6,
  116–18, 126–27,
  246–49, 255
Muslim communities in East
  Africa, 98, 105–6, 110
Muwanga, Paolo (Ugandan
  head of state), 52
Mwanda (Buganda king), 107

Nagel Institute for the Study
  of World Christianity,
  xix, 129
Nasur, Abdala Latif, 99, 127,
  173–74, 201, 214, 247, 262

National Endowment for the
  Humanities, xvii
national holidays, Christian
  and Muslim, 100
National Party (South
  Africa), 138–39
National Resistance Army.
  See NRA
National Resistance
  Movement. See NRM
NGOs (non-governmental
  organizations), 65, 192,
  195, 199, 215
Nigeria, 3, 102, 115–16
Nilotic peoples. See Bantu
  and Nilotic population
  movements in East Africa
Niwano Peace Foundation,
  175, 211
"No Place for a Rebel" (film), 201
NRA (National Resistance
  Army), 92, 122, 130, 139
  abuses committed by,
    74–75, 81–82
  as rebel force in exile,
    50, 52–53
NRM (National Resistance
  Movement), 61, 63, 85,
  234–35, 238
Nyerere, Julius, Tanzanian
  head of state 51

Obote, Milton (Ugandan head
  of state)
  first term, 39, 43–46, 49, 62
  second term, 50, 52–54, 63
Ocayo, James, 216–17, 219–21
Odama, John Baptist, 137,
  150, 212
Odong, Matthew, 126–28,
  133–34, 147, 161–62,
  203, 229, 231, 247–48,
  250–53, 255
Okello, Moses Rubangageyo,
  54–55, 64, 68, 87,
  200–201, 205, 209,
  211–12, 221–29
Omony, Julius, 135, 156, 176, 266
Ongwen, Dominic, 166
opposition parties, nominally
  allowed after 1995, 62,
  64–65, 234–35, 260

Orthodox church (in Uganda),
    125–26, 129, 188, 264
Otonnu, Ogenga, 144
Otti, Vincent, 176
Otto, Caesar Acellam, 136

Pader (town), 130, 225
Paraa (village and traditional
    shrine), 66–67, 76
Parliament of Uganda, 38, 44,
    63, 241
    enactment of amnesty law,
        134, 160, 225
    proposed anti-
        homosexuality law, 183
    removal of presidential term
        limits, 65, 168
"Patience" (pseudonym),
    14–18, 242
Perry, Alex, 5, 8
Perry, Tony, 7
Pew Research Center, 115–16
Postlethwaite, J. R. P., 20, 22
protectorate (status under
    British rule), 23–25,
    34, 37, 39
purification
    Acholi rituals, 207
    advocated by Alice
        Lakwena, 67–68, 72
    advocated by Joseph Kony,
        77, 172

Qur'an, 100, 104, 112, 127,
    244, 249

railway, Mombasa to
    Kampala, 28, 33
Ramadan, 99–100
rebel movements (other
    than LRA)
    in CAR, 166, 182
    in DRC, 94, 165, 182
    in northern Uganda, 73–75
    in Sudan, 259
reconciliation
    Acholi rituals promoting,
        206–9, 212
    as ARLPI priority, 129, 159,
        236, 239, 254–58
    rehabilitation camps,
        199–200, 225

religion and public life in
    African society, 111–12
religious affiliation
    in Africa, 114–16
    in Uganda, 47, 63, 116
Republic of Uganda, 46, 54,
    57, 134, 169
"Resistance Councils" in
    Uganda, 63
Resolve LRA Crisis
    Initiative, 181–82
Rodriguez, Carlos, 128, 132–33
Rome Statute (creating
    ICC), 165–67
Rubongaya, Joshua, 62–63, 69
Russell, Jason, 8
Rwanda, 58n3, 81, 92, 94,
    100, 116

"Sam" (pseudonym) (US
    Special Forces), 184–86
Sant'Egidio, Community of,
    170, 175, 254
schools, as targets of LRA
    abduction, 17, 87, 223, 232
Second World War, 37, 66, 230
self and community, African
    conceptions, 113
Sese Seko, Mobuto (DRC
    head of state), 51
Seventh-Day Adventist
    church, 110, 116, 125, 195
Severino Lukoya. See Lukoya,
    Severino
slavery
    British efforts to end,
        28–29, 32
    changing attitudes in
        Europe, 3–4
    East African, 4, 29–31
    linked to ivory trade, 31
    in pre-colonial Africa,
        3, 29, 31
    in Sudan militia, 32, 92
South Africa, 25, 35, 138–40
South Sudan, 122–23, 170,
    177–81, 190
spirits, individually named
    invoked by Alice Lakwena,
        66–69, 71–72
    invoked by Joseph Kony,
        77–79, 82, 172

    invoked by Severino
        Lukoya, 76
Stanley, Henry M., 2, 4, 27
"Stepping on eggs". See Acholi
    tradition: reconciliation
    rituals
Sudan
    alliance with Uganda,
        122–23, 156
    conflict with Uganda, 224
    as refuge for LRA,
        54–55, 190
    role in LRA
        negotiations, 154
    role in regional conflict,
        92–93, 251
    role in slave trade, 31–32

Tanganyika (now Tanzania),
    32, 36, 38, 42
Tanzania, 1, 42, 46, 110, 234
    as refuge for NRA, 50, 52, 55
    support for Amin
        ouster, 51, 55
Tempels, Placide, 113
Ten Commandments, 1, 5,
    69, 77, 79
traditional beliefs and
    practices, persistence of,
        112, 114, 116, 207
TRC (Truth and Reconciliation
    Commission), 137, 139, 141
Tripp, Aili Marie, 58, 60
Truth and Reconciliation
    Commission. See TRC

Uganda Land Act, translation
    into Acholi, 195, 204
Uganda martyrs (1886),
    36, 106–10
Uganda Martyrs
    University, 117
Uganda National Liberation
    Army. See UNLA
Ugandan Constitution
    enacted after consultation,
        allowing opposition
        parties (1995), 62, 122, 235
    rewritten without
        consultation by Obote
        (1966), 44–45
Ugandan Supreme Court, 52

Uganda People's Congress. *See* UPC

Uganda People's Defence Army (rebel militia), 74, 80

Uganda People's Defence Force. *See* UPDF

Uganda People's Democratic Army. *See* UPDA

UNESCO, 261

UNHCR (United Nations High Commissioner for Refugees), 191–94

UNICEF, 151, 153, 258

UNLA (Uganda National Liberation Army), 51

UPDF (Uganda People's Defence Force)
abuses by troops, 97, 123, 144, 157, 162, 166, 170

ineffective protection of IDP camps, 143, 145, 161, 189

mistrust of Acholi, 123, 245

USIP (United States Institute of Peace), 65, 139–40

U. S. Special Forces, in Uganda, 11, 183

Village Savings and Loan Associations, 228

VSLAs. *See* Village Savings and Loan Associations

"War Dance" (film), 97

wa'Thiongo, Ngugi, 24

West Nile (district), 31, 44, 53, 55, 111, 117, 146

Whitmore, Todd D., 57, 97, 122, 147

witchcraft, 67–68, 77, 84

women
assignment to LRA officers, 80, 89, 255
in East African slave trade, 30
empowerment as ARLPI priority, 204, 215
increased numbers in Parliament, 63
victimization in LRA conflict, 162

World Bank, 60, 64–65, 95

World Renew, 215, 218, 220

Zanzibar (now part of Tanzania), 30–31, 42, 102, 105